and support over me
years
Margaret-A

A BOLD VISION

A BOLD VISION
Women Leaders Imagining Canada's Future

Foreword by Dr. Roberta Bondar

Editorial selection by A Bold Vision Steering Committee

WOMEN'S LEADERSHIP CONFERENCE
A moment in time – 150 years in the making.

Women's Network Inc.
Charlottetown, Prince Edward Island, Canada

A Bold Vision: Women Leaders Imagining Canada's Future
Published by Women's Network Inc.
Charlottetown, Prince Edward Island, Canada
Editorial selections by A Bold Vision Steering Committee

ISBN 978-0-9695419-7-4 (paperback)
Printed in the United States of America

Library and Archives Canada Cataloguing in Publication

A bold vision : women leaders imagining Canada's future / foreword by
Dr. Roberta Bondar ; editorial selection by A Bold Vision Steering Committee.

Includes bibliographical references.
Issued in print and electronic formats.
Text in English; two essays in French.
ISBN 978-0-9695419-6-7 (bound).--ISBN 978-0-9695419-7-4 (pbk.).--
ISBN 978-0-9695419-8-1 (epub).--ISBN 978-0-9695419-9-8 (mobi)

1. Women--Canada--Social conditions--Forecasting. 2. Women--Canada--
Economic conditions--Forecasting. 3. Social prediction--Canada. 4. Economic
forecasting--Canada. I. PEI Women's Network, issuing body II. Bold Vision
Steering Committee, editor

HQ1453.B64 2014   305.420971   C2014-905429-7
                                            C2014-905430-0

CONTENTS

FOREWORD
The Bold Vision Project

It has been 150 years since the Charlottetown Conference set 23 men *sans femmes* on a course of action that would lead to a vision of what the country could be. Since then, we have witnessed vast changes in our physical and psychological selves. Exploration, exploitation, the good, the bad, the shameful, and the ongoing struggles move us by tectonic shift, eruption, landslide, drought, and flood. We become a people who try and fail, yet try again more wisely in light of the ethics and moral standards not just of today but prescient for the future. We are people of the present, learning from the past while trying to impact the future. Our country is not perfect; otherwise, we would not need a Bold Vision for the next 150 years.

In this anthology, thoughtful Canadian women reflect on what for them would be a vision that each could endorse. The visions are more than nebulous thoughts and whimsy, and the authors identify more than the irksome and more than frivolous fantasies. They tug at the very fabric of the definition of a Canadian. The theme is more than being bold enough to dream. We may not have it right yet, but the message is that we must try to do better. These visions share the value of hope.

With themes of gender equality, diversity, and justice expressed through poetry, story, and essay, the authors grant us a living, contemporary insight into what we were and what we still need to be. Economic, ecological, and social justice should be sustained values upon which we build our visions for the future. As our actions are shaped by our values, why would we not work towards recognizing and celebrating those things that we value most?

None of us claims to be clairvoyant, and there is no palm- or tea-leaf–reading here. The Bold Visions set forth in this book are based on education, experience, historical fact, insight, and the desire to make Canada truly strong and free. We owe it to ourselves and to the rest of the world. We should be an example within to be the reflection outside.

Roberta L Bondar

O.C. O.Ont. MD PhD FRCP FRCS ICD.D

INTRODUCTION

About the Project

This year, in 2014, Canada is celebrating the 150th anniversary of the Charlottetown Conference. This meeting, held in Charlottetown in September 1864, enabled 23 Fathers of Confederation to create a bold vision, form relationships, and begin conversations about what our country could be. It is remembered as an exciting step towards establishing a union of British North American colonies into a dominion known as Canada. It was the beginning of a three-year journey to Confederation in 1867, a year that saw a union of four colonies. It was an important historical moment in a process of nation-building that began long before 1864 and that continues to the present, as we negotiate the Canada of 2014 as a confederation of many nations, spread across ten provinces and three territories.

In the fall of 2012, PEI 2014 Inc. announced a community grant fund inviting groups to develop innovative projects to celebrate this momentous time in Canadian history. As a group of women's organizations, we wanted to celebrate the historic accomplishments of the Charlottetown Conference but acknowledge that in 1864 the voices and experiences of women, Aboriginal peoples, racialized people, people with disabilities, and many more groups were excluded from the formal discussions.

It is *our* bold vision that a diversity of women's voices is included in the ongoing discussions of nation-building that a country as young as Canada must have. So, in this context, we asked, what would a vision for Canada look like that includes the voices and experiences of women from across Canada?

Our project is ambitious: We've selected 23 women from more than 200 nominated by their peers from across the country. When she accepted her nomination, each nominee made an extraordinary commitment that, if selected as a visionary, she would set aside time to contribute to this anthology and be available for a three-day conference in Prince Edward Island. More than 200 said yes. The final selection process was intense, as we worked to ensure representation from all ten provinces and three territories and to ensure that, as a group, the 23 Bold Visionaries would stand in the starkest possible contrast with the 23 men who attended the Charlottetown Conference. The visionaries would include English-speaking and French-speaking Canadians, as did the Charlottetown Conference, but go beyond linguistic and cultural differences. Not men, but women. Not only settlers, but Aboriginal peoples. Not only political leaders, but leaders from many spheres. Not only white men, but people of colour. Not only men who own property, but people of a variety of incomes and backgrounds. The diversity of age, ability, sexual orientation, and family backgrounds and experiences represented among the visionaries is deliberate; in fact, it is the whole point. And what these diverse women envision individually and collectively is astounding.

Far more than 23 of the nominees have bold visions for Canada; 200 and more women leaders continue to stand ready to put forward their visions for the future and are actively making their visions count in their communities across the country. We hope the final list of visionaries pays tribute to the quality of nominees.

The 23 amazing women represented in this book have generously given their time and ideas to our project, each writing a vision for Canada's future, collected in this anthology. As part of the project, these 23 inspiring women of vision will also join others in a women's leadership conference and will join together for a collaborative vision session to be held at Province House, the Prince Edward Island legislature, the very building where the Fathers of Confederation met. At the end of their historic meetings, the public will have an opportunity to hear their shared and individual visions.

A Bold Vision is a unique opportunity to reflect on the changes that have happened for women in this country over the past 150 years, to celebrate the accomplishments of trailblazing women, and to imagine Canada's future.

The partner organizations involved in A Bold Vision include Women's

Network PEI, the PEI Coalition for Women in Government, the PEI Advisory Council on the Status of Women, the PEI Interministerial Women's Secretariat, and the PEI Business Women's Association. It is our hope that 150 years from now, not only will some of the visions presented by the women in this anthology have come to fruition, but that the Bold Vision conference will be recognized as another moment in history when diverse leaders met in Prince Edward Island, engaged in relationship-building, and discussed the future in committed, collaborative ways to create new pathways in the territory we presently call Canada.

....

About the Anthology

The visions in this anthology are, indeed, bold. They complicate historical and contemporary ideas of "Confederation" and "Canada"—and radically charge the ideas that are possible for our peoples sharing an unwritten future, where social and political change will unfold amid lands and seas facing uncertain ecological transformations. We are so proud to present these visions to you.

It is said that the Fathers of Confederation "builded better than they knew." So reads a plaque in the Confederation Chamber in Province House in Charlottetown. But, of course, the fathers also "builded" worse than they knew, enshrining institutions that in the name of the public good privileged the few, particularly the land-holding white male colonizers. Instruments of cultural genocide such as the Indian residential schools followed hard on the heels of Confederation. Confederation did not usher in universal suffrage: Women, Aboriginal peoples, and other groups had years of struggle to have a vote in the Canadian form of democracy—and many still struggle to have a voice and place.

For these reasons, the bold journey of vision in this anthology begins with an invitation to listen. Jessie Housty, of the Heiltsuk First Nation in British Columbia, reweaves the stories of beginnings and takes us to the roots of storytelling and sacred stories in a luminous, compassionate, and poetic call for radical listening: "To listen, and to speak. To our ancestors, to ourselves, to each other, to our children. To the children still to come." She is unflinching about the injustice we will hear together if we accept her challenge; but this is necessary, she says, to create "a country in which a shared narrative is possible."

Jessie Housty gently urges readers, "If this is uncomfortable to read, be patient, and make space for it," and this is a valuable guide for reading many of the bold visions in the anthology. For there is difference among these visions. And there is the pain of injustice. A clear, precise, and rigorous history lesson grounds the Gwich'in woman Crystal Fraser's vision, presenting her own traditional Aboriginal knowledge and what she is learning as a promising doctoral candidate in Canadian history. She asks the unsettling question, "How can Indigenous communities flourish and find solace in a 21st-century Canada that continues to openly oppress them through rhetoric, state policy, and the ongoing intergenerational effects of residential schools?" The solutions, including education that acknowledges injustice and dialogue about the ongoing effects of colonization, are urgently needed. A successful future together is not possible, she says, without the full, active, and engaged leadership of Indigenous individuals and communities.

In an interview for *A Bold Vision*, Member of Parliament for Churchill Niki Ashton brings her personal and political experience as a woman from Northern Manitoba to a bold vision focused on justice. Her broad view of justice in Canada encompasses social justice, economic justice, and ecological justice — themes that ring throughout the essays in this anthology. She also talks about the vital role of communities in creating her vision, where "people in their communities have a key role in deciding what is best for them" — another theme that recurs in many essays. Guided by her firm conviction that Canada can be a leading light for all forms of justice in the world, Niki Ashton puts forward a vision of gender equality founded on values of justice.

What happens — or doesn't happen — in Canada to promote gender equality is, indeed, a matter of global justice, and leading feminist human rights expert Shelagh Day of British Columbia recounts her "longing for an egalitarian state" in an essay that puts a fine point on the consequences of dominance and domination. Her woman-centred vision convincingly makes the case for immediate action to remedy growing income inequality, rampant gender inequality, and exploitation of natural resources. A true, egalitarian democracy, built with respect for founding relationships with Indigenous peoples and respect for the environment, can preserve Canada from social and environmental collapse, she argues. And yet, human rights are a tool of hopefulness. "Governments matter," she insists, and the tools and functions of governments, their budgets and speeches from the throne, communicate social values. When fresh thinking is needed, women and groups that have been excluded from the halls of power hold vast potential to renew democracy.

Questioning the values on which our democracy is built is the theme that Mina Mawani of Ontario takes up in her contribution to the anthology, providing a set of questions about our values to inspire self-reflection. "Our actions are shaped by our values," she says, so to move to a future beyond the "values that promoted hierarchy and inequality" in 1864, then our first action is to question our assumptions and disrupt our own privilege — and then to revalue the strengths and assets on which we can found a more inclusive and egalitarian future.

From halfway across the country and from the vantage point of an artist, Prince Edward Island visionary Becka Viau creatively takes up the challenge of unpacking privilege in an activist, artistic experiment: She practises radical revisioning and collaboration with a group of co-authors on her essay. With Helaina Lalande, Josie Baker, Merray Gerges, Diana Hosseini, Mireille Eagan, and Marie Fox, Becka Viau's contribution to the anthology celebrates the "unstable" identity of Canada, inviting readers to "acknowledge the complexity of a truly multi-peopled culture, look to the silenced, and listen for possibility."

A living part of what she calls "Jigsaw Canada," Eman Bare of Saskatchewan talks about her own experience as a puzzle piece, negotiating identity and representation as a young Muslim woman from a Somali family. The question "Where are you from?" dogs her, a daily reminder of "otherness" and a rejection of the future of equality that she envisions. Eman Bare eschews soothsaying about the future in favour of action, committing herself "to making my vision of Canada my life's work, my legacy and passion."

The personal is political for Kluane Adamek of the Kluane First Nation, Yukon Territory, as well. She outlines her vision for reconciliation and a path forward built from treaty relationships—founding agreements that long preceded Confederation talks. "This is our true, shared history," she says. Just as her understanding of her familial and cultural past informs her vision of the future, she sees *education* as the central tool to rebuild broken relationships. Despite the failures of the past, learning our shared history can lead to a future in which benefits from the land and its resources are justly shared.

Civics education is central to Nazanin Afshin-Jam MacKay's bold vision for a Canada where the institutions of democracy are not taken for granted. The Iranian-born international democracy activist envisions a Canada where young people are actively engaged voters, equally renewing civil society and government. Formal politics need young people, and, she argues, youth "*are* interested in politics generally, are active in alternative ways, and are eager to play a more active role." She proposes provocative, concrete projects to engage youth in Canada's political institutions.

No one in this anthology has demonstrated her love for Canada's political institutions more publicly and unmistakably than former Prime Minister, The Right Honourable Kim Campbell. She knows and understands Canadian democracy intimately as a politician who has held office at three levels of government and as a social scientist who has studied the challenges of democratic institutions. Her evident love for Canada leads her to a bold conclusion that gender parity is needed in Canada's parliaments, and that it is practically, concretely, and immediately possible. She clearly sets out the steps that she sees as most practicable.

Equally committed to greater gender equality in political institutions is

Maritime-raised Toronto business lawyer Libby Burnham, who has had a significant role supporting numerous of Canada's most successful women political leaders in their campaigns and their careers. Like so many of the visionaries in this book, she challenges the monolithic assumption that the "Fathers of Confederation" created Canadian democracy by retelling the stories of some of Canadian history's heroines for democratic change and women's political rights, drawing a dotted line between the challenges they faced a century ago and the challenges women face today.

Libby Burnham points out the highs and lows of women in political leadership across Canada; one of the few women who has lived the experience of territorial leadership is Eva Aariak, who served a term as Premier of Nunavut during a brief historical moment when six of thirteen provincial and territorial leaders were women. In a far-reaching interview, Eva Aariak offers a passionate voice for Nunavut and the North, with a vision that includes infrastructure and development alongside vibrant Inuit language and culture. Eva Aariak reflects on the incredible changes her culture and society have faced in the past decades — and the tremendous example of adaptability that the people of Nunavut can offer to the rest of Canada as they live at the vanguard of climate change.

Motivated by love for her grandchildren and their future descendants, scientist Dr. Catherine Potvin researches ways to mitigate climate change. In a series of intimate letters *en français* to her future descendants and their fellow citizens, she speaks painfully, joyously, and hopefully of the legacy of our era and her dreams for the future. Whether she is writing to them about the elimination of violence, about peace founded on tolerance and equality, about "*un français vivant, un français vibrant*," or about the philosophical and scientific roots of climate change, she does not waste a word of the opportunity to plead with her fellow citizens for the future she desires for her descendants and ours.

More young women in science, technology, engineering, and math careers is the focused goal of the determined, ambitious rocket scientist Natalie Panek of Ontario. In her rocket-powered essay, she energetically embodies what she espouses — as a visible role model for women in non-traditional STEM careers, as a willing mentor to young women, and as an advocate engaging media to represent more women doing exciting, out-of-this-world work in technology and engineering.

Spanning a long and successful career in science, Dr. Margaret-Ann Armour of Alberta has been living the non-traditional STEM career and promoting and supporting similar choices for other women. To her, science with a social conscience, science undertaken "as if people matter," requires the innovative thinking of women as well as men. Having seen the incredible power of community-driven science and collaborative research, she yearns for a future with "a strong societal recognition of the fundamental human need to belong to supportive, interacting communities where we are nurtured and fostered."

Communities as manifest in municipalities: Those are the cause of Mississauga's longest-serving mayor, Her Worship Hazel McCallion. In an interview for *A Bold Vision*, this non-stop nonagenarian calls for communities that meet the needs of the people, as she envisions reforms to governance that ensure local government, the government closest to the people, can thrive into the future.

Mayor McCallion's experience is with cities. Guided by similar principles of people-centred development, Irene d'Entremont of Nova Scotia, a community-minded Acadian businesswoman, argues the place of rural communities. Through a lived history, rural communities provide a deep connection to resource-based industries on land and sea, but rural Canadian communities are changing — and must change more, if they are to survive. According to Irene d'Entremont, rural Canada's challenge will be to demonstrate to the rest of the country how to "become a more culturally diverse and tolerant society while maintaining the core values, freedoms, and institutions that make us uniquely Canadian."

Examining similar challenges of change and inclusion, union leader

Lana Payne of Newfoundland and Labrador has a vision for a "progressive Canada," with progressive and egalitarian values clear to the world outside our doors and transparent in policies covering everything from how we share and distribute income, to how we develop resources, promote equality and equity in our society, and create democratic systems and institutions "that act as an equalizing force."

Writing her vision of unity and solidarity *en français* and from the perspective of her Quebec community, Member of Parliament for Ahuntsic Maria Mourani asks Canadians to *se lancer un défi*, take on a challenge, "*d'être un peuple de sœurs et de frères*," where Canada is a leader in human rights, in support for the least fortunate, and in sustainable development.

Member of Parliament for Toronto-St. Paul's and family doctor Carolyn Bennett has come to understand "going forward in a 'good way'" as learning to incorporate the knowledge and wisdom refined by Indigenous people over millennia living in and loving this territory—and after decades of their learning to survive and resist colonization and assimilation. Expanding the story of "two founding nations" to include the First Nations, Inuit, and Métis foundations of the country must, she argues, come first for the country to learn and grow in good health.

The principles Dr. Carolyn Bennett has come to learn from an outsider's perspective are part of Mi'kmaw lawyer Dr. Pamela Palmater's very identity; what she knows is what Dr. Bennett implores readers to learn. Exploring the history and the future of the treaty relationship between Indigenous peoples and settlers, Pamela Palmater argues for action and commitment on promises that have never been superseded or retracted—even if they have been repeatedly and unjustly broken. Despite broken promises, she astoundingly continues to extend an offer of peace and friendship, because, she says, "Addressing outstanding land and treaty rights would benefit Canadians and Indigenous peoples alike. We all win if justice is restored in Canada."

Singing out the rhythm of justice and her great hope for social change, Halifax Poet Laureate El Jones sees a future where resilience is valued, resistance is celebrated, and reconciliations and second chances are the norm. Her vision for Canada is for a place that builds bridges among people of all races, cultures, and economic situations, and where the future is full of hope not just for the privileged few but for those who struggle, those who are incarcerated, and those who today face staggering inequality.

Finally, Bonnie Brayton of Montreal takes readers 150 years into a brilliant future to look back on today's challenges. With hopefulness and imagination, she envisions the Bold Vision conference of 2014 as a turning point for social change and social justice, the beginning of a collaborative and inclusive movement that leads to the transformation of Canada into a more just and equal society where the social determinants of health provide a framework for ensuring that all people's needs are met.

Bonnie Brayton's vision is not speculative fiction, but we can borrow a famous phrase from sci-fi and conclude of her vision, and of all the visions in this anthology, "Make it so." Together, collaboratively, let us aim to make women's bold visions come true.

A BOLD VISION

JESSIE HOUSTY

Jessie Housty is an Indigenous community leader from the Heiltsuk First Nation in Bella Bella, British Columbia.

She received her BA in English from the University of Victoria and is currently pursuing her MA in English at the same institution.

Her work is based in the heart of the Great Bear Rainforest and focuses on capacity-building for social and environmental justice; land and marine stewardship; Indigenous governance; and leadership and collaboration. She is an elected member of Heiltsuk Tribal Council with portfolios related to stewardship and governance. She also works as the Communications Director for *Qqs* (Eyes) Projects Society, an Indigenous-driven non-profit with an open mandate related to Indigenous community development and intergenerational models for learning and leadership.

Her independent community organizing focuses on topics such as food security, energy issues, deforestation, sovereignty and self-determination, trophy hunting, and anti-oppression work.

She has worked as a teacher, facilitator, coach, and collaborator to help Indigenous and non-Indigenous individuals and organizations develop authentic, values-driven approaches to joint work. Her own work is rooted in the principle that sustained social change requires cultural shifts, meaningful collaboration, and a commitment to community-building.

Jessie Housty is a published poet, a contributor to numerous works of environmental literature, and a writer in *The Tyee*'s national pool. She was a finalist for the 2010 Ecotrust Indigenous Leadership Award, and an inaugural recipient of the University of Victoria Provost's Advocacy and Activism Award in 2013. Jessie Housty's motivation for change is rooted in both the past and the future — living by the principles and customs that are the legacy of her ancestors and honouring the generations to come by fighting to make this a world where they can flourish.

Jessie lives in Bella Bella, British Columbia, with five generations of family surrounding her.

RECONCILIATION AND RADICAL STORYTELLING:

A Vision for Transformation in Canada

"Storytelling makes grieving and healing a responsibility that is shared with everyone who hears the story. The process requires trust. It requires that we all be tender and brave, and above all, gentle with one another. It requires that we honour one another and make space for what is so generously given, even (and especially) if the thing that is shared is pain."

Beginnings

The First-Generation stories of the Indigenous peoples across Canada have many common narrative threads. Among them, we consistently see the figures of "Creator," "mother," and "trickster." Givers of life force. Women who give birth to Nations. Wise and wily figures whose magic brings us light and knowledge. While remaining clear that this continent has hundreds of distinct peoples, it is still arguably simpler for us to find those common narrative threads among ourselves than to find them in the predominant colonial culture whose "First-Generation" stories instead privilege and are constructed around archetypal characters who are conquerors and heroes. The figures central to the plot of Canada's colonial narratives are portrayed as righteous and mighty. From the very first, they are "discoverers" and "civilizers"— roles that imply an absence or deficiency of stories extant in this geography at the time of European contact.

One story meets another. One storyteller meets another. And from the time of contact to the modern day, we see a natural but destructive impulse at play: Indigenous and Settler people have simply been characters and plot devices in one another's stories. We have catalogued one another in our systems of knowledge and narrative. But we have not yet learned the act of telling stories together.

The Starkness and Silence of Winter

As an Indigenous woman in Canada who lives in service of her people and her communities, I know at the root of my heart that the issues we face are abundant and real. They are embedded in the legal, institutional, and policy framework of this country. They relate to the social and economic situations of Indigenous peoples; the space for Indigenous peoples to participate in society; the integrity of treaty and other claims processes. They are tied to health, education, justice, stewardship, and self-government. They are issues of principal human rights.

At one time, this continent was criss-crossed by the traplines and moccasin trails of many sovereign peoples. They had their own languages and govern-ments, their own relationships to place and one another, and a scale of time that measured progress and change in generations — in millennia. From the time of contact, that timescale has rapidly shifted. Physical violence — wheth-er in the form of warfare or waves of disease — caused deaths in such stag-gering numbers that the ceremonies of burial and mourning could no longer be adequately practised by those left behind. Since then, the narratives and policies of erasure in this country have subjugated the stories and histories of the Indigenous people whose collective knowledge, passed generation to gen-eration, itself represents the fullest and longest story to come from this land.

One of my elders has teaching tools she has developed to help Settlers work-ing in our territory to understand the values, stories, and history of my peo-ple — the Heiltsuk people, whose territory stretches through that threshold space where the mainland of central British Columbia scatters into islands that seed the Pacific's edge. One of her tools is an image. It represents the con-tinuum of Heiltsuk history to the present day, and it marks known incidents of great importance: Creation, the founding of the first villages, the Great Flood. There is also a marker that denotes European contact; it is situated so close to the end of that long continuum that it seems a tiny speck.

This is the Heiltsuk worldview. We have tens of thousands of years of history as a people, and only a couple of recent centuries are shared with Settler peoples. In the stories our elders pass down to us, there was a point in pre-contact history when our Heiltsuk people were as numerous as the trees. Certainly, there were tens of thousands of us stretched across the span of our territory. After contact, and after waves of disease that nearly exterminated us, there were fewer than 200. But we are still here.

Today, Indigenous people make up a little over four per cent of Canada's population, and we are the fastest-growing segment. The demographics are dry but informative: There are 617 bands, around 50 cultural groups, and around 1,000 centralized Indigenous communities in this country (with many Indigenous individuals also residing in cities and towns where they represent a minority). But beyond the demographics, what is perhaps more compelling and powerful is the fact of the social and cultural fabric of our lives within Canadian society.

If this is uncomfortable to read, be patient, and make space for it:

This country has seen episodes and alarming patterns of unjust and devastating human rights violations against Indigenous peoples from the time of Settler contact. The Indian Act, a statute originating in the 19th century, is still used as a tool in attempts to control many aspects of our governance and identity, and with only minimal reforms since its first articulation. My parents' generation still remembers the Potlatch Ban, a period stretching into recent history when expressions of culture and ceremony were made illegal. My grandparents' generation still remembers the Indian Agents who controlled whether our people were allowed to leave the reserve. Policies were enacted that stripped people of their Indigenous identity and membership before they were permitted to participate in institutions such as the military or the academy. A history of Settler-Indigenous relations recounts exclusions of our people from voting or jury duty, blocked access to lawyers and legal remedies for land-related grievances, and the imposition of colonial governance structures intended to supersede our own millennia-old institutions of governance. Some of these practices are ended, yes. But together, the patterns and episodes add up to an attempt at erasure, and this is a reality we must confront.

If you're about to tell me "It's in the past," if you're about to say "Let it go, move on," you're not the first. But what you need to know is that I am the sum of all the stories that brought my people, my great-grandmother, my grandmother, my mother, to the point at which I entered the world. My stories, whether collective or individual, are my identity. And many of those stories are more current than you might think. If you're uncomfortable right now, ask yourself why it's so important that this narrative of racism and oppression be rooted in the distant past. Don't worry—this conversation is a safe space. It's easy to insist that these narratives have ended, because then we don't have to confront the fact that the effect of those narratives is still felt today — and that many of them are, in fact, still unfolding.

There is a dark century in that history of Settler-Indigenous relations. The residential school era. Indigenous children were forcibly removed from their homes, families, and communities with the explicit intent of "killing the Indian in the child." Hear the story: These children were whipped for speaking their mother tongue. Hear the story: These children were stripped of their names. Hear the story: These children felt their bonds with family and community and culture deliberately and systematically beaten out of them. I don't need to hyperbolize. The survivors have been generous with their painful stories. We all need to hear them and make space for that pain.

Thousands of Indigenous children did not withstand this assault on their bodies and their identity. Many are buried in unidentified graves. Those who did survive bore the ugly scars of physical, sexual, and emotional abuse. They grew up estranged from their people, their language, their culture, and their identity. During the "sixties scoop," Indigenous youth were again removed and fostered out into non-Indigenous homes in Canada and abroad, prolonging the legacy of broken bonds and lost children. You might push this legacy away, say it's a distant past that just has a long shadow. But hear the story: I am twenty-seven years old, and in my family, I am part of the very first generation in which no child was forcibly removed.

For some people, these are historical and academic issues. For me, they are the context in which I've grown up, the story I've inherited to carry on behalf of those who came before me. I'm not describing the darkness to instill a sense of guilt. I'm giving you a window into my lived reality. I'm showing you the darkness in the hope that we can illuminate it, together. Not erase it, but open up a crack through which a beam of light might enter. This is a trailhead on the path to reconciliation. For me, these issues are a narrative not just of Indigenous peoples — but a narrative of Canada — and in my work, it is imperative that we agree to speak the truth, to know that the truth must be spoken.

If we are going to undertake work here together, we must begin by acknowledging a set of facts that is not simply academic, but vital, visceral, and still intimately tied to the policies and frameworks that guide Settler-Indigenous relations in this country today. Yes, hear the story: today.

The Song Inside the Bird Inside the Egg

There is a custom amongst my people that carries great meaning for me. It goes like this: Stories are ceremony, and ceremony is power, and power can heal. When there is a wound, whether it is physical or spiritual or any other kind, the path to healing is in the cleansing act of storytelling. Our "washing ceremonies" ritualize storytelling to create a process for grieving, for loss, for pain, and then for healing. But the healing is not possible without first establishing truth—without first telling the story. Storytelling makes grieving and healing a responsibility that is shared with everyone who hears the story. The process requires trust. It requires that we all be tender and brave, and above all, gentle with one another. It requires that we honour one another and make space for what is so generously given, even (and especially) if the thing that is shared is pain. It breaks down the false dichotomy that separates "storyteller" from "audience." Once the story is told, everyone who hears it has a responsibility to help carry it. This is the space where healing is made possible.

Storytelling is both the most powerful and the most radical act we can commit. Ask yourself what stories and histories and narratives in this country have been subjugated through time, are being subjugated now. Then ask yourself why. Acknowledge that it is time for us to come to a critical consciousness. It is time for us to be unafraid of stories. The interruption of healing narratives is a threat to our wellness. It's a threat to our wholeness. We must tell stories readily. To be radical in our healing power, to be radical in our intervention, we need to tell the stories and impart to those who listen their new responsibility to help bear the pain and the healing and the power of the telling. If you're asking yourself which stories are the important ones, it's all of them. Every story we share. Every story that is part of our identity.

And sharing them is a ritual that uplifts us as storytellers. It is a ritual that uplifts the cultures, the places, and the junctures where stories are born. It is the most radical and, frankly, the only act we can still undertake that yet has power. To listen, and to speak. To our ancestors, to ourselves, to each other, to our children. To the children still to come.

The physical space of Canada as a country is already defined. But the geography of Canada's stories is not fully mapped, and the maps will never be static. Because stories are ways of being, of knowing, and of relating. They converge, and the points of convergence are powerful. They diverge, and the points of divergence are powerful. We must learn to tell stories without the impulse to erase or supersede the stories that came before. We must learn to tell stories without the impulse to possess the stories of others. In the Canada I envision, there are no olive branches; rather, there are people who say to one another, "Let me tell you a story," and trust in their own truth, trust that their stories will be honoured and reciprocated.

The predominant archetypes in Settler and Indigenous storytelling traditions may differ, but there is an element in common: a magical story-space in which transformation is possible.

Transitions

I envision a Canada in which stories are sacred. I envision a Canada in which storytellers have the courage for their stories—and for their act of storytelling—to be radical. To be radical for as long as is necessary, until, as a culture, we recognize that stories are all that we are. The institutions of this country are not ready to make social change. They are not even designed or permitted to make social change. It will come from the people, and it will come from the community we create around the stories we share with one another. The telling of stories is the practice of freedom. The telling of stories is the practice of truth. The telling of stories is not a practice that is emergent. It is resurgent. And until the change is made, it is insurgent. Tell stories anyway. It is time to be unafraid.

What is boldness? It is conviction. It is commitment. As a young Indigenous woman and leader, I commit to two things: To knowing the stories of my people, and to carrying them with me in anticipation of the day my daughters are born. Some of those stories are cultural, and they trickle back through time to the First Generation, to the moment of Creation. Others of those stories are more recent, and narrate the violence and oppression that is a part of my identity and the legacy I've inherited. The collective stories I hand down to my daughters will be unified by a narrative thread of *hope*; that is my intention, and that is my gift to them. I commit to holding those stories, and to sharing them, to knowing their truth. And I commit to being hopeful in my storytelling.

To my Indigenous sisters and brothers, I have this to say: Know your stories, and hold them, and share them, because through the generations of violence and oppression *we are still here*. We are resilient. We have stories that belong to us, and to which we, in turn, belong.

To my Settler sisters and brothers: Sit with the truth, even when it hurts. Sit with the truth, even when you want to harden a shell, to protest, to defend yourself. Sit with the truth of the possibility that you benefit from the subjugation of Indigenous peoples and their stories. Commit to being solidary. Commit to participating in change.

To everyone, regardless of the origin of your stories: Consider this an invitation to build a story-house with me. My stories are mine; you can learn them, but they are my identity. Your stories are yours; I can learn them, but they are your identity. There is a common space we can occupy together, though. There is a story of Settler-Indigenous relations in Canada that is young; it is just beginning to unfold. Be a voice in the telling of that story. And in that singular, radical act, commit to the truth and the power of stories, and know that stories are all that we are.

Stories narrate our past. They shape our present. And the telling of stories is a fundamental act in determining our future. If there is conflict to come, let it begin with truth. If there is healing to come, let it begin with truth. Stories represent a dynamic space in which hope and transformation are possible. If the telling of truth is radical, so be it. If the telling of stories is radical, so be it. The *act* of the telling and the *possibility* of the telling create a space in which we can boldly envision a country beyond Settler-Indigenous relations — a country in which a shared narrative is possible. Not a shared story rooted in erasure, but one that begins with radical acceptance — with a moment of convergence.

CRYSTAL FRASER

Crystal Fraser is a Gwich'in woman and a PhD candidate in history at the University of Alberta. She was raised in Inuvik and at her family's fish camp on the Mackenzie River at Tree River. Her PhD research examines the history of education in the Northwest Territories during the 20th century from an Indigenous perspective, seeking to bring local Indigenous voices to the centre of Canadian historical scholarship.

A Gwich'in elder gave Crystal Fraser the Gwich'in name *"T'aih,"* which means "strength." Crystal has overcome many challenges during her lifetime, such as coming from a family that is embedded in the legacy of residential schools, leaving home at a young age, experiencing trauma as a teenager, and leaving high school in Grade 10. Despite this, Crystal has remained committed to her visions for the future by obtaining her high school diploma at the age of 23 and moving to various provinces in pursuit of post-secondary education.

Crystal Fraser brings passion to Indigenous issues and seeks social justice for marginalized populations in

Canada. By applying her expertise in historical theories about colonialism, racial constructions, and gender issues, she brings bold new perspectives on contemporary issues with rigour and criticism, as evidenced by her contributions to conversations about missing and murdered Aboriginal women, Idle No More, and environmental concerns. Engaging in debates in local, national, and international contexts, Crystal Fraser's insights have successfully reached a wide audience. She has the unique ability to bridge the gap between the local and the academic, fostering new and meaningful conversations about Indigenous rights, social policy, and local political landscapes.

Crystal Fraser is currently living in the Edmonton area while completing her PhD. She returns to the Northwest Territories several times a year to spend time on the land, engage in cultural activities, and strengthen local and familial connections.

SRUGOONCH'UU HAH TRO'OONJII:

Visions of Social Equality and Respect in Canada's Future

"*How can lasting and meaningful change be implemented in Canadian society? How can settler Canadians engage in nuanced conversations about Indigenous peoples when the intergenerational effects of colonialism continue to emerge and reinforce stereotypical images of Indigenous communities? How can Indigenous communities flourish and find solace in a 21st-century Canada that continues to openly oppress them through rhetoric, state policy, and the ongoing intergenerational effects of residential schools?*"

Fish camp teaches many lessons. My own family's fish camp is along the Nagwichoonjik (Mackenzie River), on traditional Gwich'in and Treaty 11 territory. Fish camp serves as a highly charged space for contemplating philosophical queries, engaging in cultural reproduction through fishing, actively protesting the historical removal of Indigenous peoples' land by simply being on the land, and learning about healthy relationships with neighbours (human or otherwise). Chief among these lessons that I have learned from my Gwich'in family is the notion of acceptance, but not simply acceptance: *srugoonch'uu hah tro'oonju* is the ability to embrace acceptance with happiness. I contend that by embracing the concept of *srugoonch'uu hah tro'oonju*, we, as Canadians, will obtain a more balanced society in the aim of achieving social equality and respect for all cultures.

In December 2012, a woman of the Nishnawbe Aski Nation and Thunder Bay community was walking to a local grocery store. Two Caucasian men approached her, forced her into their vehicle, and took her to a remote location where they sexually assaulted, strangled, and beat her while using racial slurs, telling her "You Indians deserve to lose your treaty rights."[1] The assault occurred at a highly politicized time in Canada. Just one month earlier, the grassroots movement Idle No More kicked off on the Canadian Plains responding to the ideological nature of Bill C-45, an omnibus bill that sought to alter environmental legislation in Canada, among other things. In the thick of peaceful and nationwide Idle No More demonstrations, Chief Theresa Spence initiated a hunger strike with the goal of meeting with Prime Minister Stephen Harper to improve the housing crisis on the Attawapiskat reserve in Ontario.

Idle No More provided new opportunities for Canadians to debate a wide variety of issues relating to colonialism, Indigenous dispossession, and the responsibility of settler Canadians. But the assault of the Thunder Bay woman — at once horrific and frighteningly common — indicates that despite a pan-Canadian rhetoric of tolerance and multiculturalism, the larger socio-political context of Canadian-Indigenous relations is deeply embedded in notions of racism, patriarchy, and social inequality.[2] My vision for Canada over the next 150 years is to educate Canadians, encourage critical dialogue, and foster new understandings of equality for Canada's Indigenous peoples, especially for Indigenous women. In doing so, I want to discuss three points to foster new dialogue between Canadians, academics, politicians, and leaders.

Indigenous peoples have maintained a strong presence on Turtle Island (North America) since time immemorial. Indigenous men and women were keepers of the land, savvy politicians and negotiators, and the producers of knowledge and practices. With the arrival of European newcomers, people entered into new relationships and agreements. Indigenous peoples were invaluable to the success and well-being of early missionaries, fur traders, and settlers, providing them with information about the land, navigational routes, and food stores. A number of factors, however, changed relationships between early settler populations and Indigenous communities. The outcome of the War of 1812 meant that Indigenous peoples were no longer desired as military allies. The formation of the Canadian nation-state led to the implementation of draconian colonial policies, such as the Indian Act of 1876. The perceived threats of the Frog Lake Massacre and Riel Rebellion, both in 1885, resulted in public executions of Indigenous people and served to fuel rhetoric based on stereotypical fears about "savage Indians." The dwindling supply of bison on the Plains, the expansion of agricultural settlement, and the establishment of poorly serviced reserves led to the imminent threat of starvation and disease among many Indigenous communities in northwestern Canada during the late 19th and early 20th centuries. There are many other developments of the same era that significantly impacted the role of Indigenous peoples in Canada: residential schools, the Pass System on the western Canadian Plains, the criminalization of Indigenous cultural expressions (such as sundances and potlatches), the implementation of new economic structures (namely capitalism), and the policy of Enfranchisement through which "Indians" lost their status and were forced to move off-reserve and away from their communities. Through these policies, and others, the Canadian and provincial governments sought to almost completely dispossess and further debilitate vulnerable communities.

Although Indigenous women were and are often less visible than their male counterparts in the telling of these events, they are undoubtedly present and active in all aspects of life, both in the past and present. A large body of literature examines the histories of Indigenous peoples. Academic researchers investigated the histories of Indigenous women in terms of "pre" and "post" contact, theories of social and progressive evolution, and the plight of Indigenous women in their own communities. As historians Mary-Ellen Kelm and Lorna Townsend note, many Indigenous women found these research agendas "unsatisfying and homogenizing." Scholars went on to question how "official" historical records effectively silence Indigenous voices and are instead embracing oral histories while probing imperial and colonial settings as gendered phenomena. Kelm and Townsend write that "good women's history will change the way we see society, will illuminate the relations of power, [and] will challenge our assumptions about 'how things are.'"[3]

A critical part of A Bold Vision is to question hegemonic ideals of "how things are" by challenging existing narratives about Indigenous women, perceptions of what it means to be Canadian, and what the fabric of our nation might look like over the course of the next century. Understanding how Indigenous women have been historically constructed and pointing to the ways in which Indigenous women in Canada are currently leading our country into new conversations about Indigeneity and colonialism will starkly demonstrate how the nation-state and larger settler Canadian populations seek to further silence Indigenous peoples. We need to move beyond these marginalizing narratives.

Historians such as Sarah Carter and Adele Perry show how negative images of Indigenous women became intrinsically embedded in the consciousness of settler Canadians as early as the nineteenth century.[4] Since then, the bodies of Indigenous women have been overtly sexualized, criminalized, and served as objects of polarized rhetoric about Indigenous people. Other historians, such as Joan Sangster and Robin Brownlie, demonstrate that state policies, often executed by Indian Agents, were used to marginalize Indigenous peoples, especially women, in the twentieth century.[5] For instance, Indigenous women lost their Indian Status, as regulated by the federal legislation of the Indian Act, when they married non-Indigenous men. Ironically, white women gained Indian Status by marrying Indigenous men. In 1985, the federal government passed Bill C-31, allowing women to retain their Indian Status regardless of whom they marry. Despite this, there continues to be gender inequality in the Indian Act.

Through times of epidemic, residential schools, political oppression, and cultural alienation, Indigenous women have remained steadfast in their efforts to protect their families, communities, culture, and beliefs. The era of the mid-20th century spurred a change in Canadian politics. During the post-war decades, Indigenous people secured the right to vote in Canada and the Civil Rights Movement fuelled new questions about equality and freedom. The White Paper of 1969 politicized Indigenous people in new ways and Canadians witnessed the rise of Indigenous political groups seeking meaningful and lasting social, political, and economic change. Canadians, in more recent decades, have witnessed the furthering of Indigenous issues through the debates over *Calder v. British Columbia* (1971), the failed Meech Lake Accord (1990), and the events that transpired near the Town of Oka and the Mohawk community of Kanesatake (commonly referred to as "the Oka Crisis" of 1990).

Although there have been important self-determination and sovereignty milestones for Indigenous peoples since the 1960s, the marginalization of Indigenous women continues. In May 2014, The Royal Canadian Mounted Police released a report confirming the documented cases of nearly 1,200 missing or murdered Indigenous women in Canada between the years of 1980 and 2012. From British Columbia's Highway of Tears, to the highly publicized 1990s Vancouver murders, to the unsympathetic streets of Saskatoon that Christine Welsh shows in her film *Finding Dawn*, Indigenous women in Canada continue to be victims of colonization, racism, and patriarchy. Successive Canadian governments, both Liberal and Conservative, have failed to prioritize this important issue. The current Canadian government continues to reject the idea of a national inquiry for missing and murdered Indigenous women and has worsened the situation by ceasing funding for projects and programs designed to support women in national and international contexts. In doing so, it continues to demonstrate the patriarchal and oppressive nature of the Canadian state.

How can lasting and meaningful change be implemented in Canadian society? How can settler Canadians engage in nuanced conversations about Indigenous peoples when the intergenerational effects of colonialism continue to emerge and reinforce stereotypical images of Indigenous communities? How can Indigenous communities flourish and find solace in a 21st-century Canada that continues to openly oppress them through rhetoric, state policy, and the ongoing intergenerational effects of residential schools?

First, the multiple and varied histories of Indigenous peoples must be taught both in school and to the public. As Canadians, it is our responsibility to make an attempt to understand our nation's past. Currently, primary and secondary school teachers are recognizing this need by implementing new curricula that include Indigenous histories, the history of the nation-state, and the impact of residential schools on both Indigenous and settler Canadian populations. For example, new curricula were implemented in the Northwest Territories in 2011 focusing on the history of residential schools. While there are questions surrounding who should teach this material and what kinds of historical debates should be shared with children, changes are being made, though at a relatively slow rate. By understanding our colonial history of oppression, Canadians will be better equipped to comprehend how issues like residential schools and forced Indigenous relocation are directly linked to current day social developments and the status of Indigenous women in Canada.

Second, although some people argue that colonialism and oppressive state policies are elements of the past, there is an urgent need for settler Canadians to recognize that their histories are present in the continued dispossession and marginalization of Indigenous peoples. Without provoking guilt or ascribing personal blame, historian Paige Raibmon asserts that settler Canadians should seek to understand how their lives are embedded in colonial narratives and achieve a deepened understanding of their current responsibilities in the effort to subvert the mundane practices of colonialism.[6] Some Canadians are contributing to new understandings of what it means to be settler Canadian on "Indian land." Recently, the City of Vancouver formally acknowledged that it rests on the unceded territories of the Musqueam, Squamish, and Tsleil-Waututh Nations. Indigenous peoples themselves are also contributing to these exciting new conversations. Canada is witnessing a generation of youth who are highly politicized and immersed in many of the current debates of what it means to be Indigenous and what it means to be Canadian. In late 2013, a Saskatchewan Cree student wore a hoodie to her local school that read: "Got land? Thank an Indian."[7] This statement sparked spirited debates about land ownership and treaty rights across Canada. A key part of making Indigenous peoples equal players, once again, in Canadian society includes encouraging youth, women, and other marginalized groups of people to spark conversations and engage in meaningful dialogue, controversial or otherwise.

Third, and finally, Canadians must build political momentum and insist that the federal government take Indigenous politicians, political bodies, and socio-political movements, such as Idle No More, seriously. In December 2012, as tens of thousands of people engaged in peaceful protest at public events, and more quietly in their homes, online, and on the land, Prime Minister Harper and his government addressed the nation through silence and disregard. His and their silence erodes the very fabric of a supposedly democratic nation. Meanwhile, the Conservative government continues to demonstrate a blatant disregard for Treaty agreements, inherent land rights, Indigenous-environmental concerns, and the socio-economic status of Indigenous people. But there are other concerns too, such as the vexed and uncertain course of events initiated by the Truth and Reconciliation Commission as demonstrated by the question of what to do with confidential personal testimonies, the question of whether financial compensation has actually helped survivors, and the question of how to engage in further healing practices once the Commission comes to an end in 2015.

There are many unresolved land issues initiated by First Peoples nationwide. Calls for an inquiry into missing and murdered Indigenous women continue to be unheeded. Further, while a growing number of Indigenous people, and especially women, pursue post-secondary education, we continue to represent a very small minority of graduates. The fields of academia, healthcare, policy studies, law, politics, and social work (to name a few) are in desperate need of an influx of Indigenous academics and content. And support is needed for these endeavours at local, provincial/territorial, and national levels. Until Indigenous people have our own people working on our behalf, identifying our own goals, and utilizing our own practices and methodologies, few benefits will be gained. As the fate of Bill C-33, the proposed First Nations Education Act demonstrates, in-depth and wide understandings of Indigenous debates are necessary.

The assault on one Nishnawbe Aski Nation woman in Thunder Bay in December 2012 is not unique. The safety and flourishing of Indigenous women and Indigenous peoples is an onerous task. We must tackle the ongoing effects of colonization and patriarchy in a society that was built on racial discourses, social inequalities, and oppression. By engaging with Indigenous peoples themselves through critical dialogue and a heightened awareness of historical and contemporary colonial developments, perhaps Canadians can achieve *srugoonch'uu hah tro'oonju* — a happy acceptance of not only Indigenous people, but of *all* Canadians. It is my vision that Canadians, in the next 150 years, will make an effort to learn about our nation's past, embrace expressions of cultural respect, and engage in conversations that contribute to the resilience of Indigenous communities and Canada's First Peoples. Although not all Canadians will be familiar with "fish camp," I am optimistic that they are capable of understanding the fundamental essence of *srugoonch'uu hah tro'oonju*.

---

1. Tanya Kappo, "Hate Crime Against First Nations Woman in Thunder Bay: Family Urges Idle No More Movement to Remain Peaceful," December 30, 2012, accessed July 2014, http://www.media.knet.ca.

2. Indigenous women are 3.5 times more likely to experience violence than non-Indigenous women. Native Women's Association of Canada, "Fact Sheet: Violence Against Aboriginal Women" (Ottawa, 2010).

3. Mary-Ellen Kelm and Lorna Townsend, eds. *In the Days of Our Grandmothers* (Toronto: University of Toronto Press, 2006), 5, 7–8.

4. Sarah Carter, "Categories and Terrains of Exclusion: Constructing the 'Indian Woman' in the Early Settlement Era," in *In the Days of Our Grandmothers*; Adele Perry, *On the Edge of Empire: Gender, Race, and the Making of British Columbia, 1849–1871* (Toronto: University of Toronto Press, 2001).

5. Joan Sangster, "Domesticating Girls: The Sexual Regulation of Aboriginal and Working-Class Girls in Twentieth-Century Canada," in *Contact Zones: Aboriginal and Settler Women in Canada's Colonial Past*, ed. Myra Rutherdale and Katie Pickles, (Vancouver: UBC Press, 2005); Robin Brownlie, "Intimate Surveillance: Indian Affairs, Colonization, and the Regulation of Aboriginal Women's Sexuality," in *Contact Zones*.

6. Paige Raibmon, "Unmaking Native Space: A Genealogy of Indian Policy, Settler Practice, and the Micro Techniques of Dispossession," in *The Power of Promises: Rethinking Indian Treaties in the Pacific Northwest*, ed. Alexandra Harmon (Seattle: University of Washington Press, 2008), 57, 77.

7. Joana Draghici, "First Nation Teen Told Not to Wear 'Got Land?' Shirt at School," January 14, 2014, accessed July 2014, http://www.cbc/news/canada.ca.

NIKI ASHTON

Niki Ashton is the Member of Parliament for the riding of Churchill, Manitoba. She was first elected in 2008 and re-elected in 2011. At 26 years old, Ashton was the second-youngest woman ever to be elected at the time.

Niki Ashton was born and raised in Thompson, Manitoba. She holds a BA in Global Political Economy (University of Manitoba) and a MA in International Affairs (Carleton University). She is completing her PhD in Peace and Conflict Studies at the Arthur V. Mauro Centre for Peace and Justice at the University of Manitoba.

Niki Ashton has always been passionate about human rights and social justice. As the daughter of immigrants, she has believed in Canada's ability to be a model of diversity and equality. Active in her community, she has worked with others to eradicate racism, sexism, and homophobia. As a college instructor and researcher with the University College of the North, she brought into her classroom the teachings of shared progress and inclusion. In her work and time abroad, Niki Ashton has pursued avenues for justice at the global level.

As MP for Churchill, Niki Ashton has been a strong voice for social justice in Parliament. She has spoken out on poverty and has called for action to end the third-world conditions facing Northern and Aboriginal people. She has also been a leading voice in fighting for value-added jobs, sustainable economic development, and building an economy that empowers Northerners, women, and all Canadians.

Niki Ashton currently serves as the Status of Women Critic in Canada's Official Opposition. As Status of Women Critic she has focused on the call for a National Inquiry into Missing and Murdered Indigenous Women, a need for a National Action Plan to end violence against women, and the importance of supporting reproductive justice.

Niki Ashton lives with her partner Ryan in Thompson, Manitoba.

A VISION FOR JUSTICE:

A Conversation with Niki Ashton

"In 150 years, Canada will be a model of diversity, for the way we pursue justice, and the way we will have achieved equality."

In early June 2014, Niki Ashton spoke about her bold vision for Canada with Dawn Wilson, Executive Director of the Prince Edward Island Coalition for Women in Government and Bold Vision steering committee member. Dawn reached Niki Ashton at her office on Parliament Hill in Ottawa to ask the MP about what she envisions for the next 150 years of Canada's future, the origins of her vision, and how it connects to her current work as a Member of Parliament.

....

DW: What are your hopes and dreams for what you hope Canada will be, going forward into the future?

NA: I believe Canada can be a model for the world. We can be a model of diversity.

A country that out of an often racist past has built a nation-to-nation relationship with Indigenous peoples and people from all over the world.

A model of gender equality.

A pioneer of full equality for all citizens, regardless of sexual orientation.

A leader in socio-economic equality and the elimination of poverty.

The key element is *justice*. As a woman in politics, I have seen first-hand how critical it is to fight for justice for the people I represent and for all Canadians.

There are various aspects to the justice that we seek and that will be key to our future.

We need *economic justice*, making sure people are respected for the work that they do and the diversity of talent that they contribute to our economy. This includes the right to collective bargaining and the right to control our destiny economically.

Ecological justice will be critical. We need to change course and ensure our environmental well-being is sustainable. This will start with Canada taking a lead role in tackling climate change, and this is particularly important to Canada's North.

Also, *social justice* will be important. We will need to ensure, for example, that we live in communities and in a country which seeks to eliminate sexism, homophobia, racism, transphobia, and ableism, so that our diversity is fully celebrated.

I believe these are the critical concepts to Canada's future. They are inherent in the way we live our lives as Canadians and in the kinds of institutions that we have built and will build in the future as a country.

I think we have to be careful that we don't lose sight of that critical value of *justice*. That we recognize ways that we're falling behind.

DW: So you see Canada as a model for the world. And the three themes that are emerging for you are around economic justice, ecological justice, and social justice that are critical to our future. So where does that commitment come from for you? What is it about those three things that really speaks to you?

NA: I believe in diversity, and I believe in political action and activism. It has a lot to do with where I come from. I was raised in a northern mining town in northern Manitoba. Both my parents are immigrants. My first language was neither English nor French, but I was able to learn Greek, both official languages, and four other languages.

I grew up with people who work very hard to make a living in challenging conditions, people who built the wealth of our country. Around me — my neighbours, communities close by — I had an acute understanding from a very young age of the injustice my neighbours faced, particularly the First Nations people, the first peoples of this country. How could so many of them live in third-world living conditions in a country as wealthy as Canada?

I grew up in a community that is all about diversity, with the highest urban Indigenous population in Canada. More recently, it became one of the first Northern communities to host a full Pride celebration to celebrate the importance of our LGBTQ community.

From a young age, I had an acute understanding of injustice and the fights that people have, whether it was in terms of the labour movement, whether in terms of Indigenous rights, whether in terms of women's equality. I understood that we have to fight for rights to be recognized.

Out of my own experience coming from a family of immigrants, I have always had a sense of striving for something better, a sense that people look out for each other, in a place where community is very important. These are the values I was raised with: The sense that we all have to contribute to build better communities and a better country, a more just country. I'm very proud of my heritage, and I'm very proud that those values are something that I was raised with. They're values that I continue to hold in my work now.

DW: I wonder if we imagine looking back at 2014 from the perspective of 150 years from now, the year 2164, what justice would look like for you? How do you hope economic justice, ecological justice, and social justice will be reflected in the future?

NA: It starts with the very idea that Canada can be a model for the world.

In that sense, I see 2017 [the upcoming anniversary of Confederation] as a key turning point in our history. I see it as a time of transition, from a history of racism and inequality to a future of equality and justice. A time in which Canada has made progress in respecting ethnocultural diversity and has become a leader in terms of LGTBQ rights, but also has recognized that much more needs to be done, especially in the area of gender equality and decolonizing our relationship with Indigenous peoples.

As a model for the world, Canada would reflect the fact that people in their communities have a key role in deciding what is best for them, that economies have to be respectful of the environment, that people must be able to make a living and be able to live in dignity, that equality for women has to be a fundamental fact — and where we no longer see discrimination based on who people are or what they look like or who they love.

I would say that future Canada is a place where, yes, there are still struggles because there are always people who will try to roll back the clock and even dismantle key elements of the model, but it is a society where there is a social consensus that people are always aiming to do better, to build better communities, and to build a better country and a better world. I see a Canada where we are all truly equal. That we're healthy. That we are happy.

I know this won't happen overnight. It will require constant efforts to move towards this goal, that Canadians continue to be a beacon in the world for the way we pursue justice, the way we achieve equality, and the way we look out for each other and eliminate discrimination. We must start now.

Many have struggled to make Canada a better place. I hope that Canada regains the kind of leadership that we have shown in the past, that we break away from our colonial approach, and that we move forward in playing a leading role in building a better world.

DW: I'm wondering what role you feel federal MPs can play in helping to create this vision that you are talking about.

NA: We must recognize that our fundamental responsibility is to build a fairer, more just Canada for all.

For MPs, this starts by being a strong advocate for our constituents, a voice for those that are often not heard. It means building connections in our communities and sharing struggles, sharing ways of building better communities, and building partnerships — within our North, but also with other communities and other parts of the country.

Our communities must have greater control over their destiny. I feel it is very important as MP to support the direction they choose — that *we* choose — and to see that the federal government doesn't stand in our way in building that better future, but that it supports us.

In my role as Opposition Status of Women critic, my priority is to advocate on women's issues, to push our country to really achieve women's equality, and to hold the government to account when it is clearly falling behind.

We cannot lose sight of the fact that Canadians do not want to fall behind in reaching women's equality. I take it very seriously that my role is to fight for fairness, justice, and equality for women by working with women of all generations — activists and leaders in their communities and in their workplaces — to really build a country with conditions and opportunities that allow for women's equality.

DW: I'm wondering, is there anything particular around that going forward that you have some hopes for? In terms of women?

NA: Yes. There is a great deal of hope. Where do I start? I would say that more people are recognizing that despite the fact most Canadians *want* to see women as equal in so many ways, it's clear that we're not. There are so many things that we need to do, so many areas we need to address in order for us to achieve equality. And these require a strong federal role and leadership at the national level. We need a feminist politics that addresses the sexism and misogyny that exists in our society.

Key today and in the future is to end violence against women. Violence against women is a reflection of the inequality that women still face. We know that violence is a major obstacle that affects women and that prevents us from realizing our true potential. It scars us, and, in the worst of situations, it takes women away. We need to address the national epidemic of missing and murdered Indigenous women. We need to call a national inquiry, and we need to understand why Indigenous women are four times more likely to be killed than non-Indigenous women. The federal government must take action and address the systemic sexism and racism that Indigenous women in our country face. We also need to create a national action plan. I put forward a motion to do that — M-444, to create a National Action Plan to Address Violence against Women. This involves the understanding that to end violence against women, we need a comprehensive approach. We can learn from other countries that have taken this approach.

Addressing violence is critical, but it's not the only thing we need to do. We need to make sure that women have control over their own destinies, and that includes women having control over their own bodies. That means women have to have the ability to choose what to do with their own bodies, including their reproductive health. There must be full access to sexual and reproductive rights.

It means meeting women's needs in terms of our health system, in terms of our wellness. A different approach to wellness needs to be recognized, because women have different experiences and often face health insecurity in ways that men don't.

We need to face the pay inequity that women experience. Canadian women are still at 71 cents to the male dollar. That means that women don't have the same economic security as men do — in terms of their working lives, but also in terms of their retirement — and that's wrong. Women in both their paid work and their unpaid work contribute immeasurably to our economy. Their unpaid work needs to be recognized, the pay equity gap needs to be closed, and we need to ensure life is affordable for women across the board.

That includes understanding the reality of younger women, where costs like tuition fees and costs of living are increasing, leaving many young women (who are also adjusting to making less than men) at a disadvantage in terms of their wellbeing.

In the future it is critical that we have national programs, like a national childcare plan, that advance equality. This is critical to both women and men, but we know from our own country in provinces like Quebec, children and women are better off when we have affordable and accessible childcare in our country. In the future, childcare must be a comprehensive social program equivalent to medicare today.

I would say as a final point that women's voices need to be heard. We need to address the discrimination that women still face in terms of women in politics, women in the workplace, and women in their homes. In the future we need to not only elect more women, but to elect feminist women whose voices will be heard — and women who will strive for equality, because we have a lot of work to do.

DW: Thanks, Niki, and that is comprehensive vision for social justice. What are your additional thoughts on economic justice and ecological justice?

NA: In terms of economic justice — income inequality is increasing in our country in ways we haven't seen in decades, and we know that countries that are more unequal are countries that are less healthy and where people are worse off.

I think we can look to the Nordic countries, for example, where labour rights are very strong, where people's pensions are strong, where people are able to balance their work and their life in a way that allows them to be healthier, to raise a family, to contribute in many ways.

We must end the fact that Indigenous peoples are marginalized and their lands are often exploited in our country. Many Canadians — depending on where they live — have much greater or lesser economic opportunity than others. We're not realizing the potential of local economies. The fact that women are paid less because they are women. Those are the kinds of issues we need to tackle as a country today and in the future.

And it very much connects with ecological justice. We can't keep exploiting the natural wealth at the expense of our future. We need to apply the notion not just of sustainability, but also ecological justice. We need to respect our environment and work within that environment because only then will be able to talk about "150 years from now…" and not just tomorrow.

DW: Good points. So, looking forward 150 years, ecological justice looks like what to you?

NA: Coming from the North, I can say that our natural environment is an important part of who we are.

The Prairie landscape, the Boreal forest, the Arctic tundra are an important part of how I see Canada. As MP representing Churchill, known around the world for its polar bears, I have seen how polar bears exhibit in very real ways the damaging effects of climate change. A very real measure of our success in 150 years will be the degree that they continue to be a living symbol of this great country and not an extinct species.

We need to tune in to the ways our ecosystems, our wildlife, and our people are being affected adversely by climate change. Indigenous peoples are sounding the alarm on this front in many ways.

We need to take action, and it means taking leadership at the national level. It means working with communities to create economies that work for our environment. And to create good jobs that will contribute to our communities and to our country and that exist within a sustainable economy.

I can't imagine a Canada where we don't have the clean lakes that we do, or the blue sky that we do, or the ability to get out on the land. We have so much to learn from Indigenous peoples who have been stewards of the land for such a long time. We can't just think of profit; we need to look at the next seven generations. We need to look at the next 150 years and make sure we have an earth that we can live with and live on.

DW: It's really clear that you have really strong points for your vision. I was just wondering if there was anything else that you really wanted to talk about to add to your vision?

NA: The one thing I would emphasize more in terms of the three pillars I mentioned is the voice of women in shaping all of those three pillars. Women in our history have been excluded from shaping our economy, our government, our future. It is critical in the future to ensure that women's voices are heard, that women are at the decision-making table in communities — and I don't just mean elected leadership. Women must be equal in all walks of life.

In general I am optimistic about Canada's future.

We can be a model for the world, a beacon of hope.

A country where we can all live and work together in harmony with each other, with our environment.

This is our Canada. This is our future.

SHELAGH DAY

Shelagh Day is an internationally respected expert on human rights, with many years of experience working with governments and nongovernmental organizations. She is a thinker, writer, leader, and activist.

She is currently a Director of the Poverty and Human Rights Centre and the Chair of the Human Rights Committee of the Canadian Feminist Alliance for International Action. She is also the President and Senior Editor of the *Canadian Human Rights Reporter*.

Since graduating from Harvard University in 1965, Shelagh Day has worked in the area of human rights. She has been a major contributor to shaping anti-discrimination law in Canada. She has also been one of Canada's leaders in the development and articulation of the concept of substantive equality, which has influenced equality jurisprudence in Canada and internationally.

She has been a founder and leader in many of Canada's most important women's and human rights organizations, including the National Action Committee on the Status of Women, the National Association of Women and the Law, and the Women's Court of Canada. She was the first Human Rights Officer in the Province of British Columbia, the Director of the Saskatchewan Human Rights Commission, the first President of the Women's Legal Education and Action Fund, and a founder of the Court Challenges Programme of Canada.

For 20 years she has worked internationally, appearing before United Nations bodies when Canada's compliance with its human rights treaty obligations is being examined.

Shelagh Day is co-author of two influential books on women's equality in Canada, *One Step Forward or Two Steps Back?* (1989), and *Women and the Equality Deficit* (1998), and author of numerous articles on statutory human rights law and constitutional equality rights. She has received many accolades for her work, including the Governor General's Award in Commemoration of the Persons Case. She is a Member of the Order of Canada.

Shelagh Day lives in Vancouver, British Columbia, with her partner, Gwen Brodsky.

TOWARDS AN EGALITARIAN FUTURE

"One hundred and fifty years ago, when the Fathers of Confederation met in Charlottetown, they had no idea of equality. They believed in dominance: the dominance of settlers over Indigenous peoples; of men over women; of humans over the natural world.

"If Canada is to still exist 150 years from now, and to become a model of democracy, human rights, and women's equality for the rest of the world, as I believe Canada can, these false premises on which Canada was founded must be abandoned."

I long for an egalitarian state, and I am not sure that Canada will survive for another 150 years unless it becomes one. The future cannot be left to simply unfold; it needs urgent attention.

Like other countries in the world, Canada faces three central challenges: increasing income inequality, entrenched sexism, and overuse of natural resources.

A bold vision for Canada's future must face into and grapple with these big challenges. It must also be woman-centred, in order to put equality at the heart of the design.

Because women have been excluded from power and subordinated to men for centuries, it is essential to start from the reality of women's conditions, many different women's conditions, with a view to imagining a state and a world that is more egalitarian and more secure. If a state delivers equality for women, it will be more egalitarian and secure for everyone. So it is time to shift the paradigm, to allocate both natural and human resources to fulfill the basic human rights of Canada's people, and to make a woman-centred economic model, which values adequate food, clothing, and shelter for everyone, adequate incomes, child care, access to the use of rights, and the safety that comes with collective responsibility for everyone's well-being.

One hundred and fifty years ago, when the Fathers of Confederation met in Charlottetown, they had no idea of equality. They believed in dominance: the dominance of settlers over Indigenous peoples; of men over women; of humans over the natural world.

If Canada is to still exist 150 years from now, and to become a model of democracy, human rights, and women's equality for the rest of the world, as I believe Canada can, these false premises on which Canada was founded must be abandoned.

Inequality

Income inequality is increasing in Canada, with the richest group gaining a larger share of national income while the poorest and middle-income groups are losing. On income inequality, among 17 peer countries, Canada ranks 12th.[1] This increase in income stratification is happening in large part because governments have chosen policies which favour the already rich, including lower tax rates on the highest income earners and lower corporate taxes. Women's persistent income inequality is a key component of the larger picture of income inequality in Canada. Eleven per cent of Canadian women live in poverty, and for particular groups of women—single mothers, Indigenous women, racialized women, and women with a disability—poverty rates are much higher.[2] At the same time, and as a consequence of regressive tax policy, governments have withdrawn from redistributive social programs, and women have been particularly harmed by this governmental withdrawal.

Professor Kathleen Lahey reported to the Parliamentary Committee on the Status of Women in May 2014 that women's equality has deteriorated rapidly in the 21st century. "From 1990 to 2000, Canada was ranked 1st in almost every United Nations *Human Development Report*. Canada was also ranked 1st in the UN sex equality rankings from 1997 until 2001. Since 2001, Canada's sex equality rankings have fallen rapidly —from 1st to 20th in the UN gender indices, and as low as 31st in recent years in the new World Economic Forum gender rankings."[3]

The neo-liberal restructuring of the last twenty years has affected women in so many profoundly negative ways. I did not think that women could move so far backwards so fast. The post-1980s brand of capitalism is deeply antithetical to the value of egalitarianism—as well as to the rights to security of the person and an adequate standard of living that Canada has embraced both in its Constitution and in international human rights instruments which it has ratified. In 2014, the neo-liberal erosion of the foundations of women's equality—strong social programs and investment in the "care economy"—is now paired with an overt hostility to women's human rights, the shrinking of space for dissent, and the erasure or weakening of institutions designed to hold government accountable to the values and standards it has endorsed.

Canadian women have developed some common understandings over the last forty years of activism. Not the thin, formal version of women's equality, but the full, fat version of equality, which we call "substantive," has material conditions at its centre. This version of equality, which the Supreme Court of Canada says it embraces, commits us to looking at women's real conditions and asking whether women experience equal outcomes. In the language of international human rights, that means that social and economic rights are an integral part of the "substance" of substantive equality, and inseparable from it. Women who are the most materially disadvantaged, many of whom are Aboriginal, racialized, or have a disability, do not enjoy equality, and their sexual autonomy, security, political participation, and liberty are all constrained.

The fat version of equality cannot be delivered by a stripped-down version of the state, which is understood to deliver freedom by its absence. It requires attentiveness, intervention, action, and spending by governments to create conditions of equality for women, not withdrawal from social policy and deference to the market, which have both characterized the pattern of recent years.

The general erosion of social programs and social protections has negatively affected both men and women. But it has particularly harsh impacts for women because social programs give tangible reality to the right to equality. They level the playing field by turning illness, unemployment, childbirth, single status, disability, and old age into affordable — or at least not catastrophic — incidents of being human, or female. For women in particular, social programs have been fundamental creators of equality. Income security programs soften our economic dependence on men, and health care, home care, and child care, have shifted some of the burden of caregiving from individual women's shoulders to the state, permitting us to move in greater numbers into paid employment and higher education.

The erosion of social programs has also negatively affected women in particular because it accompanies the failure of government policies to address ongoing employment inequality for women and the continuing unequal division of unpaid household labour.

Women in all social groups face inequalities compared to men, but there are also significant differences among women, and, again, the impacts of social program erosion hit the most disadvantaged women the hardest.

How far backwards we have moved because of provincial and federal government withdrawal from social policy was demonstrated to me when the Poverty and Human Rights Centre undertook to canvass those doing front-line work with women in British Columbia.[4] Front-line workers described a "vicious circle" of bad policies and abandonment, a circle that women may enter at any point and for different reasons. But, however it happens, once a woman enters the vicious circle, the likelihood of other harmful events in the circle occurring is greatly increased.

The connected events described by front-line workers include male violence, lack of adequate housing, welfare that is insufficient to meet basic needs, lack of access to legal aid, child apprehension, and depression or addiction. For many women, these events are caused by, and are a consequence of, both sex and race discrimination. They are difficult to escape, especially without significant supports.

One participant described the vicious circle for Aboriginal women this way: sexual abuse in childhood, addictions, male violence, inadequate welfare income, loss of housing, loss of children.

Another woman described the circle this way: A woman seeks to leave a violent relationship, but there are few adequate supports. Often, a woman needs social assistance so that she can support herself and her children independently from the violent partner. Once she is receiving social assistance, inadequate rates mean finding and maintaining adequate housing for herself and her children is difficult, if not impossible. Children may be apprehended because they have witnessed male violence, or because living conditions are considered poor enough to constitute "neglect." Once children are apprehended, it is often hard for women to get them back. Shelter allowances are cut when children are not present, but a mother has to show that she has an adequate place for children to live before the children can be returned. Lack of legal aid to deal with separation matters (and legal representation *before* children are taken away), inadequate welfare entitlements, and poor housing make it difficult to break out of the circle.

As a feminist and a human rights activist, it is unacceptable to me that women in Canada are caught in conditions that stand so starkly in contradiction to our declared commitments to equality. What creates the vicious circle is the absence of adequate, basic social programs — affordable housing, civil legal aid, and income security — that can change these conditions and prevent the harms.

It is clear that Canada cannot claim a commitment to ending violence against women, here or in any part of the world, unless it faces into the connection between women's social and economic inequality and the violence they experience. As the Poverty and Human Rights Centre's research shows, women's poverty makes them vulnerable to violence and unable to escape it and its disintegrating effects.

A bold vision of the future for women in Canada and around the world requires an end to their poverty and a commitment to redistributive programs and policies that ensure that women will have adequate food, shelter, health care, sexual autonomy, and security.

Canada's Founding Relationship

Another central component of inequality in Canada is the oppression and entrenched disadvantage of Indigenous peoples in Canada — First Nations, Inuit, and Métis. As James Anaya, the UN Special Rapporteur on the Rights of Indigenous Peoples has said in his recent report:

> It is difficult to reconcile Canada's well-developed legal framework and general prosperity with the human rights problems faced by indigenous peoples . . . that have reached crisis proportions in many respects . . . The most jarring manifestation of these human rights problems is the distressing socio-economic conditions of indigenous peoples.[5]

The distressing socio-economic conditions are an effect of colonization, particularly over the last 150 years, a period which includes not just the creation of the nation-state of Canada, but also the construction of Canada as a colonizer, controlling Indigenous peoples through racist and sexist laws and practices; including the banning of cultural practices, denial of voting rights and access to courts; forced assimilation through "enfranchisement," residential schools and the "sixties scoop"; and legalized discrimination against Indigenous women, which stripped them of personhood and the ability to transmit Indigenous identity and status to their children and grandchildren.

Despite the Royal Proclamation of 1763 and modern constitutional recognition of the treaty and inherent rights of Aboriginal peoples, and despite the residential school apology and many statements of intent to improve the conditions of Aboriginal peoples, Canada persists in treating Aboriginal peoples as threats and burdens, not partners. Canada fails to respect the original treaties which opened Canadian territory to use by settlers, to treat Aboriginal women as equal persons, to negotiate land claims with respect to unceded territories expeditiously and in good faith, and to make Indigenous peoples full partners in decisions when their lands will be affected by resource development and extraction. The "history of misdealing and harm"[6] continues.

The human rights crisis of hundreds of murders and disappearances of Indigenous women and girls is a result of the sexism, racism, and brutality inherent in colonization. Non-Indigenous women have a significant role to play in remaking the foundational relationship between settlers and Indigenous peoples on which Canada rests. As Gordon Christie said at a recent Idle No More teach-in, "in Canada, whether we are indigenous or non-indigenous, we are all treaty peoples." Canada's settlers are not honouring the terms of our founding partnership with Indigenous peoples.

Climate Change

The 2013 report of the Intergovernmental Panel on Climate Change tells us that warming of the climate system is unequivocal and … unprecedented. … The atmosphere and ocean have warmed, the amount of snow and ice have diminished, sea level has risen, and the concentrations of greenhouse gases have increased.[7]

It also tells us that "human influence on the climate is clear … from the increasing greenhouse gas concentrations in the atmosphere."[8]

But Canada is accumulating "Fossil of the Year Awards" because of its refusal to act on climate change, and, as things are going, Canada will not meet even the modest 2020 targets for emissions reductions to which it agreed in 2005 when it signed the Copenhagen Accord. Canada apparently wishes to have no constraints on its development of tar sands and gas resources, despite known risks and already evident harms. On environmental protection, Canada ranks 27th out of 27 of the world's wealthiest countries — at the bottom.[9]

For Indigenous peoples in Canada, the impact of global warming and of environmental negligence is particularly harsh. Their lands, and the animals, fish, plants, and whole ecosystems around which their cultures and ways of life have been organized are vanishing or threatened. For Inuit and other circumpolar peoples, as the ice melts away, so does their world. Indigenous peoples in other parts of the world are similarly threatened. And, generally, climate change affects the poorest and most vulnerable first and worst, whether entire countries or groups within countries.[10]

As climate change increases the number and intensity of "natural" disasters, it has become evident that women are extremely vulnerable in a disaster-prone world. As with poverty, disasters increase women's vulnerability to violence, their caregiving responsibilities expand, and female headship of families rises, as men leave to find work away from disaster-hit areas.

Most Canadians understand that addressing climate change is of key importance to generations to come and that serious action is required in order to pull the world back from catastrophe. We understand that some climate change is already irreversible, but that collective human action can keep it from becoming much worse.

Social Collapse

The necessity of urgent collective action on a broad scale is underlined by new cross-disciplinary research by natural and social scientists.[11] This research uses thousands of years of historical data to study the rise and collapse of civilizations. Two interrelated factors were identified which cause civilization decline: "unsustainable resource exploitation and increasingly unequal wealth distribution."[12]

The scientists explain that these two factors interact, and "high levels of economic stratification are linked directly to over-consumption of resources."[13] When the wealth which the mass of people create is not distributed equitably, the rich consume too much of available resources; even in wealthy and sophisticated societies, deprivation in the lower stratas of society ultimately causes collapse. The study concludes that under conditions "closely reflecting the reality of the world today … we find that collapse is difficult to avoid."[14]

The warning is shocking, but useful. We can already see that widespread concern about politicians' incapacity or unwillingness to come to grips with inequality and with the current unsustainable exploitation of resources creates political disaffection and a dangerous contempt for government — of any stripe. This is a recipe for social disintegration.

The social and resource collapse that the scientists predict is not inevitable — the right political and structural changes can ensure that we avoid it. But avoiding it will require bold steps to shrink income inequality and dramatically reduce use of natural resources. We do not have endless time. Can Canada do it? Can the world do it?

If we are thinking forward 150 years, here's what Canada needs:

1. The nation-state matters, as it is the locus of democracy. Governments matter. The redistribution that both women and men need in order to have an adequate standard of living and security cannot be

accomplished by private corporations through charitable giving or by non-governmental organizations through erratically funded services. It can only be accomplished by governments through laws, policies, regulation, taxation, and spending. Widespread support for government and robust participation in democratic life are essential to any future. That means that political restructuring is essential to permit women and men who have a longer view than the next election cycle to serve successfully in politics and to design and implement laws and budgets that will give Canada a viable future. Canada needs to be able to elect governments that are dedicated to the well-being of Canadians for the next seven generations, not the next four years.

2. A nation's economic model and its budgets are statements of values. Canada is redistributing wealth upwards and income inequality and poverty rates have increased rapidly;[15] at the same time, we are spending money on fighter jets and new prison cells. This economic model must be reshaped. Canada needs a long-term plan that connects responsible and sustainable use of resources to the realities and imperatives of partnership with Canada's indigenous peoples, and to redistributive strategies and programs that will ensure equality. What would this look like, in detail, over fifty years?

3. Women need to be a driving force for change, for change in Canada and for change around the world. If we are not, the deeply rooted structural inequality of women will simply remain. But to be a driving force for change, we must be more connected to each other. Over the last twenty years, women's organizations have become siloed, focused on particular groups of women, or on a particular area of expertise or need — housing, health, poverty. Now, we cannot afford this separation; the challenges and dangers are too great. Women need connectedness and solidarity.

4. Canada has a democratic problem. Space for participation in law reform and policy development, and capacity to use constitutional and

statutory rights to equality, have shrunk for women, particularly over the last decade. This is not simply an issue of the long-standing under-representation of women in formal politics in Canada. It is even more significantly an issue of the closing down of democratic participation for women's advocacy organizations that speak for women, including the most disadvantaged women in the country. In 2014 Canada's governments continue to be male-dominated, with diminishing space available for women to influence law and policy. At the national level, Canada has a government where power is concentrated not in Parliament, but in the Prime Minister's Office. This current thin version of democracy represents a real danger for Canada, and for women; it signals an inability to face the real challenges that Canada's future holds and to solve them in democratic and egalitarian ways.

Canada needs a new start on a democratic, feminist future.

1. Conference Board of Canada, *Income Inequality*, accessed July 2014, http://www.conferenceboard.ca/hcp/details/society/income-inequality.aspx.

2. Statistics Canada, *Women in Canada: A Gender-Based Statistical Report, 2010–2011*, accessed July 2014, http://www5.statcan.gc.ca/olc-cel/olc.action?ObjId=89-503-X&ObjType=2&lang=en&limit=1.

3. Kathleen Lahey, Consultation Brief to the House of Commons Standing Committee on the Status of Women, Study on Economic Leadership and Prosperity of Canadian Women, *Women's Increasing Inequality in Canada: Economic and Fiscal Dimensions*, May 12, 2014, testimony accessed July 2014, http://www.parl.gc.ca/HousePublications/Publication.aspx?DocId=6589080&Language=E&Mode=1&Parl=41&Ses=2.

4. Gwen Brodsky et al, Poverty and Human Rights Centre, *The Vicious Circle*, April 2010, accessed July 2014, http://povertyandhumanrights.org/wp-content/uploads/2012/11/The-Vicious-Circle-Report.pdf.

5. James Anaya, Report of the Special Rapporteur on the Rights of Indigenous Peoples, *The Situation of Indigenous Peoples in Canada*, A/HRC/27/52/Add.2, 7 May 2014, par. 14 and 15.

6. Anaya, par. 58.

7. Intergovernmental Panel on Climate Change, "Summary for Policy Makers,"

Climate Change 2013, accessed July 2014, http://www.climatechange2013.org/images/report/WG1AR5_SPM_FINAL.pdf.

8. Ibid., 15.

9. Lawrence Martin, "On Climate Change, Obama Just Turned Up the Heat," *Globe and Mail*, 3 June 2014, accessed July 2014, http://www.theglobeandmail.com/globe-debate/on-climate-obama-just-turned-up-the-heat/article18951307/.

10. Center for Global Development: Climate Change, accessed July 2014, http://www.cgdev.org/topics/climate_change.

11. Safa Motesharre, et al., "Human and Nature Dynamics (HANDY): Modeling Inequality and Use of Resources in the Collapse or Sustainability of Societies," accessed July 2014, http://www.sesync.org/sites/default/files/resources/motesharrei-rivas-kalnay.pdf.

12. Nafeez Ahmed, "NASA-Funded Study: Industrial Civilization Headed for 'Irreversible Collapse'?" *The Guardian*, 26 March 2014, accessed July 2014, http://www.theguardian.com/environment/earth-insight/2014/mar/14/nasa-civilisation-irreversible-collapse-study-scientists.

13. Ibid.

14. Ibid.

15. OECD, "Country Note: Canada," *Growing Unequal?: Income Distribution and Poverty in OECD Countries*, Geneva: OECD, 2008, accessed July 2014, http://www.oecd.org/els/social/inequality. The OECD said: "After 20 years of continuous decline, both inequality and poverty rates have increased rapidly in the past 10 years, now reaching levels above the OECD average." Inequality in household income increased significantly and poverty increased for all age groups. The OECD further noted that taxes and transfers do not reduce inequality in Canada as much as in other OECD countries or as much as they previously did in this country.

MINA MAWANI

Mina Mawani is a resilient, collaborative leader. Born in Uganda, Mina Mawani and her family fled the country in the early 1970s and spent a year in a refugee camp in Vienna, Austria, before settling in Thunder Bay, Ontario.

Mina Mawani graduated with a Bachelor of Administrative Studies from York University and graduated from the Nuclear Medicine Technology program at the Southern Alberta Institute of Technology (Calgary) and the University of Alberta (Edmonton). She completed a Master's degree in Health Science/Administration from the University of Toronto.

Mina Mawani began her career in 1998 as a healthcare practice consultant for KPMG and PricewaterhouseCoopers. She went on to work as a senior policy advisor for the Ontario Ministry of Health and Long Term Care. In 2009, Mina Mawani was appointed the Chief Executive Officer for the Aga Khan Council for Canada. She was the first woman to occupy this senior strategic position. More recently, she served as the chief development officer at CivicAction and president and CEO of the Canadian Women's Foundation.

A strong believer in giving back to the community, Mina Mawani volunteers much of her time to organizations that are at the forefront of empowering women and girls. She recently completed her two-year term as the chair of the governance and nominating committee at Women's College Hospital. She is an advisory board member for the United Nation's Women's National Committee, and a member of several organizations including Equal Voice, Catalyst Canada, and Women of Influence.

Mina Mawani currently resides in Toronto, Ontario, with her husband and two children.

QUESTIONING OUR GUIDING VALUES:

Building a More Inclusive and Equal Canada

"A more inclusive and equitable future will only emerge if we are guided by values and actions grounded in inclusion and equality. That means we must inherently address the root causes of violence and poverty and challenge gender, racial, and other stereotypes. Our work must be driven by a set of ethics, morals, and values that speak to all — not just certain privileged groups in society."

In 1864, the same year twenty-three men met in Charlottetown to discuss the political union that would eventually become Canada, a woman named Rose Fortune died. She was 90, but her longevity was just one of many remarkable things about her.

Rose had been born into slavery in Philadelphia and came to Canada when she was ten, escaping with her family to Nova Scotia as part of the Black Loyalist migration. To earn a living, she worked on the ferry wharves, transporting luggage for passengers in a wheelbarrow. Rose had a big personality and knew everyone, including the town's leading citizens. In time, she became a self-appointed, one-woman police force, wielding a small stick to keep order on the wharves and enforce the curfews she herself created. One observer called her "an authoritative person," adding, "She was evidently a privileged character."[1]

Today, Rose is recognized as Canada's first female police officer. She was also an entrepreneur who launched a family business that lasted almost 100 years: After her death, her grandchildren expanded her baggage-handling business, graduating from wheelbarrow to wagon to truck, until it finally closed in 1960.

So have women in Canada come a long way, or do we only think we have because we don't know enough about women like Rose?

If Rose was this empowered 150 years ago, why are we still fighting for women's basic rights? Why do so many of us — especially racialized women — remain trapped by violence, poverty, and ridiculous stereotypes that limit our potential as human beings?

With Rose as our yardstick, we can immediately see we may not have come as far as we think. Why not?

We are not on an inevitable path to a more inclusive and equal society. Everyone says they want a better world, but the 23 men who met in Charlottetown in their silk top hats and cravats were not interested in improving the lives of people like Rose.

Although these fathers of pre-Confederation may have told themselves they were building a better future for everyone, they were driven by values that promoted hierarchy and inequality. These values were also behind one of the most tragic policies ever created in Canada's history: Just six years after the Charlottetown Conference, the first residential schools for Aboriginal children opened.

The processes and policies shaped by these values would ensure that political power in the new country of Canada would remain with propertied white men, and the impact of this legacy can be seen to this day.

Our actions are shaped by our values.

The collective values of a society run invisibly under its surface, much like the unseen currents in a wide river. We might not even notice they are there, but they push and pull us every day, influencing what we do and say, what we believe to be true and correct—even what we believe to be possible. Each society's values carry it inexorably to one future and not another.

As Canadian history clearly shows, many attempts to engineer a "better" future have either virtually ignored marginalized groups or caused them tremendous harm.

That is why in this bold vision I do not ask, "Where should we go?" but "How will we get there?"

In other words, "What values should drive our collective actions?"

A more inclusive and equitable future will only emerge if we are guided by values and actions grounded in inclusion and equality. That means we must inherently address the root causes of violence and poverty and challenge gender, racial, and other stereotypes.

Our work must be driven by a set of ethics, morals, and values that speak to all—not just to certain privileged groups in society. Our work needs to focus on those who are marginalized and vulnerable in society and should not be driven by self-interest.

One possible road map to a bold vision is to use questions to guide our thinking and our work, as illustrated in the following examples.

Each question is designed to open a dialogue—within ourselves and with others — and to encourage us to reflect upon the often unconscious assumptions and motivations beneath our work.

These questions are expected to change over time as we continue to learn and grow, and they will be refined and improved in collaboration with the other Bold Vision participants.

I. Am I Using a Gender Lens?

During my time as President and CEO at the Canadian Women's Foundation, our vision was to "invest in women and girls, change everything." When I was CEO at the Aga Khan Council for Canada, we believed in improving the quality of life of women and girls. Research has shown that improving women's equality actually helps everyone. It has a ripple effect.

It's interesting that we have to keep reiterating that women are not a special interest group: We are 50 per cent of the population. When we reach our full economic and social potential, everyone benefits.

When a woman gets the help she needs to escape violence, right away she and her children become safer. But, in addition, there are ripple effects. Her children are also less likely to experience violence when they grow up, and so are their own children. And when we also teach children to build healthier relationships, we stop the violence before it starts, and the entire community becomes safer.

At the Aga Khan Council for Canada and the Canadian Women's Foundation, we knew that when you help a woman to move out of poverty, you not only improve her quality of life, but you improve the quality of life of her family as well. Her children become healthier — both physically and mentally — and do better in school. Not only that, the whole family becomes less reliant on government assistance and can pay more taxes and contribute more to society. Again, the effect ripples well beyond the family.

As you read this, you may be thinking, "But men need help too." Men have always been at the centre of societal thinking, and now it's time to be bold and focus on women and girls. This focus needs to directly challenge patriarchy — patriarchy that has kept women and girls from achieving their full potential.

Using a gender lens means looking at the world through women's eyes — at least 50 per cent of the time — and reviewing decisions in light of their potential impact on women and girls.

For example, when you view part-time work through a gender lens, you immediately see that 70 per cent of all part-time workers in Canada are female. Research shows that most women work part-time because they cannot successfully juggle their domestic responsibilities plus a full-time job. At first glance, their work arrangements appear to be based on personal choices, but seen through a gender lens, we see there is actually a systemic gender issue based primarily on the chronic lack of affordable childcare and the absence of family-friendly workplace policies.

Canadian employment practices and government policies are still mired in the outdated family model of a male breadwinner and a female homemaker. Creating policies and practices informed by a gender lens will have a ripple effect: It will help women reach their full economic potential, improve the lives of all working parents, and strengthen Canada's entire economy.

2. Am I Addressing the Greatest Needs?

It's true women and girls in Canada have come a long way. Most of us enjoy freedom and opportunity that Rose Fortune probably would have found hard to believe. In almost every aspect of our lives — family, career, and education — most of us make our own choices. We have taken on leadership in business, politics, and community life. Thanks to the hard work of the women who have come before us, we have a lot to celebrate.

However, there is still much work to do. Half of all women and girls experience physical or sexual violence in their lifetime, income inequality in Canada is growing, and the devastating impacts of residential schools continue to harm the first peoples of this land. Thousands of women across Canada are raising their children alone in poverty. Certain groups of women — including newcomer women, Aboriginal women, racialized women, single mothers, and women with disabilities — are especially likely to be poor.

Progressive social change does not occur when we focus on those at the top of the social heap; that just protects the status quo. Achieving social inclusion and equality starts with focusing on those who are the most marginalized.

Rosemary Brown, the first Black woman in Canada to be elected to a provincial legislature, put it this way: "Until all of us have made it, none of us have made it."[2]

3. Am I Listening More Than I Am Speaking?

Those closest to social and economic problems create the best solutions to those problems. Yet, too often, those who hold social power make decisions without involving the people who are or will be most affected. As we organize for change, we must not only actively recruit their participation but also actively address any barriers to their meaningful participation.

For example, at the Canadian Women's Foundation, we created a 24-member task force on the trafficking of women and girls in Canada to develop recommendations to end sex trafficking in Canada. Survivors of sex trafficking were members of the task force, and more survivors were also invited to a full-day round-table discussion to share their expertise; their input will be instrumental in shaping the task force recommendations. However, making the invitation was not enough. Ahead of time, we had to identify potential barriers to the full participation of survivors — everything from lack of childcare to food allergies to no access to transportation — and create strategies to address them. We provided honoraria to recognize the value of participants' time. If we asked the survivors to share their personal stories, we also provided counselling and follow-up support.

Marginalized groups must be a genuine part of decision-making processes not out of sentimentality or even because it's the right thing to do, but because their voices are essential to creating good solutions.

However, the people who are closest to the problems are also the ones most likely to question the validity of organizers' processes, to name hard truths, and to challenge our underlying values. It is essential we engage as genuine partners and listen with an open heart.

4. Am I Building on Assets?

Women should not be seen as victims, but as powerful people who are being temporarily held back by systemic discrimination.

As in all oppressed groups, the impact of systemic discrimination often manifests in personal behaviours that appear unique to individuals. For example, many individual women exhibit a chronic lack of confidence and tend to focus on their flaws rather than their strengths. But, as a group, women also have many inherent strengths, including listening, collaboration, and emotional intelligence. It is only recently, however, that these traits have been valued by society. We must counter the impact of systemic discrimination by taking a strength-based, positive approach.

For example, for a woman living on a low income, learning to recognize her "hidden" assets is often the catalyst for taking those first difficult steps towards financial independence. Poverty alleviation and economic development programs must focus on a woman's assets — not just on how much money she has, but also things such as social networks, education, physical health, and parenting skills. For many women, beginning with strengths is a tremendously empowering process. The next step is a woman in low income learning how to leverage each of her assets in order to reach her financial goal. It is encouraging to see that this asset-based approach is being utilized in many organizations and communities globally.

Building on assets isn't about being overly optimistic or ignoring problems. It isn't even about offering a "hand up," which can sometimes be experienced as disempowering.

Building on assets is about creating processes that empower marginalized individuals and groups to recognize and leverage their existing strengths and to take control of their own lives. In the end, that allows us all to create stronger solutions to economic and social problems.

5. Am I Thinking Holistically?

The best way to solve complex economic and social problems is to look at them from multiple angles. To create genuine change, we must address issues along their whole continuum.

Complex issues such as violence against women can't be addressed with simple solutions. To stop the violence, we need to fund emergency shelters so women and their children can escape immediate danger, but we also need to fund programs that teach teens — both boys and girls — to create healthier relationships over the long term. We need to encourage governments to create stronger anti-violence policies and fund research into best practices for service providers.

Considering another complex problem, that of poverty, in order to help women move out of poverty, we must fund programs that provide "wraparound" services that help women address whatever issues are keeping them from achieving financial independence. These can include factors such as domestic violence, lack of childcare, inadequate education, isolation, and low self-confidence. We need to fund programs that help women to identify the most immediate barriers to their economic independence and then to get connected to relevant community services.

Thinking holistically means acknowledging that many women experience complex and interconnected challenges. For example, if a woman is experiencing violence, it will likely be very difficult for her to focus on an employment search. However, once she and her children are safe and stabilized, it is usually easier for her to think about building a new future. Although at first glance helping a woman find shelter and supportive counselling may not seem related to helping her to move out of poverty, it is often the essential first step in her journey to financial independence.

To create a better future, we must acknowledge the complex roots of social and economic inequality and ensure the solutions we promote address the realities of women's lived experiences.

6. Am I Sharing Power?

Patriarchy has been called "the religion of power."[3] Its central concept is hierarchy, in which people are sorted into categories of higher and lower worth. Both men and women receive many messages — both blatant and covert — that men deserve more social status than women.

Besides gender, hierarchies also apply in categories such as race, age, income, education, sexual orientation, physical and mental ability, appearance, religious beliefs, and language. Within a patriarchal, hierarchical framework, those deemed to be of lower worth are subject to formal and informal control through all manner of abusive behaviours: sexual, physical, emotional, financial, and spiritual.

We have all absorbed patriarchal messages about worth, and it takes hard work to unlearn them. The first step, as always, is to become conscious of them. As the saying goes: "A fish doesn't know it's in water."

Sharing power means designing programs that empower those for whom — and with whom — the programs are designed. We must empower women and girls to not only design the programs but then take on leadership for those programs in many other ways. Evaluation shows this strategy is highly effective with many different populations, and we must fund empowering types of programs so that approaches built on power-sharing become the rule and not the exception.

We know that sharing power with girls requires overcoming our bias that adults know best and should be in charge. It also demands that we let go of the adult's desire to control everything. Although this urge for control is usually driven by a genuine desire for things to go well, it can be very disempowering to program participants.

Creating a more inclusive and equal future requires us to become more aware of the dynamics of power in actions both large and small. When we organize a community meeting, for example, we express power through decisions such as who creates the agenda (an act of power and influence) and who takes notes (an act that carries much less social power).

When power is genuinely shared, participants are much more likely to feel ownership of the process, and a spirit of collaboration is more likely to flourish.

7. Am I Building a Community?

Women are different from each other in so many ways, but we all experience discrimination based on our gender. Ending this discrimination can be the common goal we share.

But in order to work together, we must honour both our commonalities and our differences.

For example, at one recent workshop an Aboriginal woman who worked at a community organization was sharing the barriers that often prevent Aboriginal women from accessing services. In response, a staff person from a different organization that serves a non-Aboriginal population stood up and said excitedly, "Yes, this is exactly what the women in my community experience!" In our eagerness to find common ground, it can be easy to unconsciously erase our differences. In doing so, we may marginalize the experience of others.

We must take on the hard, ongoing work of becoming aware of our privilege, whether it's based on race, income, sexual orientation, physical ability, or other factors. We must also resist the emotional urge to retreat into either guilt or defensiveness about our privilege. We don't choose to have privilege; it is simply assigned according to the dominant values of our culture. Neither can we refuse to accept it, nor choose to give it away. We can only choose how we use it.

Privilege gives us the power to describe problems, create strategies, shape solutions, and access resources. When it comes to community building, the question becomes: Are we using our privilege to maintain the status quo, or to work for genuine change?

....

Our society must enable every woman and girl to live free from violence, poverty, and stereotypes that limit her potential.

The Bold Vision project is a tremendous opportunity to begin the process of building a more inclusive and equal Canada that can help us to reach these goals. But first we must bring our assumptions and motivations to the surface, ask ourselves in whose interests we are acting, and whether we are guided by values that promote inclusion and equality.

Our combined values — using a gender lens, addressing the greatest need, listening deeply, building on assets, thinking holistically, sharing power, and building community — must guide all our work.

These values are respectfully offered as the elements of one possible roadmap to a future Canada where political, social, and economic power are equally shared.

In that future, every woman — even a woman who today is as disenfranchised and as empowered as Rose Fortune was 150 years ago — will have the opportunity to achieve her full potential.

....

1. Annapolis Heritage Society, "Rose Fortune — A 'Privileged Character,'" Community History: Notable Personalities of the Past, accessed July 2014, http://www.annapolisheritagesociety.com/history-pers-fortune.html.

2. Heroines.ca, A Guide to Women in Canadian History, "Quotes from Famous Canadian Women," accessed July 2014, http://www.heroines.ca/features/quotes.html.

3. Allan Johnson, *The Gender Knot: Unraveling Our Patriarchal Legacy* (Philadelphia: Temple University Press, 2005).

BECKA VIAU

Becka Viau is a Canadian artist, arts administrator, and community advocate in Charlottetown, Prince Edward Island. She is program director of the artist-run centre this town is small inc., a non-profit organization dedicated to supporting the growth and sustainability of the contemporary arts on PEI.

After a few years of exploring the liberal arts at McGill University and the University of Prince Edward Island, she received her Bachelor of Fine Arts in 2008 and Master of Fine Arts in 2013 from NSCAD University. She has committed her professional career to the rigorous study of contemporary art and theory. She has exhibited in many galleries throughout the Maritimes and the United Kingdom and was long-listed for the prestigious Sobey Art award in 2011 and 2014.

Strengthened by the challenges and beauties of her rural upbringing, Becka Viau has remained committed to community service and volunteering since establishing the Kids Help Phone Student Ambassador Program on PEI in 1998. She has worked as a curator, educator, and coordinator of arts collectives, an artist-run centre, and an arts festival. Much of her artistic activity engages with questions relating to institutions, dissemination, and social networks of art and culture.

Her artistic practice is grounded in the research of historic and contemporary media techniques, theories of the everyday, and social research methods. The histories of documentary, portraiture, cultural presentation, and anthropological research influence her creative studio process through various explorations of people, place, and identity. The forms of artwork Becka Viau produces generally appeal to a popular audience. They draw people in with inviting architecture and welcome the viewer to wander a variety of conceptual paths.

Becka Viau lives in Charlottetown, Prince Edward Island, with her partner, Scott Brown, and infant Meike.

POSSIBILITIES

"To open the dialogue and advocate for a discourse that is created between multiple voices of varied backgrounds and situated circumstances . . ."

Written by Becka Viau, co-authored by Helaina Lalande, Josie Baker, Merray Gerges, Diana Hosseini, Mireille Eagan, and Marie Fox[1]

....

"Because imagination is not constrained by the boundaries of reality that frustrate traditional political action, it is a space that allows subjects to explore possibilities that reveal themselves only within fantasy." – *Ralph Ellison*[2]

Canada: A country, a nation, a landscape detailed in waterways, forests and plains, a natural and cultural ecosystem, a place, a name, a collection of stories bound with a common history. Canada is a construct, a myth built from these parts. And what is a myth but a powerful and pervasive narrative, an imagined reality perpetuated by a desire to live out a dominant fantasy?

The question I ask is who has written, decided, and preserved the prevailing Canadian narrative? Considering the colonial and predominantly white, english, and male control of the Canadian ideal, the national myth is essentially homogeneous. However, this homogeneity is hidden behind a strategically woven story, a deceptive narrative neatly integrated into civil structures, institutions, and government processes— described, listed, and lived within the supposed ideals of multiculturalism, plurality, and benevolence.[3]

What would be an effective way to rupture this homogeneity? To interrupt the dominant story and influence the Canadian narrative in a radical and truly disruptive fashion? How can we reveal potential and possibility in Canada and its future without breaking down the barriers that exist within the psychic and physical infrastructure of the nation?

I was paralyzed by these questions when confronted with the task of articulating my vision for Canada over the next 150 years. I felt trapped ... as I often do, when considering my place within Canadian national identity and the institutions that govern its environmental and cultural systems. It is easy to become apathetic and lost in a situation dominated by a voice that is ignorant to its own prerogative and far removed from personal experience.

I can't continue to blindly play along and circle back into the dominant structure of the national narrative. I want to break out of that cycle. As a self-identified queer, feminist, white, english, cis female, eighth-generation Canadian, I don't want to continue taking up space. I want others to speak, to vision, to imagine, and to create a new fantasy we can stumble about in together. Of course, I have a voice too (in this case and in many other opportunities I have been presented). While my voice is privileged in many ways, my voice is also enabled by its varied privileges to step aside: To open the dialogue and advocate for a discourse that is created between multiple voices of varied backgrounds and situated circumstances.

The questions of where Canada will be, what Canada should do, and how we should proceed should be answered through discourse powered by the voices of people who currently live in and around the borderlands of the dominant narrative. Search for Canada, the imagined reality, through the voices of people who already live on the edge of the dominant reality. Who really, one could say, already live in the realm of fantasy — a courageous place of possibility.[4]

Listen to the borderlands. Be present in their imaginings, their desires. Be silent, my privileged voice, and listen ...

Helaina Lalande

The year is 2164. The last fifteen decades or so have been rather trying for humankind. Canadians have had an especially hard time of it, what with the beaver fever outbreak of 2081 and the 2142 U.S. invasion of Fort McMurray and ensuing Martial Law. Thankfully, that was put to an end with the development of bovine methane power. This, in addition to greatly lowering greenhouse gas emissions globally, is what has made Canada one of the most influential (wealthy) countries in the world. Its vast expanses of forest and meadow have been mowed down to golf-course standard and now serve as pasture for billions of cattle.

In the sports world, we have recently been celebrating Quilla-daughter-of-Mabel's zirconium medal win in four-armed backstroke at the 2164

Olympic Games. Corporeal enhancements have made it a good time to be in athletics, along with the fact that athletes are now the highest wage-earners in the country.

Since paper was banned in 2150 to conserve Canada's few remaining trees, artists have been searching for alternative forms of hard media, which some believe to be more authentic than digital art, however primitive they may seem. Most recently, the trend has been toward lino cut, a technique that has been facilitated in modern times by precision-cutting laser pointers.

Of course, it's impossible to talk about the state of things without mentioning the latest fad to sweep the nation—analog watches. This isn't the first time an archaic technology has become popular among "mode-ites," and it almost certainly won't be the last. So-called fad-augurs are predicting a return to eyeglasses might be next, but, really, who knows what the future holds?

Josie Baker

I am not proud of Canada right now. We seem to be governed by the ideology that government's role is not to build and maintain a stable, just society, but to facilitate corporate profits and to ensure a compliant workforce ripe for exploitation. As a nation we are actively ignoring the threats posed by climate change and increasingly desperate poverty. We are actively criminalizing First Nations, Métis, and Inuit activists, migrants, refugees, immigrants, and environmentalists. Canada today is embodying the worst of what our history has to offer: a history of colonialism, imperialism, and genocide.

The bold vision I would suggest for the future of Canada is to work to better embody a Canadian ideal — that of democracy. A truly democratic system could nourish vibrant, resilient communities across Canada. To be truly democratic, we need to fundamentally change the power balance of our society.

We need to reshape our economy. Eliminating poverty has been within our power as a country for a long time, but it has not been considered profitable. The economic system that we have creates and profits from poverty. It creates and profits from environmental destruction. However, poverty and extreme wealth are not acceptable, and they demand a price that we cannot afford. No one should have to choose between paying for medicine and buying food. No one needs to stay with their abuser because they can't afford to leave with their children. No one should work full-time and still have to rely on food banks.

We need to take steps to build resilience and abundance in our communities. We need to empower and enable communities to put their human creativity and ingenuity to work to face our common problems. To truly fulfill our democratic ideals, to work towards social and environmental justice, we need to build relationships of trust and collaboration with those on the margins. The voices of a few have dominated for too long. We cannot afford to continue to marginalize people — we need the voices and perspectives of everyone to meet our common problems. The change needs to come through community — we need to do the hard work of recognizing the wounds that we have inherited from our history and build alternatives that don't repeat the mistakes of our ancestors. Inclusion takes a lot of work, and it is challenging, but in the process of building inclusion we learn about ourselves and our assumptions; we build relationships, and we build trust. To create a democratic Canada, we need to face the wounds of our history, and we need to recognize the blind spots in our world view. As a nation, we must work towards our common survival, and we need a vast spectrum of human creativity and wisdom to succeed.

Merray Gerges

From:	Merray Gerges	Sent: Tue, May 27, 2014 at 2:52 AM
To:	Becka Viau	
Subject:	future Canada?	

Hi Becka,

After I messaged you last, I went back through previous bits of research and transcribed conversations, and it became clear to me that I must use this opportunity to give space for someone who's considerably more frustrated than I am. I spoke with Pamela Edmonds, a Toronto-based curator of colour, a few months ago for a piece about tokenism in the Canadian art world that I was working on. I selected a few quotes from our conversation that I feel respond to the question at hand far more eloquently than I ever could. Feel free to pick and choose according to your needs. I've also attached the resulting piece for context.[5]

"I strived to bring art that connected to different ethnic and cultural communities. I felt somewhat tokenized, and I still do even now, 15 or so years later. But that's just the place that we're at. We're still not there. I learned that you take three steps forward and then there's two back. But at least you got one ahead. That's the price that you pay to be within the mainstream. I always try to be somewhat subversive within the programming that I do.

"You can't just pick and choose and have everyone in this equal place because that's not how it is in reality. You have to recognize that there's discrimination that's not being recognized. It's sort of disingenuous. People don't really believe it. I don't think they really believe the exoticisation of cultures. On multicultural day, you sample the food. It's not an understanding of that culture in terms of their contributions. It's a nice idea. I wouldn't want to give it up. But it has to be a critical multiculturalism somehow.

"It's important to reach diverse communities but vital to reach the art world too to say, 'I'm sorry but you're gonna have to give up some of your power.' People have to be ready for that dialogue at some point. It's gotta happen. Recognition of that oppression is not easy to deal with. But I think it will happen because people will change over the generations. Might not be in my lifetime. That foothold of the white middle class male? It can't keep up. It's too multicultural of a world for that to stay. I don't see it staying that way. We have to look at what art is in a different way, because the west-centric art idea has changed. I don't want to be in response to you, or intervening anymore. I just wanna go in and do stuff.

Why do you have to reinterpret European art? Just forget about it. It's tired. I don't wanna respond to that anymore. I just wanna go about my business."

Talk soon,

M

Diana Hosseini

My Vision of Canada

The Canada of tomorrow, the one that perhaps my great grand-children will grow up in, will be a place where they will never feel culturally alienated. No one should ever feel "other" and thus strive to strip away and reject their home culture(s). I do not think that our society fully understands either the potential social and psychological damage of today's form of assimilation or the fact that it even exists. We may not be in a situation where assimilation is forced; the process at hand is different than that used in the shameful part of our history. However, it peeks its ugly head when people introduce themselves with alternate names or when a mother tongue is lost from one generation to the next. Names may seem like very simple things; however, they are our very first markers of identity. When a person provides a different name or a different pronunciation of a name, they do so because they sense that this is a requirement in our society, which means that their true self is excluded. Step by step, there are changes in the self, some of which are unfortunately irreversible or take years to heal. In terms of the mother tongue, its loss is a loss of knowledge and a sort of break in communication between parent and child. Remember that a translation may always have deficiencies.

There needs to be a superior level of understanding among us. At the end of the day, besides the Indigenous population, we are all immigrants. Some of us can trace our Canadian lineage far back, while some of us have just begun creating one. Being Canadian may mean something different for each of us, but we are all here because our parents, our ancestors, or we sought something better. Let us not be ignorant of differing languages, foods, and perspectives on life.

Instead, we should embrace the greatest privilege that we have, and that is to be able to live among a multitude of cultures. We should be aware and respectful of our differences; it is by doing so that no one is excluded or feels "other." In the Canada of tomorrow, I would hope that we will have finally reached a stage where we can without hesitation claim to be a true model of multiculturalism.

Marie Fox

Hagia Sophia
Medium: digital photography
Year: 2013

Mireille Eagan

"Under the eye of God, near the giant river,

The Canadian grows hoping.

He was born of a proud race,

Blessed was his birthplace.

The sky has noted his career

In this new world."

– *Translation of the original version of "Ô Canada" (1880)*

It is said that Walt Disney is cryogenically frozen at the point just before death, under the Pirates of the Caribbean ride at the theme park that bears his name. When science is willing, Disney will be revived. The story may be a rumour, but it is far more interesting to imagine that it's true. It speaks to the quality of our time—a result of 150 years of fluctuations between the apocalyptic and the romantic.

In Canada, for instance, a robust optimism informed the late-1800s to mid-1900s. It was predicted that Canada, with its harsh climates and vast natural resources, would forge a hardy people, a "True North, Strong and Free." An indicator of the time is found in its art, in the celebration of (some of) Canada's rugged landscapes. The whole thing was a myth, of course, intended to provoke a national identity. The next 50 years would assert the errors found in this approach, that just beyond the frame of the painted solitary trees were people—among them First Nations, Métis, Inuit, immigrants, and women.

It is the nature of progress that we respond to what came before. Future people will, therefore, find us misguided, confined by the ideologies of our time. It is humbling to consider that all our current predictions, fear stories, and saccharine antidotes may be charming relics.

If all goes well in terms of science and rumour, Walt Disney will be our ambassador to the future. A product of his time in many ways, he adapted old stories and fairytales to eliminate the macabre and invoked happy endings where they may not have been before. As Disney hobbles around the future in his freezer-burnt body and antiquated moustache, I hope that he will realize that he has become what he gave us, what we want—a reminder. In his words: "People look at you and me to see what they are supposed to be. And, if we don't disappoint them, maybe, just maybe, they won't disappoint us."

....

The voices represented by the co-authors Helaina Lalande, Josie Baker, Merray Gerges, Diana Hosseini, Mireille Eagan, and Marie Fox represent a small selection of people. I acknowledge that some key demographics and communities are missing, including but not limited to Indigenous, senior citizens, Francophones, persons with disabilities, and varied genders ... This essay is an attempt to present a theory in practice and is not claiming to be all-encompassing. I actually feel that this essay's approach is reflected in the *A Bold Vision* anthology's structure and very existence.

My vision for Canada for the next 150 years requires that, as a nation, we forgive ourselves for eagerly consuming a diluted sense of ourselves. Our story has been simplified to invoke happy endings for a powerful few. A homogeneous wash over a complex and difficult history. But this isn't the end: the Canadian narrative continues, and we all play a part its creation. Let us embrace our failures, acknowledge the complexity of a truly multi-peopled culture, look to the silenced, and listen for possibility.

To be Canadian shouldn't be comfortable. It should be unstable, disruptive, and unrelentingly challenged by difficult discourses that are propelled by the far reaches of accepted reality.

....

1. Co-author biographies:
    Helaina Lalande is a(n):
    tenth grader
    Trekkie
    cat person
    human
    Bicycles fan
    doodler

Moomintroll lover

cheese connoisseur

ordained minister of the Universal Life Church

Beatles aficionado

sister

amateur felter

narcoleptic

mediocre saxophonist

Studio Ghibli devotee

Tolkien buff

atheist

dumpling addict

Joni Mitchell enthusiast

francophile

Pisces

Josie Baker is a feminist community organizer in Charlottetown, PEI. She works on issues of food sovereignty, migrant worker rights, anti-racism, reproductive justice, and queer visibility in the smallest province in Canada. In her spare time she is an avid vegetable gardener.

Merray Gerges recently graduated from NSCAD with a BA Art History and a minor in Journalism Studies from the University of King's College. She is interested in cultural studies and postcolonial theory and spends her time trying to reconcile her genuine interest in identity politics and anti-oppression practices with her superficial but irrevocable attraction to Minimalism and other art-historical movements notorious for not being the most welcoming to women, people of colour, and queer people.

Diana Hosseini is a Toronto-based artist. Her practice explores ideas surrounding cultural hybridity through the use of cultural objects reinvented with electronic and mechanical materials. She holds a Bachelor's Degree in Medical Anthropology and Studio Art from the University of Toronto as well as a Master of Fine Arts degree from Nova Scotia College of Art and Design.

Mireille Eagan is a curator, art historian, and art critic based in the Atlantic provinces. She is currently Curator of Contemporary Art at The Rooms in St. John's, NL, a position she has held since 2011. From 2008 to 2010, Eagan was curator at the Confederation Centre Art Gallery in Charlottetown, PEI.

Marie Fox is a painter, an observer, and an eye-twinkling voluptuary.

2. Ralph Ellison, Introduction to *Invisible Man* (New York: Vintage International, 1995), xx.

3. To read more about my perspective on Canadian identity and historical presence please read my essays "Sovereignty" and "Assimilation," collected in the

"Sovereignty" exhibition catalogue. You can download this catalogue from my website, accessed July 2014, http://beckaviau.com/press/.

4. Many of these ideas have been expressed/explained in an artistic writing piece I created as my MFA thesis statement which can be found on my website, accessed July 2014, http://beckaviau.com/press/.

5. To read the essay mentioned by Merray Gerges, please visit http://beckaviau.com/press/ and download the essay "Major Feature," found listed in the writing section alongside this essay.

EMAN BARE

Eman Bare is a journalism student and activist whose philosophy, belief, and vision all point to global human rights.

Eman Bare was born in Regina, Saskatachewan, in 1992, to a family that had immigrated to Canada from Somalia. Growing up as a first-generation Canadian and a Muslim, she felt she was living two separate lives: A life at home with her family and a life with her friends. It was only when she began to explore what it meant to be Canadian that she realized she had the ability to combine the knowledge and perspective of two entirely different cultures. Further, this diverse ethnicity underscores, for her, the importance of acceptance, multiculturalism, and equality.

Eman Bare was 17 years old and on an out-of-province exchange program when she happened to see coverage of the famine in Somalia, a catastrophe during which more than 250,000 people died between 2010 to 2012. She was hit with the stark realization that she shared a language, history, and culture with those who were literally starving to death. Before the segment ended, she was on her phone organizing what would become her first fundraiser, an event that raised $10,000 for famine relief.

Now a third-year journalism student at the University of Regina, Eman Bare successfully draws attention to those whose rights are being violated, either by laws, those in power, or even their fellow citizens. After graduation, she aspires to work for CBC national, to produce educational documentaries on the long-term effects of colonialism, and to begin an eco-friendly clothing line that generates incomes for women in countries still suffering from the impacts of colonization.

Eman Bare lives in Regina, Saskatchewan, with her parents and siblings.

JIGSAW CANADA

"*Otherness. That's what I was. I was reminded every day. I would flip on the news, and I would see how women who looked like me were oppressed and those who had dark skin like mine were subject to discrimination.*"

One of my earliest memories is of a trip to Calgary. My mother and older brother and I spent a week visiting my great-aunt. I was four and my brother was five. What I remember vividly about this trip isn't silly family photos or even meeting part of my extended family for the first time. What stands out so clearly is being asked, "Where are you from?" I would always answer "Canada" — mostly because to my five-year-old self, Calgary wasn't *in* Canada — Canada was home, and I wasn't at home. My mom would add in that we were from Somalia. Ahh, Somalia. The country I had heard so much about but that to me was nothing more than bedtime stories of long ago. Somalia was the phone ringing Sunday mornings, with the woman who was my grandmother on the other end of the line. I knew of Somalia, but I also knew I was not of Somalia. How could my home be somewhere I had never experienced?

Throughout my childhood and teens, that million-dollar question "Where are you from" was asked of me more times that I can count. As a child, the question confused me — but I learned to answer with "Somalia," because I felt like that was what the stranger was expecting from me. I never understood society's constant need to "figure me out." It was as though they would see me, see the scarf on my head and the colour of my skin, and immediately put me in a box. I was labelled a "foreign." I remember Mrs. Dennison in Grade Three who said, "We were all foreign, every one of us, except those who were Indigenous to this land." Except it was never an Indigenous person trying to "figure me out."

In my teens, my responses to "Where are you from?" became more defiant and laced with aggression.

"Where are you from?" they would ask.

"Regina," I would say.

"No, but where are you *from*?"

And then I would say, "I don't know, ma'am. My ancestors were brought over during the trans-Atlantic slave trade. Because of colonization, and the ideology that one person's life was somehow worth less than another's simply because of the colour of the skin, I don't know where I am from."

They would soon walk away, leaving me with a sinking feeling in my stomach. Because none of what I had so defiantly said was true, or, at least it was not true of me. Like most Somali youth, I could trace my ancestors back ten generations. But what made me physically ill was the tug-of-war that I was playing. You see, the rope was Canada. And on one side, I stood with everyone who was Canadian and a visible minority, and on the other side stood the questioners. The people who felt they had more of a claim to Canada because of the colour of their skin or because of their religion.

I felt like I needed to try extra hard to fit in. I needed to sing "O Canada" a little louder at every hockey game, speak English as obviously as possible, and live up to every Canadian stereotype.

Those were my teens — when, like most teenagers, I was trying to figure out who I was. But instead of trying to make the cheer team or find my clique in high school, I was standing with my feet on two sides of a tug-of-war line. The outside world was pointing fingers yelling foreigner, and my inner voice was doing everything possible to "fit in."

Otherness. That's what I was. I was reminded every day. I would flip on the news, and I would see how women who looked like me were oppressed and those who had dark skin like mine were subject to discrimination. And so every time the guy at the gas station looked at me a little funny, I couldn't help but wonder if he thought I was being forced to wear this scarf on my head. I also couldn't help but wish that he would just ask. And the only reason I had to wonder that is that we've created a belief that everyone who looks a certain way, is a certain way. We decide, because we know.

And somehow, I, the 21-year-old feminist who poured sand down a boy's pants in pre-school for being mean to my brother, who played rugby all through high school, who teaches yoga every weekend was oppressed.

Of the boxes that we have created, the "oppressed" box was mine.

Slavery is not dead. We have just transformed it. We have created the "Other."

Somehow, we have convinced ourselves that those who do not look like us somehow do not feel what we feel and do not hurt like we hurt. We have told ourselves that other mothers do not cry over their children (who have been killed by our guns) like we would cry over our children. They are different.

And different is bad.

Colonization believed this, slavery believed this, and the foundations this country was built on believed this.

But that was the past, and we have moved on. But have we? Or have we created new "Others"?

They say history repeats itself, and they say this because it's true.

And as activist, I say I will not let that happen. My vision for Canada is understanding that there is no room for "othering." That we are one, and territorial or any boundaries do not somehow make us feel less or feel more.

My vision for Canada is understanding that no matter that we can give billions in foreign aid, by allowing our clothing to be made in sweatshops, we are paying for the deaths of others. What is a sweatshop but a factory meant to break dreams and remind people that they are worthless?

Canada is changing. Canada's reputation on the world stage is changing. Where we were once considered peacekeepers, we are now being looked at as guilty in turning a blind eye to missing and murdered Indigenous women. We have turned our backs on the environment. We have a prime minister in power who this past year gave a speech in the Middle East that screamed of ignorance. We have stopped being Canada.

My vision for Canada is to be Canada: The Canada we have been and, better yet, the Canada that we can be, and no "Others."

This country was not built in an honourable way, but we have the power to create bright futures for all of our children.

It's not enough simply to say what my vision for Canada is, because visions like that are often short-lived.

I commit to making my vision of Canada my life's work, my legacy and passion.

Equality is something that we have fought and died for over the years, but when it is someone else's turn for equality, we think of a million-and-one reasons why they do not deserve equality.

All women, all men, created equal. That is equality. That is my Canada.

That is the understanding that we need to have. No religion, no sexual orientation, no skin colour, no country of origin makes anyone bleed any differently, hurt any differently, or feel their heart beat any differently. And that's it. All I've ever wanted this country to be is a place of understanding and acceptance of others.

Sixteen-year-old me tried desperately to change to be Canadian, and it wasn't until much later that I realized that I didn't need to change. Everyone else did.

KLUANE ADAMEK

Kluane Adamek has experience living in rural, urban, northern, and southern communities. A graduate of Carleton University, she is fluent in English and French and continues to learn her traditional languages of Southern Tutchone and Tlingit. A citizen of Kluane First Nation, Yukon Territory, and from the *Dakhl'aweidí* — Killerwhale Clan, she dances traditionally with the *Dakhká Khwáan* Dancers — Inland Tlingit Dance Group. Kluane is proud of her ancestry, Indigenous and non-Indigenous, which she believes has given her the ability to view the world with different perspectives.

Kluane feels most at home in Yukon and believes her values and abilities have been tremendously shaped by her experience working with community organizations such as the Skookum Jim Friendship Centre and the Council of Yukon First Nations and serving on various boards including the Aboriginal Healing Foundation, Yukon Aboriginal Women's Council, Yukon Aboriginal Sport Circle, AFN National Youth Council, and, most recently, the Kluane Development Corporations. Kluane has represented the Yukon at the Vancouver 2010 Olympics as a Youth Ambassador and torch-bearer. She was asked to represent Canada as a flag-bearer for Commonwealth Day Celebrations in 2012, held at Westminster Abbey. Kluane was also recently selected as a Global Shaper as part of the World Economic Forum. Kluane worked with the Assembly of First Nations in the role of First Nation Liaison and Advisor to former National Chief Shawn A-in-chut Atleo and is currently a Fellow through the Walter and Duncan Foundation — Northern Fellowship. She has been instrumental in the development of the Yukon Indigenous Emerging Leaders and their upcoming gathering, "Our Voices," that brings together Yukon First Nation Emerging Leaders from across the Territory. Her passion for supporting community development and leadership and supporting emerging leaders and youth is demonstrated through both her personal and professional experiences.

KNOWING THE DEPTH
OF OUR HISTORY

"My grandparents, similar in age, have had two completely different experiences of being 'Canadian.' This offers a perfect example of the depth of our history and shows why it is so important to share their stories. All of our grandparents' stories need to be told, honoured, and respected."

"To know where we are going, we must always know where we have come from." – *Yukon First Nation Elders*

Kluane First Nation citizens: Elder Lena Johnson, Pauly Wroot, Late Elder Rita Joe, Elder Margaret Johnson, Kluane Adamek, Silver City, Yukon 2012

When we think of Canada forming as a nation, many of us think of a time-line dating back just 150 years. This is how we have been taught to consider the past: We consider time in years, history written by pen on paper, and a Canada formed out of a conference attended by 23 settler-men who met to unite British and former French colonies.

When I think of Canada, I reflect on the original relationships with the Indigenous peoples of the lands. The original inhabitants were the Indigenous peoples, who governed their lands and maintained tradition-al practices including languages, customs, and protocols within their own communities and nations, as well as holding relations with other nations for trade and commerce, including exchanges of art and culture. Children were educated in their traditional ways by family and the community with language and culture at the root of their identity. Treaties, agreements, or dealings between communities and other Indigenous nations were achieved and recognized through ceremony, tradition, and consensus-building. When the first settlers travelled and arrived on what we know as Turtle Island (North America), they formed agreements and thereby entered relationships with the Indigenous people. These agreements have continued to exist over centuries and lead us towards what will be recognized as "Canada's 150th Year Celebrations."

In their very nature, settlers' agreements and relationships with Indigenous peoples were formed on principles of true respect, partnership, sharing, economic and military alliance, and equal opportunity. Some of the original agreements forged include the Royal Proclamation of 1763, Peace and Friendship Treaties, the Robinson Huron Treaties, the Douglas Treaty, and numbered Treaties across Canada.

Formal agreements were made by way of trade relationships, mutual understanding, and respect among the Indigenous and non-Indigenous peoples. This is our true, shared history, and far too often this part of our history is not what is spoken of; rather, it is often ignored. Over time, this original relationship changed drastically. New government policies emerged causing the imposition of paternalistic governance models, the removal of Indigenous peoples from their lands, Government-attempted "control" of Indigenous peoples through legislation and policy, and specific programs of control and assimilation as evidenced by the creation of residential schools. Indigenous peoples were given "lesser-than" rights within the lands that they had always inhabited. These policies are also part of our shared story, a dark chapter of Canadian history. The conversation about negative aspects of the past is not an easy one, for we often shy away from it in discussion. It is an uncomfortable conversation based on misunderstandings and over a century of mistrust between the Canadian state and Indigenous peoples.

"In order to see each other, we must first understand each other." – *Shawn A-in-chut Atleo, Hereditary Chief, Nuu-chah-nulth, Ahousaht, former Assembly of First Nations National Chief*

When we talk about "reconciliation" in Canada, what it really means to me is *seeing and understanding* each other. We need to see each other and understand each other and our shared history and backgrounds.

As is our custom, I will share a little about who I am, in an effort to explain how my own unique identity stems from a diverse cultural background and informs my perspective today.

My grandparents: on my father's side, my grandmother, a First Nations residential school survivor; on my mother's side, my grandfather, a German refugee who immigrated to Canada after the Second World War. Both have experienced trauma and abuse and have lived their entire lives dealing with the impacts of these experiences. My grandmother was taken from her family at the age of five and given a number in residential school. While growing up as a child, she rarely saw her parents or went home to her community. She was abused in the residential school and taught that everything about her, her traditions, and her way of life, everything about being Southern Tutchone, was dirty and immoral. My grandfather, who grew up in Germany, was fortunate to survive the Second World War and as a young boy worked incredibly hard to make just enough to provide basic food and shelter for his family. He was fortunate to immigrate to Canada in efforts to start a new life — and, to this day, he is incredibly proud of his Canadian citizenship.

My grandparents, similar in age, have had two completely different experiences of being "Canadian." This offers a perfect example of the depth of our history and shows why it is so important to share their stories. All of our grandparents' stories need to be told, honoured, and respected. Neither of my grandparents had the opportunity to attend university; neither was educated in a way that respected their culture, nor did their education reflect who they were. But they both carried determination, resiliency, and a desire to live better lives. This is Canada, and more of the stories of our deep history need to be acknowledged and understood.

When we think about how our children learn, what they learn, and where they learn, we must critically think about how our forthcoming generations will be educated and socialized, and what this means for their future. Today, I see our students in public and private education systems. I see First Nation students attending on-reserve schools that are majorly underfunded with minimal access to secondary and tertiary resources. In 2014, there are still schools on-reserve without gymnasiums, music rooms or instruments, libraries, playgrounds, computers, or special-needs supports. This past year, the United Nations Special Rapporteur on the Rights of Indigenous Peoples visited Canada and reported that Canada is currently in a crisis situation.[1] This injustice cannot continue for the next 150 years.

Kluane Lake School — Muskrat Camp. Students learning how to skin Muskrat, Yukon 2014

We must work now, together, to ensure that Indigenous peoples and their rights in Canada are fully respected in relation to the UN Declaration on the

Rights of Indigenous Peoples as well as our own Treaties, our Constitution, and the Charter of Rights and Freedoms. First Nation people have the right to be educated in their traditional languages and in a manner that reflects culture because this is at the root of who they are; this is their identity.

Student Mentors and Elder Frances Woolsey, Whitehorse, Yukon, 2012

For the last 40 years, First Nation leaders in particular have been fighting for control of their education — "Indian Control of Indian Education." Education was the tool used to assimilate and remove culture and language from our communities; thus, it must now be the driving force to help our communities rebuild and enable all First Nations peoples to thrive and revitalize language and culture. I have experienced visiting communities where five-year-old kindergarten students are fluent in their language. I have been to public schools where all students, Indigenous and non-Indigenous, are welcome to join traditional dance groups and learn the language, the songs, and the dances. To me, this is part of reconciliation and part of the opportunity we have in the next 150 years to change and create stronger relationships and understandings. It is truly an incredible opportunity.

I want to see this for all our First Nations communities: language fluency among our Indigenous peoples, curriculum that includes our true history, students learning our original relationships, the truth told about the history of cultural genocide in the form of residential schools, and understanding of the challenges this posed to Canada's Indigenous peoples. But these aren't things that only Indigenous children should be taught. In order for us to cultivate the significance of our Indigenous traditions, this history must be taught to all Canadian students.

Every child should be proud of a Canada that works with Indigenous nations and respects the nation-to-nation relationships as originally agreed to, centuries ago. They should be proud of a Canada that prioritizes education for all, beginning with early childhood and onto post-secondary education, where we recognize the holistic, lifelong learning process. University and other post-secondary education should not in a classist way represent only one section of the Canadian population. It should reflect all of our history together. Everyone should be given the opportunity to pursue a higher level

Kluane kids — hosting a sleepover with the local youth, Kluane Traditional Territory, Burwash Landing, July 2013

of learning, if they so choose and desire. With Indigenous peoples grossly over-represented in the justice system, in care, in unemployment, and in poverty, investments in education should remain the priority. Making a fundamental shift in education comes from recognizing that the Western classroom model in many cases does not support the most effective education outcomes for all our students. Student success needs to be the priority. This will, in turn, create the most positive change not only among Indigenous communities, but beyond. As Nelson Mandela reminded us, "Education is the most powerful weapon which you can use to change the world."

The next century should be spent focusing on our future generations and what it is we will leave them as a legacy. Canada currently has two national languages: French and English. Indigenous languages must be honoured and respected in Canada, in the same way that we acknowledge French and English. We need to move towards a more collaborative system of governance at the federal level. There are examples of territorial and Indigenous governments in Canada's Northern regions, including the Yukon, Northwest Territories, and Nunavut, where consensus models are used and are more effective. The structure in itself could be one that welcomes discussion as opposed to fostering hostility and aggression as it does currently. An example could include a circle structure, which enables a less aggressive, non-confrontational way to conduct parliamentary proceedings.

By infusing Indigenous characteristics and representation into the foundation of the House of Commons and the political structure in the way that is stated above, a more harmonious and inclusive precedent could be incorporated into the Canadian governmental system. We must recognize that other states have included Indigenous seats as part of their governance structures. We look to New Zealand, where the Māori have reserved elected seats in their federal parliament.[2] We need to start exploring options for Canadian Constitutional reform to ensure that Indigenous peoples are represented and included appropriately.

"Concerted measures, based on mutual understanding and real partnership with aboriginal peoples, through their own representative institutions, are vital to establishing long-term solutions." – *James Anaya, UN Special Rapporteur on the Rights of Indigenous People*[3]

Natural resource development can be a collaboration or a collision between the interests of Indigenous people and others.[4] We are in a time where we must start doing things differently in relation to natural resource development in Canada, especially when we look to decision-making processes and Inherent and Aboriginal Rights. By working with Indigenous nations and communities, industry and government have the opportunity to look at ways in which responsible development can occur. When we think about the mining industry, hydraulic fracking, or oil and gas development, there are concerns that all Canadians share. It is clear, these are not solely Indigenous concerns: These are Canadian concerns. We have the opportunity to make decisions now that pave the way for responsible and sustainable development—and any decisions must include Indigenous peoples. As mentioned earlier, the UN Declaration on the Rights of Indigenous Peoples should be used by all levels of governments in relation to setting the standard for Indigenous peoples and their roles in decision-making processes, assessments, and approvals. Indigenous people must be equal partners in development that affects their territories. Free, prior, and informed consent must be the path forward.

In terms of royalties and natural resource development and extraction, far too often we see shareholders and companies benefitting from increased wealth while the Indigenous communities most affected by development continue to experience poverty, poor housing and water conditions, lack of opportunity and employment, and high levels of suicide. I want young people to know that there is more for them out there—and that the status quo is not the only way forward.

We must recognize that in order for us to all benefit from development and growth, we have to be open to creating new relationships and agreements and understand that Indigenous peoples need to benefit from these projects in a more sustainable and equitable way than we see today. I want to see those who have benefitted from the resources and opportunities of the North always give back to the families and communities where development has taken place.

In Canada's true North, we see three orders of government, a rich resource-development industry, and a high population of Indigenous people. Canada's North in the next century will see and experience major changes in relation to climate change, development, and industry. Northerners and those who are currently impacted by these changes are quite often absent from the decision-making table. Industry remains the leader of development, and communities are now, more than ever, voicing their concerns and issues with development and the growth of the North. Communities that are rural may not want road access, and the Arctic sovereignty issue remains a discussion among international states. The rate of change and the impact that development and growth have already had on rural Northern communities remain major concerns, alongside equitable support for health care, food access, and housing. Joint decision-making needs to be recognized, and appropriate policies need to be developed that include the voices of local communities. Their needs should be at the forefront of this work.

For Canada to truly be successful, we must, in the future, see Canada working in true partnerships with Indigenous peoples, a true nation-to-nation relationship. This concept requires Canada, the state, to recognize the unique Aboriginal rights and title of Indigenous peoples in Canada. It requires all Canadians to understand the past and present relationship between Canada and Indigenous peoples, and it requires us all to do the hard work, in resetting the current relationship, to one that fosters mutual respect and recognition. I have a vision for the implementation of all Treaties and agreements forged with Indigenous peoples past, present, and future. I want to see Canada as a proud nation with strong understanding of who we are and where we have come from, including the history of Indigenous peoples. We

*Healing totem-raising event: IRS Healing Totem Project,
TRC Reconciliation Commission, Whitehorse, January 2013*[6]

must work together to achieve reconciliation and continue to hold the vision of our ancestors, for we all want our children to be successful and have every opportunity. This is our Canada, and in the words of Elders from the Yukon, we must stand "Together today for our children tomorrow."[5]

I want to see Canada as the leader of change, social innovation, and good treatment of Indigenous peoples, a country that is proud and strong. I want to see Canada where we know where we've come from and have the ability to learn from the past. Let's use this as our guide to forge a way forward: Working collaboratively, for this is the way we will all be able to benefit from Canada's wealth and prosperity. I want to see a Canada that remembers us—this current generation—as grandparents who made decisions keeping future generations in mind, who changed the way we think, see, and feel about each other—as grandparents who, like ours, remained resilient and worked hard to create a sense of pride in who we are.

....

1. James Anaya, "The Situation of Indigenous Peoples of Canada, Advance Unedited Version," accessed July 2014, http://unsr.jamesanaya.org/country-reports/the-situation-of-indigenous-peoples-in-canada.
2. New Zealand Electoral Commission, "Māori Representation," accessed July 2014, http://www.elections.org.nz/voting-system/maori-representation.
3. Anaya, "The Situation."
4. Shawn A-in-chut Atleo, Assembly of First Nations Chief, speech to the Vancouver Board of Trade, 2013.
5. Yukon Native Brotherhood, *Together Today for Our Children Tomorrow: A Summary* (Whitehorse, Yukon: Yukon Native Brotherhood, 1973).
6. Truth and Reconciliation Commission, "Residential Schools in the Yukon," accessed July 2014, http://www.yesnet.yk.ca/firstnations/pdf/12-13/trc_jan_14_15_13.pdf.

NAZANIN AFSHIN-JAM MACKAY

Nazanin Afshin-Jam MacKay is an international human rights and democracy activist, author, public speaker, and mother. She is president and co-founder of the organization Stop Child Executions and founder of the Nazanin Foundation.

Nazanin Afshin-Jam MacKay earned a BA in international relations and political science at the University of British Columbia and continued with exchanges to *Sciences Po* in Paris, France, and the International Study Centre in the UK. She later became a Global Youth Educator with the Red Cross.

In 2003, Nazanin Afshin-Jam MacKay won Miss Canada and was runner-up at Miss World, giving her the platform she sought to raise awareness and funds for charitable organizations working on issues ranging from natural disasters to fistula awareness. In 2006, she successfully ran an international campaign to save the life of a young woman sentenced to death in Iran for stabbing a man who tried to rape her. She has since co-founded Stop Child Executions to help put an end to executions of juveniles worldwide. Meanwhile, Nazanin released a multilingual album, charting hits in Canada, USA, and Europe. In 2008, she was appointed to the board of the Canadian Race Relations Foundation to help eliminate racism and discrimination in Canada. In 2011, she graduated with a Master's in diplomacy with a concentration in international conflict management at Norwich University in Vermont.

She is the recipient of several human rights awards of distinction and has given speeches at the UN, EU, UK, Canadian Parliament, and numerous universities and conferences.

Nazanin Afshin-Jam MacKay is the author of *The Tale of Two Nazanins* (Harper Collins, 2012). Half of her proceeds from the book support initiatives to counter violence against women and children and to empower young girls through the Nazanin Foundation.

Nazanin Afshin-Jam MacKay is married to Minister of Justice Peter MacKay, and together they have a young toddler named Kian.

A BOLD VISION FOR RENEWING CANADIAN DEMOCRACY

"I have come to learn the importance, benefits, necessity, and fragility of a democracy. A real democracy. A strong democracy. While Canada has a great democratic system, I believe there are ways to ensure it stays healthy, vibrant, and inclusive and that we perpetually improve on our democratic institutions."

I was born in Iran at the start of the Islamic Revolution that transformed the country into a theocracy. Since then, an unelected Supreme Leader stands at the helm and is the top decision-maker in the judicial, executive, and legislative branches of government as well as the armed forces. The president, who has a secondary role, is not democratically elected either. Rather, he (and it is always a "he") is "selected." Presidential and parliamentary candidates are vetted by the Guardian Council made up of a dozen appointed jurists and clerics who determine whether or not the candidates are dedicated enough to Islamic principles and the constitution. From such a very narrow political selection, the population is then allowed to cast their vote, hardly free, fair, or representative of the people.

Iran's penal code, based on Sharia Law, has been imposed on the population despite the fact that the vast majority of Iranians want separation between religion and state. Any form of dissent against the rules and regulations of the regime is met with fines, imprisonment, torture, and execution. Close to 700 people were executed in 2013 alone, and over 800 prisoners of conscience are being held in Iran's jails today. Persecution of ethnic and religious minorities continues; women are treated as second-class citizens and valued at half the worth of men. A brutal and oppressive security apparatus commits grave human rights abuses on a daily basis. Contributing to the repressive environment are a state-controlled media, a cyber army that spies on citizens online, and morality police that scour the streets for violations of Islamic dress code or "promoting western culture" such as men and women intermingling or music, parties, or dancing. Civil society is suffocated, and, naturally, democratic institutions suffer. It is only a matter of time before a state with such an undemocratic system collapses. Seeing the hunger for true democracy and free votes in Iran makes me value what we have in Canada even more. We should not take it for granted.

As a result, I have come to learn the importance, benefits, necessity, and fragility of a democracy. A real democracy. A strong democracy. While Canada has a great democratic system, I believe there are ways to ensure it stays healthy, vibrant, and inclusive and that we perpetually improve on our democratic institutions. We must keep in mind that it takes work and effort to ensure that our population does not become lazy or take democracy and the right to vote for granted. Apathy, lack of knowledge, and alienating segments of our society could lead to democratic stagnation or even serious decline. As a whole, the nation could suffer and thus our quality of life could be harmed.

They say a true litmus test of a great person— or country for that matter— is how it treats its most vulnerable, particularly children. Therefore, my "bold vision" for Canada's future focuses on strengthening Canada's democracy by embracing youth involvement in national policy decisions. As well, my vision focuses on revitalizing parliamentary procedure through the help of modern technology.

These ideas are a preliminary vision, supposed to ignite thought, dialogue, and debate. By no means is this a comprehensive study or road map. The real road map should be constructed by the citizens themselves, whether youth or parliamentarians or others who have a stake in Canada's future.

First, a focus on youth and democracy. In a representative democracy, the wishes of the population are supposed to be enacted, communicated, and reflected by elected officials. With over 29 per cent of the Canadian population under the age of 24, should youth not have some kind of direct voice at the federal level?

All the studies conducted in the past decade in Canada and in other western democracies have conclusively shown that voting-age youth, ages 18 to 24, are disengaged from conventional politics. Voter turnout has declined successively over recent elections, with a noticeable drop particularly observed since the 1984 federal elections in Canada.[1] According to one analysis, "Youth voter turnout in the 2011 election was considerably below the average — just 38.8 percent of Canadians aged 18-24 and 45 percent of 25-34 year olds voted."[2]

It is commonly believed that as youth mature, so will their appreciation for politics, and, in time, they will cast their ballot. However, recent studies indicate this is a fallacy. Today's youth are not showing signs of becoming more likely to vote as they age. Rather, bad habits form and continue, and the trend indicates that low voter turnout continues into the future, so that according to Elections Canada, "Each successive generation appears to be less inclined to vote than its predecessors."[3] Another study reminds us, "This trend poses an obvious threat to the core democratic idea of popular control of government."[4]

To reverse this alarming trend, we must first understand why Canadian youth are not voting or involved in politics to the same degree as youth in the past and then figure out solutions. As it stands, many combined factors explain the decline in youth-voter turnout compared to turnout of older voters.

One factor is lack of knowledge. Before the 2008 federal election, a Dominion Institute survey found "that 43% of youth sometimes find politics and government too complicated to understand."[5] Experts such as Henry Milner find "the level of 'civic literacy' to be relatively low in Canada, compared to other Western democracies, despite our high levels of educational attainment."[6] Thereby, voter abstention increases because of a lack of confidence to make proper and informed decisions.

A second factor in lower voting numbers is little exposure to and lack of interest in formal politics. This includes youth having limited contact with political parties and candidates before and after campaigns, and, therefore, being disengaged from the whole electoral process. On the other side of the same coin, "election officials respond to the preferences of voters, not non-voters. As rational actors, candidates and parties tend to ignore the young and a vicious cycle ensues."[7]

A third factor in declining turnout among youth is "a declining sense that voting is a civic duty."[8] During my five years as an air cadet, I received an early appreciation of how generations of Canadians fought and died to defend democratic values. More than any other segment of our population, veterans understand that freedom does not come free. I am heartened by much higher public appreciation and respect for the Canadian Armed Forces as a means to also heighten awareness for youth engagement in the electoral process.

Many studies indicate that while youth are less interested in "formal" or conventional politics, they *are* interested in politics generally, are active in alternative ways, and are eager to play a more active role.[9] "The problem is therefore not political apathy but alienation from the political system."[10] One of the realities is that today's youth are marginalized. They do not have a chance to be part of the decision-making process. Indeed, a United Nations survey conducted in 186 countries found that "the main challenges for youth were limited opportunities for effective participation in decision-making processes."[11]

To reverse this, we must first accept as a nation that youth participation is a fundamental democratic right. We older Canadians must respect and respond to youth needs. The UN suggests youth "be consulted at all stages—in development and implementation of public policy as well as in its evaluation."[12] But in order to have actual input, one must participate. Democracy is predicated on being active; therefore, we must empower the young. We need to create space and opportunities for them to exercise their voices and leadership, for them to see their ideas implemented into action and witness real change as a result of their initiative and participation. In the words of the people behind the "Apathy is Boring" movement, "It is important to recognize that involving young people is not only about the qualitative idea of inclusion. Rather, it is about recognizing that youth can offer measurable benefits to organizations and individual adults."[13]

Engaging youth in all levels of politics is a win-win situation. Not only will it boost youth confidence, stimulate an appetite for politics, and prevent voter apathy from a young age, but it will also help us as a nation by strengthening democratic institutions. The government of Canada will benefit from the energy, fresh perspectives, and creativity of young minds in the country and be able to draw on their firsthand knowledge and up-to-date experience within the education system itself. Youth will also be able to keep government modern and more efficient with their knowledge and know-how on new technologies and their links with non-traditional news and media outlets. Youth representatives and spokespeople could also be conduits back to their youth peers regarding governmental matters and initiatives. Youth appreciate, relate, and listen more to information coming from one of them. Involving youth leaders, including persons from the worlds of sports, music, and entertainment to promote active involvement should be part of any strategy.

It is very important for young Canadians to be involved in the decision-making process on issues that will affect their lives and futures rather than older adults making all the policy choices for them.

How can all Canadians address the concerning matter of low voter turnout among youth and engage younger Canadians in formal politics? According to Elections Canada, various actors are responsible to address this concern: "Political parties and candidates, educators, civil society organizations—and young people themselves—all have an important role to play."[14] Because the causes of youth disengagement are so diverse, there is not one simple solution.

One solution is for politicians to ensure that issues of importance to Canadian youth receive ample attention on their political agenda. For a healthy democracy to exist and thrive in a country like ours with a significant population under twenty-four, the political agenda must speak to and be relevant to them.

It has been sensibly noted that we should be focusing efforts in schools, with focus on civics courses and practice elections. Certainly, it has been established that "civics courses do impart information and foster development of attitudes known to encourage participation."[15] Student-focused groups such as "Apathy is Boring" that educate Canadian youth about democracy are really making a difference.

Elections Canada plays an important role in that it recognizes the importance of reaching Canadians who are younger than voting age. "There is little data in Canada about the amount of civics instruction in provincial schools curricula. Comparisons are difficult because the hours of civics courses differ among jurisdictions."[16] By focusing civics education on teens or even preteens, the electoral process could become second nature and seem less foreign when students finish high school.

Elections Canada notes certain "administrative difficulties" as one reason for a curb in voting among younger voters. Making politics easier to access is as important as increasing youth knowledge of it. If we bring it to them; make it interesting, easy, and accessible; and use current technology and social media to inform and involve them, these methods will garner greater participation. While there is no true replacement for human face-to-face engagement we older Canadians must gradually bring youth to the point that they are ready for in-person engagement by meeting them on their own terms and using their preferred methods of communication. More direct communication online through modern social media is both invaluable and inevitable. Twitter, Skype, and Facebook are all platforms able to provide the most up-to-date forms of political engagement, and new popular forms are likely to emerge. As well, call-in shows and virtual town-hall meetings that use technology can help directly reach young people. We can do our taxes and banking online, and even register for voting online, but we cannot actually vote. If we can develop a safe, secure, and sure-proof method for voting online, this could increase voting across the spectrum from young to old.

The Constitution Act 1867 gives provinces almost complete jurisdiction over educational concerns. It may be time to evaluate whether the federal government should have partial jurisdiction in educational matters that pertain to elections and promote democracy. In other words, the Federal government would be responsible for promoting democracy, elections, and history, including a standard history course in all parts of Canada that teaches young people the value of citizenship and an appreciation of the sacrifices of past generations. This could result in more standardized civics education, but could also provide more equitable content in education for students who move from province to province and result in more fair assessments in provincial exams and university acceptance. In the interim, until there is a federal strategy possible, Elections Canada has suggested "a national civics education strategy be developed, coordinated by the Council of Ministers of Education Canada."[17] This could be a great national start to revitalizing youth understanding of the practical importance and operation of our Canadian democratic system.

My "bold vision" requires the involvement of a national initiative, whether enacted by a federal entity or a consortium of all the provinces and territories together. In my vision, each high school would elect a representative, either their school president or another, but preferably someone who has just finished their last year of high school. There would then be an online election in each province to choose the "youth provincial leader." Next, all the provincial and territorial leaders would compete for the top job of "youth prime minister." This could either be done through online voting or through a national televised contest similar to *Canadian Idol* but addressing numerous political issues affecting youth. The youth prime minister would have a seat in the House of Commons for the duration of a session of Parliament and would receive the appropriate resources. He or she would travel throughout the country and collect the wishes and concerns of their age cohort. It would be very helpful, for example, if this youth representative were to sit on various governmental committees, working on issues such as heritage, justice, or health — and, of course, education if such a federal committee is developed in the future.

If my vision for youth participation in federal politics gains any kind of traction, then youth should be involved from inception to conclusion in order to construct the real road map.

Not only does including youth allow their voices to be heard in federal politics, it also develops an interest in politics from a young age and promotes engagement in the long term. This positive experience of actually voting for someone they can relate to, as a direct participant in the system that represents them, should boost and reinforce their confidence in democracy. Such an initiative will produce the leaders of tomorrow. If Canada is successful and the benefits are apparent, it could serve as a model to other nations. In time, there could even be youth summits around the globe discussing matters of global concern to them.

By investing our time and energy in teaching young citizens about the electoral system and their right and duty to vote, Canadians will whet youths' civic appetites for politics in Canada and give them the needed confidence to participate and be active and engaged citizens. We must not only provide them with the knowledge, but also ensure that they feel included by providing them a space and opportunity to participate. Seeing tangible results from their input will have lifelong effects of continued civic engagement and will spill over into the next generation.

Parents who actively discuss civic responsibility, politics, and the importance of voting are far more likely to see their children taking on a sense of social responsibility and casting their ballots. Teachers, coaches, and mentors also play a key role in empowering young Canadians with a sense of duty to participate in our democratic process. We teach them now; later they will teach their own kids.

All of these matters are predicated on young people taking the lead and taking up the challenge. We often mouth the words "The youth are the future." They truly are.

....

Some have speculated that youth and some other Canadians are disengaged from politics because they do not like what they see of the political system. Often, what they see in the news is the institution of Question Period. A big part of every day for members of parliament is spent preparing for Question Period. Unfortunately, this once vibrant and relevant period of debate and accountability has fallen into disrepute. Some even describe it as "theatre of the absurd" and an affront to parliamentary decorum. Personally, I view Question Period as a charade, and abolishing it altogether would free up parliamentarians' time for other business and would allow our government to be more effective and efficient. Better means to answer true questions already exist in parliament: True questions and concerns for the government are currently submitted as order paper questions or through access to information requests. The relevant departments take the time to look into each question in detail, provide well-researched answers, and take action on concerns not already being addressed. However, if Question Period cannot be eliminated altogether, there are ways it should be reformed; alternatives do exist.

First, more order needs to established in the chambers of the House of Commons. Democracy sometimes requires discipline. We demand decorum in the workplace, in schools, in courtrooms, and on fields of play. We should expect the same of parliament. A speaker should be like a good referee and impose penalties on those who abuse the rules. A strict enforcement of decorum could end the antics of Question Period. Members of parliament who break the rules should face disciplinary action and, for example, should not be allowed to answer or ask a question for a specified period of time.

Second, part of each session should be dedicated to answering questions submitted directly from Canadians and selected by the speaker's office. This may reinstate proximity to the people and offset some of the hyper-partisan and inflammatory questions asked by the Opposition purposely to get a controversial sound bite in the news. Conversely, there needs to be incentive for government officials to answer the questions asked of them rather than simply stating their talking points.

Third, more time should be allocated to ministers answering questions. To properly answer complicated questions requires more than the thirty seconds allocated.

Beyond reforming Question Period, another way to ensure that our population on the whole feels more connected to government and democracy may be to have the Parliament of Canada sit in major city centres for even a few days a year each year or every two years. This would bring the most important institution of Canada closer to the Canadian population. Just a few days sitting in communities outside Ottawa, allowing people to experience firsthand the inner workings of government, might elevate electorate interest and engagement. This gathering could take place without much added cost, since parliamentarians already have travel to and from their constituencies paid for. Existing provincial legislatures, municipal chambers (if large enough), or even theatres in some places could accommodate parliamentarians.

To further strengthen our democracy, I believe we need to update parliamentary procedure in the House of Commons. For more effective use of time for parliamentary business and reduction of costs to taxpayers, I believe the antiquated rule of having to physically be present in the chamber of the House of Commons to vote needs to be changed. Instead, we should develop a way for MPs to vote electronically wherever they may be at the time. Many MPs cut important meetings or gatherings short or miss them altogether because of the rule that they must be present in person in the House of Commons to vote. Enforcement is particularly prevalent in minority parliaments. Some MPs have to fly all the way back to Ottawa from islands on the West Coast or villages in the North, which takes almost a full day of travel. The prime minister and ministers sometimes cut attendance short at international meetings to be present for votes. This is not only a waste of time and travel costs but can compromise regional and international business and foreign affairs.

Not only should MPs be able to vote electronically on legislation and voters be able to vote online, but governments should be able to accept petitions and public consultations online. This would also maximize use of technology in overcoming the vast distances that are Canada's geographic reality. Travel at certain times of the year, especially in the three northern territories, can be prohibitive due to extreme weather. As well, we should make better use of videoconferencing and the Internet for parliamentary committees and public consultations to increase citizen participation and confidence in government.

There are some parliamentary traditions that can remain to honour Canada's history and past; however, in the 21st century, when we have access to such sophisticated technology, it seems absurd to do without. Other democracies have adapted, and so should we.

My "bold vision" is not a comprehensive solution. It can be implemented in whole or in part. What matters is that change is healthy in a democracy and that change responds to the will of the people. Those resistant to change must be prepared to defend the status quo or compromise. Much has changed in the last 150 years since Confederation, and for Canada to truly reach the potential we know we possess as a nation, we must embrace positive change for our citizens.

Whether the change is actively involving youth in federal policy decisions by way of a youth prime minister, holding parliamentary sessions in city centres across Canada, or making better use of technology to facilitate citizen participation through online votes, electronic petitions, or direct ability to ask questions during Question Period, the goal is encouraging points of direct democracy by the people. Allowing actual proximity to democratic institutions might help renew interest and a feeling of connection and thus result in a Canada that is that much more of an inclusive, modern democracy and a more strong and stable nation.

....

1. Andres Barnes and Erin Virgint, "Youth Voter Turnout in Canada: 1. Trends and Issues," Library of Parliament, Legal and Legislative Affairs Division (April 7, 2010, revised August 2013), accessed July 2014, http://www.parl.gc.ca/Content/LOP/ResearchPublications/2010-19-e.htm.

2. David Colleto, "Political Participation and Canadian Millennials — What Gives?," *Abacus Data Insider* (June 19, 2013), accessed July 2014, http://abacusinsider.com/canadian-millennials/political-participation-canadian-millennials-gives/.

3. Elections Canada, "Youth Electoral Participation — Survey and Analysis of Canadian Trends (October 2003)," accessed July 2014, http://www.elections.ca/content.aspx?section=med&dir=youth/forum&document=survey&lang=e.

4. Stratos Patrikios and Mark Shephard, "Making Democracy Work by Early Formal Engagement? A Comparative Exploration of Youth Parliaments in the EU," *Parliamentary Affairs* (2012), accessed May 2014, doi: 10.1093/pa/gss017.

5. Apathy is Boring, "Why don't young Canadians vote?," accessed July 2014, http://www.apathyisboring.com/en/about_us/faq.

6. Elections Canada.

7. Shanto Iyengar and Simon Jackman, "Technology and Politics: Incentives for Youth Participation," *CIRCLE Working Paper* 24 (December 2004), accessed July 2014, http://www.civicyouth.org/PopUps/WorkingPapers/WP24Iyengar.pdf.

8. Elections Canada.

9.   Matt Henn and Nick Foard, "Young People, Political Participation and Trust in Britain," *Parliamentary Affairs* 65.1 (2012), 47–67, accessed May 2014, doi: 10.1093/pa/gsr046.

10.   James Sloam, "Rebooting Democracy: Youth Participation in Politics in the UK," *Parliamentary Affairs* 60.4 (2007), 548–67, accessed May 2014, doi: 10.1093/pa/gsm035.

11.   United Nations Youth, "Youth, Political Participation and Decision Making," World Youth Report, 2003, accessed July 2014, http://www.un.org/esa/socdev/documents/youth/fact-sheets/youth-political-participation.pdf.

12.   Marion Menard, "Youth Civic Engagement," Library of Parliament, Social Affairs Division (April 8, 2010), accessed July 2014, http://www.parl.gc.ca/Content/LOP/ResearchPublications/2010-23-e.htm.

13.   Apathy is Boring.

14.   Elections Canada.

15.   Iyengar and Jackman, "Technology and Politics."

16.   Elections Canada.

17.   Elections Canada.

The Right Honourable
KIM CAMPBELL

In becoming the 19th Prime Minister of Canada in 1993, the Right Honourable Kim Campbell became the first and only woman to serve in the highest office of the country.

Kim Campbell was born in Port Alberni, British Columbia. Active in student government in both high school and university, Kim Campbell holds a Bachelor of Arts and a Bachelor of Laws from the University of British Columbia and conducted doctoral studies at the London School of Economics as a Canada Council Scholar. She is an Honorary Fellow at LSE and holds ten honorary doctorates.

After serving on the Vancouver School Board, which she also chaired, and as a member of the Legislative Assembly of British Columbia, Kim Campbell was elected to the House of Commons in 1988. She held several cabinet portfolios and was the first woman to hold the Justice and Defence portfolios and the first woman to be Defence Minister of a NATO country before becoming Prime Minister in 1993.

Since leaving office, Kim Campbell served as the Canadian Consul General in Los Angeles and taught at the Harvard Kennedy School of Government. She is a founding member and former Secretary General of the Club of Madrid, a member and Chair Emerita of the Council of Women World Leaders, and a member and former President of the International Women's Forum.

Kim Campbell speaks all over the world and does consulting in the areas of governance and leadership. She chairs the steering committee of the World Movement for Democracy, is a founding trustee of the International Centre for the Study of Radicalisation and Political Violence at King's College London, and serves as advisor to several international organizations. She is the author of a best-selling political memoir, *Time and Chance*.

The Right Honourable Kim Campbell currently is Founding Principal of the Peter Lougheed Leadership College at the University of Alberta. She is married to composer, pianist, and actor, Hershey Felder.

GENDER PARITY:
Boldness Achievable

"*I believe that we need a dramatic gesture in Canada not only to bring gender parity to our governing institutions, but also to manifest a value that will support the aspirations of women in all fields.*"

The Bold Vision project aims to bring together a group of 23 Canadian women—the same number as the men who attended the 1864 Charlottetown Conference and whom we call "Fathers of Confederation"—to imagine a future for Canada in the 21st century and beyond. The challenge is great because our generation has seen such profound change, and the one thing that seems certain in contemplating a Canada 150 years from now is that we are unlikely to imagine the changes that will actually occur. Earlier in the 20th century, when people were asked to imagine the world in the year 2000, they often predicted a level of technological change (commuting about cities in rocketships) that still counts as science fiction. It is also the case that societies have changed in ways unimaginable only a decade ago, making it hard to imagine where they might go.

What I would like to contemplate for Canada's future is a change that I think would have a dramatic and positive influence on how we, as a country, learn to live with changes in technology and society: The full political and social empowerment of women.

I focus on the empowerment of women not because I think women are better than men, but because the consensus of research in the late-20th and early-21st centuries is that the status of women in a society is the best indicator of its expression of the values of modernity. Those values include everything from economic prosperity, social equality, and education to democratic values and social mobility: These have become the goals articulated by Canada and similar countries. It is beyond question that the status of women in Canada has changed enormously since Confederation—even, in fact, in my own lifetime. But there are areas where women do not hold a position of equality with men. Much of the power structure of contemporary Canadian society is still the purview of men. Government, the senior levels of business, and the professions all include women — but in numbers that lag considerably behind men. There is much discussion about why this is so, since so many formal barriers have been removed. Based on my own study of contemporary social science, I firmly believe that society still communicates messages that women do not entirely belong in the upper echelons of power.

I am not only the sole woman to have been prime minister of Canada, but the only one since 1993, to have been within striking distance of attaining that goal. I believe that we need a dramatic gesture in Canada not only to bring gender parity to our governing institutions, but also to manifest a value that will support the aspirations of women in all fields. Interestingly, this is not as revolutionary as it may sound. Many countries, including some of the newer democracies, have come to see gender parity in legislative bodies — or at least a guarantee of no fewer than 40% of either sex — as a basic principle. Increasingly, when it comes to gender parity in governing bodies, the question has become not "why?" but, rather, "how?"

In Canada, notwithstanding the protection against discrimination based on sex that is part of our Charter of Rights and Freedoms, we have not seen gender parity as a value that should be enshrined in our democratic institutions. Partly, this may be because the practical problem of grafting this principle onto our traditional, constituency-based, "first past the post" system of electoral representation seems intractable. For several years I have been arguing that it is a principle that we could achieve without a dramatic reorganization of our electoral system — say, to something such as proportional representation and party lists. My recommendation arises from my own experience in elected office and my predisposition to make the simplest changes to achieve the maximum value.

To provide some background to my plan, let me explain that not only am I the first woman to be prime minister of Canada, but I am also the only PM to have held elected office at all three levels of government and the only one to have been born and raised in British Columbia. It is to my experience as a member of the Legislative Assembly of BC that I turn. When I was elected to the Legislative Assembly of British Columbia in 1986, it was from the riding of Vancouver Point Grey. In those days, the large urban ridings of Vancouver and Victoria each returned *two* members to the Legislature. Sometimes a riding would return two members from the same party and sometimes not. I was elected along with Darlene Marzari, and we were from different political parties. As the candidate who got the most votes, I was referred to as the First Member for Vancouver Point Grey and Darlene Marzari was referred to as the Second Member for Vancouver Point Grey. So, we both served the same constituency and the situation worked quite well. Some time later, the province eliminated these two-member urban constituencies to make them consistent with the one-member constituencies in the rest of the province. Other than the desire for consistency among the province's ridings, there was no compelling reason to make the change.

I believe we could achieve instant parity in our parliament if we made every constituency a two-member constituency from which voters would elect one man and one woman. As with the provincial elections in the large urban ridings in BC, voters would get two votes. They would choose one candidate from the list of male candidates and one from the list of female candidates. They could vote a party slate or split their votes among parties, but the result would be instant parity in the House of Commons. Such two-member constituencies are not unknown in other parts of Canada, where, for example, dual-member ridings were the norm in Prince Edward Island's Legislative Assembly until 1996, or in other democracies. The United States Senate is made up of representatives of two-member constituencies.

My proposal does not require a doubling of seats in the House of Commons. A commission could develop an electoral map that would combine ridings while making adjustments for large rural areas — much as we do today. The House of Commons is considerably larger today than it was when I was in Parliament. In my day, it had 285 members, and now there are well in excess of 300. There is no hard and fast rule as to how many citizens should be represented by a single member. The U.S. House of Representatives has been limited to 425 members during a period where the American population has more than doubled. The British House of

Commons has over 600 members. The point is, we could establish a size for our House based on its capacity and work backward from there to allocate seats in the fairest way.

Such two-member constituencies would preserve the role of grassroots party organizations in nominating candidates, removing the need for leaders to parachute in candidates to create gender diversity. Men and women would not have to contest nominations on the grounds of sex or gender, and the nominated pair would have considerable incentive to run cooperatively in order to maximize the representation of their party in the House.

It may well be that there would be problems created by this system, but I cannot imagine any that would rule it out. At the moment, we have an imperfect system that is very unwieldy even where parties are committed to increasing the number of women they elect. Some suggest moving to a system of proportional representation with party lists, such as used in many countries that have increased the number of women in their legislative bodies. I have two reasons for considering this a suboptimal approach for Canada. First of all, it is hard to combine such a system with the kind of territorial constituency-based electoral system we have today. I think that the direct relationship between an MP and a constituent is a valuable feature of our democratic governance in Canada. Second, I think that proportional representation often confers power on the party leadership to determine the order of candidates on the party list. There are countries where a sort of "primary" vote sets the order. That, however, can make more difficult the alternation of men and women on the list that is the basis for its role in creating gender parity.

If Canada were to adopt the form of electoral practice I am recommending, it would make a powerful statement that in Canada, gender equality is a fundamental value. It would give powerful expression to the provision of the Charter of Rights and Freedom prohibiting discrimination based on sex and would create a political landscape in which men and women were equally present and from which people would acquire their sense of how the world works. I think if we were to make this simple but powerful change, Canadians looking back on our country from the perspective of 2164 would regard our current political arrangements with the same bemusement with which we regard our parliament before women had the vote.

The goal of gender parity is worthy and achievable. To deliver on it requires only A Bold Vision!

LIBBY BURNHAM

Libby Burnham, C.M., Q.C., DCL, is counsel at Toronto law firm Morrison Brown Sosnovitch LLP. She is currently the first woman to serve as Chancellor of Acadia University in Nova Scotia.

Libby Burnham was born and raised in Florenceville, New Brunswick. She graduated from Acadia University in 1960 and was the first woman graduate of Acadia to pursue a law degree, which she earned from Dalhousie University in 1963.

A senior, well-respected, and nationally connected legal, business, and political advisor, Libby Burnham represents businesses in their relations with governments at municipal, provincial, and federal levels. She is a skilled political organizer, advisor, mentor, strategist, and fundraiser for provincial and national party leaders, mayors, and members of various parliaments. She is a nationally known political figure, frequently providing comment on public issues.

Libby Burnham's distinguished career in law and public service has been defined, in part, by her determination to encourage greater participation by women in public life. She has been honoured for her leadership in numerous ways. She has received the Dalhousie Law School Weldon Award for Unselfish Public Service and the Metropolitan Toronto YWCA's Woman of Distinction Award for Public Affairs, is an Honorary Life Director of the Canadian Club of Toronto, and is a Life Member of the Law Society of New Brunswick. She is a member of the Ontario and New Brunswick bars. She holds an honorary degree from Acadia, is a member of the Order of Canada, and received both the Queen Elizabeth II Gold and Diamond Jubilee medals.

Libby Burnham is married to retired Superior Court Justice G. Gordon Sedgwick, and they have three children, John, Anne, and Jamie.

SEEING OUR FUTURE BY REFLECTING ON OUR PAST

"My belief in gender equality and the advancement of women in politics, law, and business has always been and continues to be a personal priority and a central part of my vision for the future of Canada. A fair, modern society does not leave the female half of its people behind."

I was raised a rural girl on a farm in New Brunswick. As a young woman, I was transformed by university and the study of law, which burnished my early and enduring love of politics—by which I mean both the noble art of good government and the nasty cut and thrust of winning.

I look at Canada and its future as one who has spent nearly 60 years organizing, counselling, strategizing, and fundraising — for mayors, premiers, members of various parliaments, and prime ministers. For them all, I devoted myself to voters' day-to-day concerns but also to thinking big about their communities, provinces, and, most of all, our country, Canada.

My perspective on our past and future is also shaped by my deep empathy for the women who went before me in the study and practice of law, and by what I have learned in the political backrooms, often with dismay, of women's experiences when they stand for election.

I was personally fortunate as a young woman to be able to attend university, and right here in the Maritimes at Acadia University. Here, I was encouraged to reach for my goal of becoming a practising lawyer, and my life was enriched by connecting with students from different cultures and different countries.

Today, I am honoured to serve as Chancellor of Acadia, an institution that boasts 175 years of being. Acadia existed for over two decades before the Fathers of Confederation assembled the first pieces of a country eventually to stretch from coast to coast to coast. Did Acadia's founders envision a university to which by 2014 students would come from more than 50 countries around the world? Not likely back then, but clearly they knew the spirit of what they wanted when they adopted a Charter providing the college to be open without regard to religious persuasion.

I said earlier I was fortunate to come here to Acadia University. That's because my roots are on a family farm, among my extended kin, where my parents and grandparents drilled into me a respect for the land, the importance of hard work, and the value of keeping my word because "your good name is your most valuable asset." Rural women then, women such as my grandmothers and my mother, were expected to pull their own weight, both on the farm and in community service.

My father and grandfather were both poll captains for Florenceville at election time, and politics was a main topic of dinner-table conversation and debate. I was expected to take part — and, truth to tell, I was a natural.

That's the mixture of experiences and outlook that make my vision of Canada a practical one, although (no doubt from all those years around politicians) I can spell out lofty hopes with the best of them. Like Jean Chrétien, I want the Canada of 2164 to be united not only in territory but also in a spirit of generosity: An example to the world of different cultures, religions, and races living and working together. A country where people have learned to cherish, not squander, the natural riches of land, forest, water, and all that we call our environment. And where children are cherished, fed properly, and sent to school from an early age.

I hope Canada will remain a stable democracy, drawing strength from its Parliamentary system, with three arms of government. The titular head, the Queen, represented by the Governor-General, is a unifying figure; the appointed Senate is intended to be the Chamber of sober second thought; and the elected House of Commons, made up of our MPs, to which the Prime Minister and his Cabinet must, in the end, report, is where the concerns of all Canadians are vigorously debated and the future of our country determined. Just down Wellington Street in Ottawa is the Supreme Court of Canada, the court of last resort and final appeal.

I try to live today as a person who respects the past but is not blinded by tradition; someone who advocates change and advancement. My belief in gender equality and the advancement of women in politics, law, and business has always been and continues to be a personal priority and a central part of my vision for the future of Canada. A fair, modern society does not leave the female half of its people behind.

I realize that feminism may be out of vogue among many young people today, but I'd like to tell you why I can still get mad just thinking about some of my own life experiences and about the treatment experienced by the brave women, the so called "first wave" feminists, who fought for me and for you. And yes, when I say "for you," I mean young men and women alike. We are all better off in a fair society.

At the turn of the 20th century, women could not yet vote, nor could they buy a homestead of their own. Anyone who thinks this is fusty old history should do the math I did this week. These are not ancient-history issues, but recent history—touching my grandmother, who would have already been 42 years old and halfway through her life—before she could exercise her right to vote for the first time in the Canadian federal election of 1921.

Not until 1927 after passage of the Alberta Dower Act establishing a widow's right to a third of her husband's estate could she escape the fate of so many Canadian women. They bore large families, worked dawn to dusk in the development of their husband's property, only to be disinherited on his death or desertion.

To me, 1921—just 93 years ago—was the real landmark year for those who fought for women's rights. That year women's voting rights were granted in most of the country, though later for Quebec women or First Nations women. It was also the year that the first woman was elected to Parliament.

Young Agnes Macphail, a rural schoolteacher from Picton, Ontario, was elected to a House of Commons seat on behalf of the Progressive Party. Although Macphail, a popular speaker, told audiences she could already hear the ghostly footsteps of all the women to come after her, this did not happen.

As you might expect, Macphail lost few opportunities to speak out for women's rights, but she also ran admirable campaigns for prison reform. She marched unannounced into prisons and returned to describe to the House the terrible conditions of inmates, and particularly women prisoners for whom she founded the Elizabeth Fry Society.

Macphail spoke for workers' rights on one hand and rural concerns on the other, winning re-election three times. But during the 1930s and 1940s only three more women were elected to Parliament. In 1957, then-Prime

Minister John Diefenbaker chose as the first female federal cabinet minister Ellen Fairclough, a Progressive Conservative. The pace picked up slowly in the last half of the 20th century. Today, in the 21st century, 77 women sit in the Commons, or 25.1 per cent of all MPs. At this snail's pace of progress, women won't make up half the House until your great-great-granddaughters are grown women.

I didn't know this history when I arrived at Acadia University as a student. I certainly didn't know about how in 1929 women finally won the right to be appointed to the federal judiciary or to the Senate. We will soon mark October 18, Persons Day, celebrating the day in 1929 when Canadian women were declared "persons" entitled to hold appointed offices. This was the seminal "Persons Case," not considered important enough in my day to be emphasized in constitutional law courses.

Here's more herstory you are still unlikely to study in school. In 1916, Albertan Emily Murphy was appointed the first woman police magistrate in the British Empire. On her first day in court in Edmonton, Judge Murphy's authority was challenged. Enraged by the stiff sentence she meted out to a bootlegger, defense counsel shouted, "You're not even a *person*. You have no right to be holding court!"

In the stunned silence, Magistrate Murphy, flushed with rage, spoke quietly: "Will defense counsel develop his argument?"

He did. "Under British common law, in a decision handed down in 1876, the status of women is this: 'Women are persons in matters of pains and penalties, but are not persons in matters of rights and privileges.' Therefore, since the office of magistrate is a privilege, the present incumbent is here illegally. No decisions of her court can be binding."[1]

Although her sentencing decision was later upheld by the Supreme Court of Alberta on the grounds of reason and good sense, Emily Murphy wanted the "persons" question settled nationally too. By 1927, she had decided to exercise a little-known and little-used right that permitted any five Canadians to petition the Supreme Court of Canada for a ruling on a constitutional question.

Murphy selected four women to join her petition, which asked: "Does the word 'Persons' in section 24 of the *British North America Act* include female persons?"

All five of the petitioners were from Alberta: All were well known and respected throughout Canada for their work in national organizations and political life and were articulate in presenting the women's side of the case. They were Emily Murphy, Nellie McClung, Louise McKinney, Irene Parlby, and Henrietta Muir Edwards.

But nine months later, in April 1928, the Supreme Court of Canada ruled against the "Famous Five." Although dismayed and indignant, the five women met again and resolved to take their case to the Judicial Committee of the Privy Council in London, England, which was, at that time, the final court of appeal for Canadians.

On October 18, 1929, after four days of deliberations, the Privy Council declared Canadian women to be persons qualified for appointment to the Senate.

In overturning the decision of the Supreme Court of Canada, Lord Sankey, the Lord Chancellor of the day, contrary to the practice of the day read the decision in full before the court:

> The *British North America Act* planted in Canada a living tree capable of growth and expansion ... their Lordships have come to the conclusion that the word "persons" in Section 24 included members of both the male and female sex, and that therefore, the question ... must be answered in the affirmative, and that women are eligible to be summoned to and become members of the Senate of Canada.[2]

A year later, in 1930, Cairine Wilson was appointed the first woman to sit in the Senate of Canada. This honour was expected to go to Emily Murphy, but Prime Minister Mackenzie King apparently shrunk from having such a determined and feisty woman in the Senate.

Over the next decades, the story of Agnes Macphail's accomplishments as a Member of Parliament and the important victories won for women by the Famous Five, began to fade.

By 1960, when I began my studies of the law, I was one of only five female students in the school. I received a quality education but also never-forgotten lessons in the challenges and barriers facing women in law. I remember being told by one professor I didn't belong in law school!

Women were few in law firms across Canada. In Toronto, most of the major firms had no women, and institutions such as the Lawyers' Club, Board of Trade, and private clubs were for men only.

At the Canadian Bar Association annual meeting in 1972, we had to put a resolution on the floor to ban official events of the association being held at clubs where women lawyers were required to enter by the back or by separate entrances.

In my first year of practice, I wrote a letter to the New Brunswick Barristers' Society regarding the Reciprocal Enforcement of Judgments Acts, recommending that the Council support seeking arrangements with other Provinces to give reciprocal recognition of provisions or orders under the Deserted Wives and Children's Maintenance Act. I had clients whose husbands or fathers had walked away and skipped to another province to avoid paying for support.

It was reported to me by my principal, with whom I had articled—a council member—that the male secretary had deliberately misread my letter to make it a joke at the council. It was more important to that secretary to seem to be "one of the boys" than to deal with an important social issue.

This setback did not stop me, but I shifted my energy to politics, hoping to influence public policy and assist with the advancement of women in New Brunswick.

Working as part of a small team, we elected Richard Hatfield as leader of the Progressive Conservative Party of New Brunswick and Premier of New Brunswick in 1970. As key advisor and strategist to his government, I take pride in his four election wins and that he appointed the first woman cabinet minister in New Brunswick's history and the first women senior public servants.

In 1972, at the request of national Progressive Conservative Leader Robert Stanfield, I had the opportunity to influence national policy by writing the policy position of the PC Party on Women in Canadian Society — enlisting the support of then-young Progressive Conservatives including Joe Clark and Brian Mulroney, both later prime ministers.

Interest in women's issues was stirring again, with a campaign mounted by 32 women's organizations led by Ontario activist Laura Sabia. In 1967, in direct response, Prime Minister Lester Pearson had appointed the Royal Commission on the Status of Women to recommend steps the federal government might take to ensure equal opportunities for men and women in all aspects of Canadian society. Under Chairwoman Florence Bird, a well-known broadcaster known as Anne Francis, the Royal Commission conducted public sessions the following year across the country. Its 395 recommendations were powerful and controversial and even now merit careful study.

The Commission heard from ordinary Canadians, women's organizations, church groups, university women's clubs, and legal associations. The Commission heard what it meant to be a woman who worked as a bank teller all her life but because of gender was never able to move up the ladder; or a woman teacher doing the same job as a man but at a lesser salary.

On the participation of women in public life, the Commission concluded:

> Nowhere in Canadian life is a persistent distinction between male and female roles of more consequence. No country can make a claim to having equal status for its women so as long as its government lies entirely in the hands of men.[3]

Few of the Commission's recommendations were implemented.

In 1982, it was a great surprise to Bay Street when the quiet Bertha Wilson was appointed to the Supreme Court of Canada by Prime Minister

Trudeau. Her judgments reflected her personal vision of fairness and equality. A Dalhousie graduate, Bertha Wilson had started her career as a research and opinion writer of a major Toronto law firm. The year of her appointment coincided with the Charter of Rights and Freedoms coming into effect, and she supported a broad application of the Charter—concurring for example in the decisions striking down Criminal Code of Canada restrictions on abortion in *R. v. Morgentaler* 1988 and acceptance of battered wife syndrome as self-defence in *R. v. Lavallee* 1990.

In 2000, Beverley McLachlin became the first woman to sit as Chief Justice of the Supreme Court of Canada. The precedent will make it uncomfortable for future prime ministers to appoint justices without considering gender balance.

But the struggle for equality is far from over.

We, the women of today, owe a big debt of gratitude to the women who led the suffragette movement and took further steps to bring equality to us. But from the time that we won the right to vote to today, it has been a long, slow, and unfinished process to political equality. Where are the women in our federal politics?

There is a clear gender gap in the political leadership in this country. This is about numbers. The issue is no longer a question of talent, ability, education, qualifications, or determination. We are spinning our wheels. There is no doubt that we have an abundance of women in our country capable of assuming leadership roles. We need to find out why they are not.

And where have all our women premiers gone?

For a brief time in the summer of 2013 at the Council of the Federation there were six women premiers and territorial leaders, and hopes were high that barriers were finally removed. Heady days now gone, as only two women premiers remain.

In 1993, Canada had its first and only woman prime minister, the Right Honourable Kim Campbell, and the first woman elected as a premier in Canada, Honourable Catherine Callbeck of Prince Edward Island. I helped both of them, and we remain good friends. It was a spectacular moment when they entered the First Ministers' meeting—Canada and a province represented by women—and it was a historic first occasion for our country.

The Globe and Mail, a national newspaper, trivialized the occasion by running on its front page a picture of the Prime Minister's purse beside her chair.[4] What a missed opportunity for people to see, and remember, a photo of the Canadian team at work—anchored by a woman.

Every federal election sees fewer people voting. The interest of our youth in participating in the public process is waning. Part of this is that young people do not see themselves represented in elected leadership. Research clearly shows that, particularly in the case of young women, they just haven't seen enough successful female role models in politics.

Our society is based on inherent core Canadian values—values of fairness, for equality and justice for all. It is important that we work to overcome this political imbalance and to have more women at the decision-making table.

Society will be better served by more women in public life. After all, we are 52 per cent of the population. Women lead in small entrepreneurship skills and in areas of education, not-for-profit leadership, and health care. Women are getting educated in greater numbers in all areas of study.

I've been a political activist all my life. I have worked within my party, the Progressive Conservative Party, to advance women and minorities. I have worked with multi-partisan groups. One organization, "The Committee for 94," pushed for ten years to attain the goal of half the House of Commons being women by 1994. We disbanded when we fell far short of the target.

I am a member of a group that launched Equal Voice, a multi-partisan organization dedicated to electing more women. We launched a bilingual online campaign school, "Getting to the Gate," designed to assist women to prepare to run for office. We monitor the nominations of women and push the political parties to do better. We know from polling that Canadian voters are ready to elect more women, but first the parties have to nominate enough female candidates to give them that choice.

The founder and first chairperson of Equal Voice, Rosemary Speirs, commissioned singer/songwriter Nancy White to compose the following song for us in Equal Voice. Nancy comes from Prince Edward Island and graduated from Nova Scotia's Dalhousie University. Recently, Dalhousie honoured her with an honorary doctorate in law. Her song, called "Ask a Woman to Run," says:

> Get a woman to run
>
> Get a woman to serve
>
> Get a woman with heart
>
> Get a woman with nerve
>
> Get a woman to speak for you
>
> Where her voice may be heard
>
> Get the very best one
>
> Get a woman to run[5]

We are not going to reach equality without a dramatic push. We must work harder and with more speed. I urge you to support the advancement of women in public life so Canadians can boast their country stands for equal status for its women.

In concluding, I would like to quote a Famous Five member, Louise McKinney: "The purpose of a woman's life is just the same as the purpose of a man's life: that she may make the best possible contribution to the generation in which she is living."[6]

That's my vision of what Canada can be, too — a country in which men and women work together to create a more balanced society. Canada will be a stronger country when the differing perspectives of the sexes are heard and heeded in our law-making and in our governments.

----

1. Jean Bannerman, *Leading Ladies Canada* (Belleville, ON: Mika Publishing, 1977), 210–11.

2. Catherine L. Cleverdon, *The Woman Suffrage Movement in Canada*, 2nd ed. (Toronto: University of Toronto Press, 1974), 153.

3. Royal Commission on the Status of Women in Canada, "Section 88: Participation of Women in Public Life," *Report of the Royal Commission on the Status of Women* (1970), 355, accessed July 2014, http://epe.lac-bac.gc.ca/100/200/301/pco-bcp/commissions-ef/bird1970-eng/bird1970-eng.htm.

4. In July 1993, Prime Minister Campbell was the first prime minister to convene a First Ministers' conference for consultation prior to representing Canada at the G7 Summit.

5. Used by permission of Nancy White.

6. This quotation and other quotations from the Famous Five can be found at the *Famous 5 Foundation*, accessed July 2014, http://www.famous5.ca/index.php/the-famous-5-women/the-famous-5-women.

EVA AARIAK

Eva Qamaniq Aariak is part of a generation of Inuit who have lived through an era of tumultuous change that transformed life in the Arctic. She served as the first woman premier of Nunavut from 2008 to 2013.

Her early years were spent immersed in the natural rhythms of a community and a rich culture sustained by the Arctic environment. Like many of today's Inuit leaders, she travelled south for higher education to schools in Churchill, Manitoba, and in Ontario.

Returning to the Arctic, Aariak led a varied career as a teacher, an adult educator, a human resource officer, a coordinator of Inuktitut children's books, and a radio announcer and television reporter for the CBC North.

She was named the territory's first Languages Commissioner, responsible for protecting the rights of three official languages. Her recommendations prompted the government to write a groundbreaking law, the Inuit Language Protection Act.

Eva Aariak took a break from public life to work as a language consultant and to assist with the creation of

Inuktitut versions of Microsoft products. She later started her own business aimed at expanding the market for Inuit-made products while chairing the Baffin Regional Chamber of Commerce.

In 2008, she was elected to the Legislative Assembly of Nunavut for then-electoral district of Iqaluit East. She was at that time the only woman in the legislature. She was elected as premier by the legislature. She continues to advocate for "completing the map of Canada" by strengthening the ties between Nunvaut and the rest of the country.

Eva Aariak is the proud grandmother of four, Tasiana, Joyce, James Aliguq, and Benjamin.

CONNECTING CANADA, NORTH AND SOUTH:
A Conversation with Eva Aariak

"*Inuit are very adaptable. And that's the benefit, and the plus side, I think, of how we take on the world. Because we can take the best of both worlds: What is working for the Arctic, in our own environment, and what we take from the southern part of our nation. We take it and embrace it and work with it, and perhaps even try and improve upon it.*"

In May 2014, Eva Aariak sat down for a telephone conversation with Kate McKenna — a journalist and Bold Vision nominee with recent experience living and working in Iqaluit with the CBC. In their wide-ranging interview, Eva describes her hopes and dreams for the youngest territory in Canadian Confederation.

....

KM: You obviously have a unique vantage point. I was wondering if we could start with what you think the challenges for the next 150 years are, and then how you think we could overcome those challenges.

EA: Nunavut certainly has challenges as a young territory, and I don't think there is another way around that than to deal with those challenges. You know, Nunavut needs unique attention, just like any other province or territory when they first started off within our nation years ago. And 150 years, I think, is a good number of years that many of the things that need to be done in Nunavut will be addressed.

I see an inclusive nation within Canada, where one part of Canada is neither neglected nor not understood nor *misunderstood.* I see the Arctic, and Nunavut, being fully part of Canada, and Canadians fully understanding their own country and the diversity of their country, including the Arctic nation, the northern part of Canada.

KM: What do you think at this point they don't understand, or *we* don't understand, about the Arctic?

EA: You know, the fact that the North is so isolated is not very much understood in many cases, especially the fact that the only way to get up to the North, at least to Nunavut, is to fly, is through air, and there are no roads connected to one another community, let alone to the rest of Canada.

KM: In your lifetime, Nunavut has completely changed and has *become*

Nunavut. So it feels things are moving a lot faster up there than they are down here.

EA: Oh, absolutely! When I was growing up, when I was six years old, there were only eighteen families in my community. [Laughs.] There were no regular planes coming into the community — except perhaps once a year, the mail would come in, in December when the planes dropped the mail with all the letters to the teacher, the Hudson Bay Company members, and their mail-order supplies and stuff like that would come in. That's the only way they would hear back from their families, of course, who were living in the south. Another time would be in the summer, through sea-lift season, where supplies would come in. So there was hardly any contact.

In fact, I was listening to the radio the other day when this individual from Iglulik was saying, "When I was a child, I thought we were the only people on earth. I didn't know there were other races. I thought we were all Inuit." And this person is maybe early seventies now! Speaking of times that have changed so much, it is indeed true.

Where it took southern Canada from horse-and-buggy stages, it took the North, Northern people, let's say forty to fifty years to catch up to where they are today. Rapid, rapid changes happened. And Inuit are very adaptable. We are very adaptable people. And that's the benefit, and the plus side, I think, of how we take on the world. Because we can take the best of both worlds: What is working for the Arctic, in our own environment, and what we take from the southern part of our nation. We take it and embrace it and work with it, and perhaps even try and improve upon it.

We have let go of many of the things that were very important to our society as Inuit, because of better transportation systems, and instead of using bow-and-arrows we are now using ammunition to catch our food, and, you know, those are modern technologies we are embracing. We are totally immersed in the technological age, and the computer age.

KM: That is one of the concerns that I heard when I was up North, the merging of white people and traditional Inuit culture. How are the Inuit going to keep their culture while also probably continuing to merge with southern Canada in the next 150 years?

EA: I see the population in Nunavut as a vibrant, strong cultural and language component in our society. The desire of our young people is to have their Inuit language strong and their culture strong, only they don't have so much means of learning it because of such a rapid change of our society, where language and culture were encouraged to be abandoned by outside forces—education and residential schools and all that.

But I see the language and culture becoming more and more strong, although we are at a stage where I guess a revitalization of both sides is needed because the expectation of not learning the language, not learning your cultural background, was very much entrenched for a while until the Inuit society, the Inuit leaders, became stronger and said, "Hey, we need a change. We need to run our own journey. We need to have our own territory." And hence the territory of Nunavut was created.

But, you know, with the education system improving, and the education system being more inclusive of our culture and language through legislation, I think that it is not too late. And it depends very much on the desires of our young generation today. As you know, maybe even 30 per cent of our population today is below age 25, and these are the people that will be responsible for making the changes in the way that is the desire of the Arctic, the desire of *nunavummiut*,[1] the people of Nunavut.

KM: While we're still on the topic of language, what would your ideal vision be for 150 years from now?

EA: Oh, I see very much a language that is used—and for every Canadian, every Northerner, every *nunavummiut*, individuals are conversant and proud of their own language—as well as English because you need that in order to be immersed in other countries and other areas, as well as French as an official language.

Learning another language should not be a hindrance. When I was a language commissioner, I used to say that North Americans have a handicap, and that handicap is their belief that it is hard to learn another language. When you go across the ocean to the European countries, that is certainly not an issue at all, where people will acquire four or five different languages.

I see the Northerners, *nunavummiut*, having a strong sense of their language and culture as well as the English language, and embracing both and working with both, but still making Nunavut a unique place, where they are showcasing their language and strong, unique culture to help educate the rest of the world. And also using the language and culture as economic vibrancy, economic development initiatives, because like one elder said, you will never take away the *inukness* of a person as long as they want to keep it.

I see young people today, and especially the elders as well, wishing that the language and culture remain vibrant and very strong, and the governments of the day, including Inuit organizations and the territorial governments, working together to help that happen.

There are the challenges we are facing today, where we need to have community-based solutions. Social ills need to be dealt with, and how we can deal with those is to look within, within our communities.[2] The communities have the solutions, if only they have the means to make their visions realized, through financial capabilities which many of them do not have right now.

Because when we come up with our own solutions, as individuals or as families or as a community, we have the buy-in, we have the commitment and the willpower to continue to build upon those beliefs. So, partnership becomes very important, including between the communities in coming up with their own solutions. And from that, then partnership comes in and our vision becomes easier to realize through support from the governments: Inuit organizations, territorial government, and, of course, the federal government. And the private sector. Partnerships more and more are very important. Whereas one entity can't look after anything alone these days, I see partnerships becoming more and more an important component in addressing what needs to be addressed in our society.

And economic development, will, of course, be a huge aspect in the North, and Canada will need to be more inclusive, so that Aboriginals are not in a disadvantaged state anymore: They are understood, and their abilities are understood and supported and working towards the developments that are equal to the rest of the nation.

KM: Where do you see economic development going in Nunavut? Do you see oil or extraction as a possibility, or something else?

EA: Yes, I think they are very viable solutions to our future development of the north. Although we do have a lot of tourism potential, and cultural industries as well, we don't have a whole lot of other areas.

Nunavut has the most potential when it comes to mining and resource development and oil and gas development, and the important point that I would like to say in that area is we need to develop *responsible development* in regards to those areas. Where we have a very fragile environment, we need to be very careful as to how we develop the natural resources, and how we use them, and how we deal with the land.

For economic development, our young people need to be trained in transferrable skills. Transferrable skills are very important so that they can partake in resource development, as well as being able to contribute in their home communities. Right now, what is hindering the opportunities and the potential of *nunavummiut* is the fact that we have such a high dropout rate in education.

We have to ensure that training and education also are included in the economic development of our territory when it comes to oil and gas and mining sectors. Again, partnership is the key there, too, where we have such a large number of young people. Once they are trained and educated, every single individual can be employed. There is no doubt about that. There will be opportunities for each young person to be employed.

Our cost of living is very high, which also means the cost of doing business is very high. As we are experiencing today, the people who are going out on the land and providing country food to the families and to the rest of the communities are the ones that are able to afford to go, because you need money to buy gas and ammunition and supplies to supplement the cost of food that we have in the North from the store-bought food. So *balance* is the word.

We need to be innovative and creative in dealing with those kinds of things. Of course, that also includes infrastructure. Infrastructure needs are huge in our territory. Let's say when I am talking about businesses and providing food, or dealing with food insecurities and so on … I see in my vision for the next 150 years, we have 25 communities, by then (I can think about having less communities, I think) but each of those communities has to be serviced with the proper ports and small-craft harbours, so the boats that are coming up to provide supplies to those communities, they are properly accommodated. And with proper infrastructure comes a lower cost of doing business. You know, we need to develop the business sector in the North, where we are not relying solely on the federal transfers.

We Inuit societies come from very strong, self-reliant communities, self-reliant societies. You know, a hundred years ago, we looked after our own medical care. We looked after our own religion. We looked after our own laws and sustaining our strong families' nucleus. All those things that departments provide today, Inuit communities were doing on their own, and that strong sense of self-reliance is still instilled within the culture. We made our own clothing and our own hunting implements, without having to go through the stores. We can not go back to sustaining our lives solely by sewing our own clothing or hunting our own food, solely, so we are accommodating and adapting to what we need from other cultures, and that will be developed up here.

We have a very comprehensive Land Claims Agreement between the two governments, the Inuit organizations and the federal government, which has not been fully implemented yet, and 150 years from now I see the Land Claims Agreement all implemented and functioning well. This includes devolution for Nunavut, where decision-making powers are upon the decision-makers of the North, *in* the North. This is all part of being on the road to be self-reliant: The Northerners making the decisions and making the economic development happen, and employing and educating the people in the North.

Of course, our governments are very inclusive. We are not striving to be Inuit members only in the Arctic. We are an inclusive society, but at the same time the culture and language will play a very important role in that, which comes to education.

KM: I know for your government, education was very important.

EA: Education is the key to accomplish all that, as education *was* the key to being able to sustain your own life and be self-reliant in the old days, before the European influence was upon us. Those people who did not learn to provide for themselves properly perished. So the same idea today: Education is the key today.

And I see, you know, we now have an Education Act within the territory, and all the other territories are building upon education legislation to come to the optimum level of looking after what needs to be taught in our society.

I am an eternal optimist. So with education, the other social issues can, I think, be addressed. We are in the midst of our many social ills right now because of the sudden change that our society has gone through — and that is evident in other countries and societies where drastic change has happened. We have a severe housing shortage; we have a high percentage of mental health issues, and hardly any childcare to accommodate everyone. But, through education we are dealing with our health. Education, again, improves all aspects of our health, mental health especially. And mental health and addictions sometimes go hand in hand, especially today. I think with better understanding of the cause and effects of what we put our bodies through, we can make better choices.

Childcare is another one. I think across the nation we need a better childcare system, because it has been proven through research and studies, once a child from birth (and even before birth) has a caring and good start through nutrition and mental health, all the better outcomes when they are adults. We need to emphasize childcare today, so that we have a healthier community in the future.

And, of course, we hear all kinds of housing problems, not just in Nunavut but across the Aboriginal community, and that needs to be dealt with. In 150 years from now, no one should be talking about the housing situation. We should have found a solution to deal with the housing crisis by then. And, of course, that ties in with economic development and education.

Everything is connected, from social and economic issues. They are all connected, if only we can come up with the tools to look at all the spokes of the wheel that are so connected in addressing social ills and all of the needs of our societies. If we are looking at the wheel and looking at all the spokes that make the wheel strong, we should by 150 years from now have addressed many of those components so that we are running a better nation and better society. And along the way there will be all kinds of new challenges that we will be coming across, but at least the ills that we need to address now should have been dealt with. Of course, we will be dealing with a whole lot of other new challenges by then. That's for the generations to deal with.

KM: It's almost like you are saying if you build a strong foundation you will be able to deal with whatever comes your way.

EA: Absolutely. It comes from strong individuals, and we need support to have strong individuals so that they become strong community members and strong society in our nation. Again, everything is connected, from childcare through proper health, proper education, and living under proper housing.

KM: I know in the new curriculum there are a lot of Inuit activities in the formal curriculum. Can you take me through how you see children learning about Nunavut and what you see about dropout rates and graduation rates in formal education?

EA: I'm very proud of the fact that we are taking our culture and language into consideration when the curriculum is being developed. When I was young, everything I was learning was so foreign to me that I could not really relate to it, so my interest was not strong, especially with some topics. Perhaps history: I was not interested in that because I could not relate the kind of history that was being taught to me, to my own history. At that point in my young mind, I could not even put into perspective my own history, because it was not taught … So, I'm not saying that history is not important other than our own history — but it's because of history that that is where we are today, so it is very important that you understand in order to have better solutions for the future.

The fact that the northern curriculum is being developed incorporating our own history and language will only help in enhancing the other areas of curriculum … We have so many young parents now that are living in their own homes that did not get enough of their own background, that did not learn their language well enough to teach it to their children, and they did not learn their culture enough to teach it to their own children. The school can help to supplement that, with help from their parents, and partnership connection with the community is very important in that.

The Education Act in Nunavut was only passed about five years ago; therefore, there is a lot of incorporation that needs to happen and it is only through enhancing what was in place that will improve it. That's the big job we have to do, ensuring that the outcome of our education is strong and vibrant within our young people. We do need to work hard on ensuring our children are educated properly up to Grade 12, in ensuring they can then go on to university. We need doctors, we need nurses and teachers. We need technicians. We need engineers that will stay up here so their generations to come have role models from their parents and their grandparents.

KM: It also all comes back to Nunavut being self-sufficient, right?

EA: Absolutely! When I talk about self-sufficiency and self-reliance, we need to have young people up here and develop up here. Sometimes there would be great solutions to the problems we are experiencing right now, solutions that would be enhanced by individuals who have come up here to help, who have strong desires to be innovative and so on. But then sometimes, that spoke of the wheel leaves town, and the situation goes back to where it started, and so you take one step forward and two steps back too many times. But if we have our workforce staying up here and *building* upon up here, then these developments and advancements can be much stronger.

A hundred and fifty years from now, we *will* have a university up here. I *will* say that. But at the same time, I'm saying that the students that we are graduating at Grade 12 level today should be able to go to any university around the world and especially Canada, Canada's universities.

KM: A lot of what we've talking about has been about equality and diversity, but do you have anything in mind for the next 150 years for women's role, particularly in Inuit culture?

EA: Oh, yes, very much so. I see women in managerial, leadership positions, many more than there are today, and the society believing in those women's abilities instead of second-guessing them; believing in their abilities, supporting them, and making them empowered with the men leaders that we have in the leadership elite.

I would like to see in 150 years — I always talk about completing the map of Canada. Because in the Confederation stages, back then, Canada was developed from East to West. East to west was all connected by railways and roadways and airways. And that still has to happen in the North, and I hope in 150 years, the North will be more connected, through infrastructure, through ports and small-craft harbours and better airports. That will mean that Canada recognizes all of the nation as one, and that includes the infrastructure as well as people, including Aboriginal people. Better understanding of our country goes both ways.

Climate change is another big issue that will affect us all in the North, and affect us all in Canada and the rest of the world, for that matter. And what we need to ensure, the world (and Canada, especially) needs to understand and believe the fact of climate change.

We the people in the North are the first people to feel the effect of climate change, and we need to find solutions to adapt to those changes. I think there will be a certain level of understanding and belief in climate change by 150 years from now, but we need to start now because it is upon us. The climate change issue is very much upon us.

The erosion of our permafrost is increasing. The water level is rising and the content of the salt level of the ocean is being very much affected. We are now getting a lot more of different species of fish. We are getting salmon up in Resolute Bay waters now that were not possible. Our hunters are finding that they are going to their usual seal-hunting spots or fishing spots, and they are falling in the water because the ice is not holding them. It is not thick enough. Adaptation is very important for northerners.

And I talked about our isolatedness and our need to connect to the rest of the nation: You know, with all these changes, I think it would be helpful if we have better connections to the rest of our country.

KM: Could you explain for people who don't know (which is probably everybody down south), what it means that the permafrost is thawing, and what the actual effects of that are for people and the environment?

EA: Of course. We live in a permafrost country, where several feet down into the ground is ice in many areas. We had a huge disaster, an emergency situation in Pangnirtung several years ago, where the bridge was washed away. All of our smaller communities do not have utilidor[3] systems. Everything is trucked in to the communities. The water is trucked in; the sewage out is by truck. And because of this bridge being washed out, because the permafrost under there was all melting and washed away through river runoff, the services could not be done beyond the bridge. They could not get any water. They could not get their sewage pumped out, let alone cross the bridge to go to the health centre or to go to the stores…And that is not an isolated case.

So many houses' foundations are affected. We hear, let's say, houses that are tilting so rapidly, and all our homes are heated by oil, and there are oil spills happening on our own communities because the foundations under the oil tanks are tilting, including the whole house. The erosion of the beaches is horrendous. So we need to adapt to better systems, looking after our foundations, building roads and airports. If the permafrost under the land starts to be affected, that's a problem.

All the homes are heated by oil. We need to come up with cleaner fuel systems and cheaper to heat our homes up here in the North, through solar or wind or other solutions to deal with our energy needs. We have aging generators that will only have to be replaced with the same kinds of generators because we have not come up with cleaner solutions. We are heating our homes and businesses with dirty oil, as I call it, but by 150 years from now, that can be different.

Again, along with that, Arctic sovereignty is another issue that by then will hopefully have been dealt with. Shipping in the Arctic is an issue that Canada has to address. It needs to be regulated and well-managed, with clear boundaries. With the rest of the world looking at the Arctic Ocean, I think Canada needs to have a strong direction and a strong sense on that.

KM: You were going to talk about balance.

EA: Yes. We were talking about the wheel and the spokes and so on that constitute a balance. When I mentioned about an inclusive nation, it's the balance as well that is needed, that one society is not less looked after than the other society, and that there is a balance of the needs of our nation. And I am mostly talking about Aboriginal communities and the North.

KM: I hope you guys in 150 years can maintain the awesomeness that is Nunavut.

EA: The uniqueness! Yes, I am a strong believer that Nunavut is very unique. And it has its unique needs in the nation, and that's why there is so much potential for Nunavut.

....

1. "Nunavummiut" refers to the Inuit people of Nunavut.
2. In Nunavut, "the communities" usually refers to the towns of the territory.
3. A utilidor system is an enclosed and insulated conduit for sewage and other utilities placed above the level of permafrost.

CATHERINE POTVIN

Together with her research group, Dr. Catherine Potvin, a professor in the Biology Department of McGill University in Montreal, searches for solutions to climate change that allow us to reduce our footprint. The banner of her laboratory is "Science for Empowerment," and they work for the study of land-use and tropical forest protections to fully respect the people that live in or are from the affected region. She is a plant biologist with a specialization in global change ecology.

For twenty years, Dr. Potvin collaborated with and learned from the Indigenous people of Panama around the importance of protecting tropical forests.

Dr. Catherine Potvin's passion for nature guides her work and has resulted in numerous awards and recognitions. In 2011, she received the Schlamadinger Prize, recognizing the best scientific paper in Climate Policy. She was awarded the Miroslaw Romanowski Medal of the Royal Society of Canada in 2012. She accepted the Trottier 2013 Fellow for the Trottier Institute for Science and Public Policy of McGill University. In 2013,

Catherine Potvin became holder of the UNESCO Chair on Sustainability Dialogues.

She earned her BSc and MSc in biological sciences at l'Université de Montréal. In 1985, she received her PhD in botany from Duke University in North Carolina and returned to Montreal for postdoctoral studies in statistics.

In 1989, Dr. Potvin broke barriers as one of the first Francophone women to become Full Professor in the Faculty of Science at McGill University. Dr. Potvin credits the birth of her grandchildren as a motivator to recently focus her work on solutions for climate change mitigation in Canada.

Catherine Potvin shares her time between Montreal and Panama where her husband, biologist Dr. Hector Barrios, lives. She has three children, Philippe, Geneviève, and Thomas, and two grandchildren, Alice and Arthur.

LETTRES AUX PETITS-ENFANTS DE MES ARRIÈRE-PETITS-ENFANTS ET À LEURS CONCITOYEN(NE)S[1]

"Mon souhait le plus cher pour vous est donc que ma génération réussisse à atteindre le déficit zéro en environnement. L'équation pour y arriver est simple, mais dans le contexte actuel du Canada, sa mise en œuvre ne l'est pas ..."

Bonjour,

Vous ne me connaissez pas, mais je fais partie de votre passé … Je m'appelle Catherine, j'ai trois enfants, je suis biologiste. Je vous écris une série de lettres, bouteilles jetées à la mer du temps, pour parler de l'avenir que je désire pour vous, et pour toutes et tous les habitant(e)s du Canada de 2164. En les écrivant, j'ai compris qu'il nous incombe de matérialiser cet avenir qui sera le vôtre. Notre façon de vivre détermine l'héritage avec lequel vous devrez composer. Votre Canada, celui de 2164, dépend du nôtre, le Canada de 2014. Je vous parlerai donc aussi de mon présent qui est votre histoire.

Mon premier souhait, pour vous, c'est la sécurité, l'équité et la solidarité. Au Canada du 21ᵉ siècle, nous sommes béni(e)s de vivre dans une société peu violente. De par mon travail, je passe beaucoup de temps en Amérique latine, là où les iniquités sociales sont criantes. Il y a des gens fort pauvres qui servent les riches. Mais les riches vivent enfermés dans des quartiers entourés de barbelés pour se protéger des pauvres. Croyez-moi, il ne fait pas bon de vivre dans la peur! Je voudrais donc que votre Canada soit en lutte constante contre la pauvreté. Qu'il soit un pays où il est socialement inacceptable de laisser l'écart entre riches et pauvres s'agrandir. C'est en effet en s'assurant du bien-être de tous et toutes les citoyen(ne)s qu'on peut le mieux assurer la sécurité. Le bien-être c'est que vos besoins prioritaires soient comblés. Je souhaite que vous vous endormiez en ayant bien mangé sous un toit pour vous protéger des intempéries. Je compte également parmi ces nécessités de base l'accès à l'eau potable, aux soins de santé et à l'éducation. Cet accès est la condition préalable à tous les autres désirs que j'ai pour vous.

Quand mes enfants étaient petit(e)s et que nous regardions des films (Savez-vous ce qu'est un film?) de cape et d'épée avec de belles princesses et de nobles chevaliers, j'aimais leur rappeler que nous descendions plutôt de manants et de servantes. La Nouvelle-France a été peuplée par des orphelines et des hommes si pauvres qu'ils ont choisi de braver l'océan plutôt que de continuer à vivre dans les conditions de misère où ils étaient. Il ne faut pas oublier ce passé difficile. J'espère donc que le Canada cultivera deux valeurs pour vous léguer la sécurité: l'équité et la solidarité. La solidarité est pour moi indissociable de l'équité car elle permet, entre autres, l'empathie, c'est-à-dire, une compréhension du besoin des autres. Selon moi, une société solidaire est une société où aucun groupe social n'est, et ne sera, marginalisé. Le Canada actuel est un pays en bonne position à ce niveau-là avec un indice de développement humain élevé[2] sauf pour nos Premières Nations qui vivent largement à l'écart de ce bien-être. J'espère que nous saurons collectivement réparer les torts que nous leur avons causés. Mais je suis préoccupée pour l'avenir parce que depuis le début du 21e siècle, l'écart entre riches et pauvres s'accentue.[3] Je souhaite de tout cœur que nous ne perdions pas nos acquis et que nous vous léguions un pays d'équité et de solidarité. Je crois que c'est assez pour aujourd'hui. Je ne voudrais pas que mon message d'outre-tombe vous ennuie…

Nous nous retrouverons bientôt,

Catherine

....

Chers petits-enfants de mes arrière-petits-enfants,

Depuis ma première lettre, j'ai continué à penser à vous. Quand je vous parlais de sécurité, d'équité et de solidarité, c'est que j'espère pour vous la paix. Le soir, nous écoutons souvent un rapport sur l'état du monde autour de nous à la télévision. Je m'imagine qu'en 2164, il faudra aller au musée pour voir une télévision… Dans le Canada de 2014, c'est à travers cet appareil, présent dans presque chaque maison, que nous appréhendons le monde. Nous voyons trop souvent des lieux où les gens se battent, se tuent. Actuellement, dans beaucoup de pays, il y a des attentats, des attaques-suicides. Ces tueries, ces agressions, à quoi cela rime-t-il? On donne la vie en cadeau aux enfants pour la vie, ce n'est pas pour qu'ils se fassent tuer! Du côté de leur père, mes enfants (donc vos ancêtres) viennent de France, d'une famille juive qui a vécu la Deuxième Guerre mondiale. Je m'imagine qu'on enseigne encore cette guerre horrible dans vos cours d'histoire même si le temps a passé. Puisse cela vous être épargné.

Votre avenir s'écrira dans le contexte des autres pays de la planète. Pour moi c'est clair, sans doute parce que je passe ma vie entre le Panama et le

Canada. Il n'est pas réaliste de penser que votre Canada puisse être un pays de paix si des conflits règnent dans la majorité des autres pays. Je rajoute donc une valeur à ma vision d'avenir : la tolérance. Je vous souhaite de vivre dans un pays et une époque de tolérance qui utilise une vraie démocratie, respectueuse, pour bâtir un consensus social sur le présent et l'avenir. Pourquoi la tolérance? Parce qu'il me semble que c'est elle qui permet de régler les différends de façon mature et non violente. Parfois je pense que cette valeur prend ses racines dans la confiance en soi qui permet de ne pas avoir peur de l'autre et de se respecter tout en respectant les différences. Je crois que le germe de la paix nait avec la tolérance. À notre époque l'intolérance, particulièrement religieuse, est un réel problème et il est important d'assurer les conditions pour en éviter une montée.

À la fin du 20e siècle, le Canada a joué un rôle important quant au maintien de la paix dans le monde en décidant d'utiliser des soldats pour aider et protéger les populations vulnérables. On appelait ces soldats les Casques bleus, un magnifique projet canadien dont j'ai été fière. Malheureusement, au début du 21e siècle, le Canada s'est désolidarisé des Casques bleus. Je me demande ce que cela veut dire pour votre avenir. Il me semble que le Canada actuel devrait revisiter les institutions qui nous ont été léguées, il y a 150 ans par les Pères de la Confédération. Ceux-ci ont tracé notre route, tout comme nous traçons la vôtre. Il est temps pour nous de faire un bilan. Les institutions canadiennes ne correspondent peut-être plus aux aspirations démocratiques des Canadien(e)s du 21e siècle, car les gens votent de moins en moins. Pour vous faire comprendre mon époque, je vous fais part de quelques questions qui m'apparaissent importantes. Quels sont les grands débats de sociétés qui soulèvent les passions dans le Canada de 2014? Y a-t-il des rêves qui unissent les Canadien(ne)s? En ce moment au Canada, la population est vieillissante. Cela pose un vrai problème pour l'avenir proche car les jeunes auront à assumer un lourd fardeau social. Comment nous assurer que la voix des jeunes soit entendue? De quoi ont-ils besoin maintenant pour se préparer à cette responsabilité future? Faudrait-il réévaluer le mode de scrutin? Devrait-on, par exemple, modifier notre système parlementaire pour avoir deux tours de scrutin afin de permettre l'émergence d'alliances entre partis politiques? Comment nous assurer que les gouvernements pensent premièrement au pays et non pas aux membres de leurs partis politiques? Peut-être devrions-nous tenir une assemblée constituante? Un exercice apolitique et pancanadien permettrait-il d'explorer les réponses à ces questions afin de recentrer le Canada autour d'une vision et d'un avenir qui préparerait 2164? Mais cet exercice pourrait-il avoir lieu? Comme vous voyez, j'ai plusieurs inquiétudes quant à l'avenir et à la façon dont ma génération et moi le préparons… Mais, il se fait tard, je continuerais donc demain.

Dormez paisiblement,

Catherine

....

Chères descendantes, descendants et futurs concitoyen(nes),

Au cœur de l'avenir du Canada, je vous souhaite le français, cette belle langue que nous maintenons en Amérique du Nord. Un français vivant, un français vibrant… C'est fragile une langue, une culture, une identité. Il y a deux ans, je suis allée en Louisiane. En l'espace d'une génération, les Cajuns ont presque complètement perdu le français. Les gens me disaient « *My grandmother spoke French, but I don't speak it.* » Cela m'a fait peur. Saurez-vous lire cette lettre que je vous écris? Le mal-être du Québec au sein de la fédération canadienne au 21e siècle ne peut pas être passé sous silence quand je pense à votre avenir. Il y a un symbole qui me frappe toujours pour ce qu'il représente et c'est celui d'Ottawa. Actuellement, en 2014, il est largement impossible de s'y faire servir en français. Pourtant, c'est la capitale du Canada et seule la rivière des Outaouais sépare Ottawa de Gatineau où on parle français. Comment se sentir chez-soi dans un pays où la capitale dédaigne le français?

Comme j'aime les symboles et que je rêve à votre avenir, j'espère que d'ici 150 ans le Canada aura su se faire garant du français au Québec, mais aussi ailleurs au Canada. Pourquoi ne pas transformer Ottawa en un territoire national, comme Washington aux États-Unis ou Canberra en Australie? Ce territoire serait officiellement bilingue afin de clamer haut et fort l'attachement du Canada à la langue de Molière. Mais est-ce que cet attachement existe? Je me demande si pendant les années qui séparent nos générations, les Canadiens(e)s et Québécois(e)s sauront trouver un modus vivendi pour que les différentes identités puissent cohabiter en harmonie. Il est pourtant possible de vivre de multiples identités. Par exemple, moi je suis femme, mère, scientifique, Québécoise et Canadienne.

De tout cœur,

Catherine

....

À vous tous, les Canadien(ne)s d'aujourd'hui et de demain,

À force de penser à vous en 2164. Cette lettre est la dernière que je vous écrirais et je la veux transgénérationnelle... Vous rappelez-vous que je suis biologiste? J'ai passé toute ma carrière de scientifique à travailler sur les changements climatiques pour éviter de laisser en héritage un territoire blessé par un climat rendu incontrôlable. La nature est donc au centre de mes préoccupations pour votre avenir. J'aime marcher dans la forêt, écouter les oiseaux, voir et sentir les fleurs. J'espère que vous aurez accès à de grands espaces sauvages ici, mais aussi ailleurs dans le monde. J'aime aussi voir tomber la neige. Je me rappelle, petite, le plaisir de rester à la maison les matins de tempêtes de neige... Et l'hiver suivi du printemps, cette redécouverte de la vie avec bien sûr le temps des sucres. Je vous souhaite de tout cœur des hivers blancs de neige pour le plaisir et pour que vous puissiez comprendre le pays que nous sommes. Allez dans les archives nationales, et cherchez la chanson « Mon pays ce n'est pas un pays, c'est l'hiver », elle est un peu l'âme d'un peuple, de notre peuple.

En bonne professeure, pour vous faire comprendre les défis auxquels nous avons fait face aux 21e siècle, je vais maintenant vous entraîner dans l'histoire des idées. Les courants d'idées qui ont façonné la société du 21e siècle contribueront sans doute à façonner votre siècle, le 22e siècle. Dans la civilisation occidentale, l'importance accordée à l'individu augmente à partir du 16ᵉ siècle, on parle ici de philosophes comme Montaigne (1533–1592) et Descartes (1596–1650) qui mettent le « je » au centre de leurs pensées. La notion si importante des droits humains prend sa racine dans cette idée de l'importance de l'individu. Cependant, de l'individualisme nait une tension entre droits collectifs et droits individuels.

Puis le 18ᵉ siècle nous a donné Smith (1723–1790) et son livre « La richesse des nations ». C'est en se penchant sur la façon d'augmenter la richesse des nations qu'il évoque la notion de croissance économique devenue un dogme au 21ᵉ siècle. Smith met de l'avant la notion de marché dont le moteur est bien sûr un bénéfice personnel. Il reconnaissait cependant le rôle important des États comme garants du bien-être des citoyen(ne)s. Ici se retrouve la tension entre individu et collectivité…

Suivant Smith de près, Malthus (1766–1834) utilise les mathématiques pour démontrer que la croissance des populations est plus rapide que la croissance des ressources. Il faut attendre le début du 20ᵉ siècle pour qu'à partir des idées de Malthus, émerge un nouveau concept : celui de la capacité de charge, qui exprime le nombre maximum d'espèces qu'un habitat peut soutenir. Nous devons la notion de capacité de charge aux modèles mathématiques de Lotka (1880–1949) et Voltera (1860–1940) qui permettent de comprendre comment la taille d'une population évolue en fonction des ressources disponibles dans l'environnement. Je crois que c'est la contribution la plus importante que l'écologie mathématique a fait au monde des idées. La capacité de charge indique que la croissance des espèces est limitée par l'environnement et ne se concilie pas facilement avec l'idée d'une croissance économique perpétuelle. Dans ce contexte, un des défis les plus importants du 21ᵉ siècle est de reconnaitre qu'il est impératif de donner autant d'importance à l'état de l'environnement qu'à l'état de l'économie. Je ne sais pas si nous réussirons. Vous trouverez peut-être risible que les idées d'un homme, Adam Smith, qui a vécu au 18ᵉ siècle, structurent encore le Canada 300 ans plus tard! En fait, de tout temps, les personnes au pouvoir ont résistés aux idées nouvelles. C'est dans ce contexte, qu'actuellement l'économie domine le pouvoir politique. J'espère que le Canada saura évoluer loin du 18ᵉ siècle et s'adapter aux nouveaux concepts proposés par le 20ᵉ…

Grâce à l'immense territoire du Canada, à l'abondance de ressources naturelles renouvelables et non-renouvelables, nous pourrions vous laisser un grand héritage. Malheureusement, il existe au Canada actuel une tendance lourde visant à exploiter frénétiquement ces ressources sans penser à votre avenir. Vous savez sans doute que le passé du Canada est un passé de colonisation et de défrichement : coureurs des bois et expansion vers l'ouest. Je parie que quand vous étudierez l'histoire, vos professeur(e)s vous parleront de la ruée vers l'or au 19ᵉ siècle puis de la ruée vers le pétrole au 21ᵉ siècle. Il semble en effet que la vision d'avenir du Canada actuel se conjugue avec pétro-économie : sables bitumineux, oléoducs, pétrole de schiste dans l'île d'Anticosti, pétrole au large de Terre-Neuve. Et malgré tous les avertissements du monde scientifique, les dérèglements climatiques sont déjà là, à notre porte. Sachez que cette ruée vers le pétrole a été le fait de ma génération et que je l'ai combattue pour mes enfants, mes petits-enfants, pour vous et pour tous et toutes les habitant(e)s de l'avenir.

Si je vous ai écrit ces lettres, c'est parce que cette année un groupe de femmes a décidé de célébrer les 150 ans du Canada. J'ai eu l'honneur d'être mise en nomination comme une de ces 23 femmes visionnaires du Canada. J'ai accepté cette nomination qui me donne l'occasion de parler à mes concitoyen(ne)s et de faire un plaidoyer pour l'avenir que je vous souhaite. Je ne veux pas que dans 20 ans, ma petite-fille, qui a aujourd'hui trois ans, et son frère de neuf mois, possiblement vos ancêtres, me disent « Grand-maman, tu étais une spécialiste des changements climatiques, pourquoi ne t'es-tu pas battue pour défendre notre avenir? » Je ne veux pas que vous regardiez notre époque en disant que nous avons abimé votre avenir. Les avenirs se confondent, le mien, celui de mes enfants et le vôtre. J'espère que les visions des 23 femmes qui ont accepté la responsabilité de visionnaires pendant cette célébration des 150 ans du Canada deviendront notre miroir et nous permettront de rediriger notre société afin de rendre possible l'avenir dont je rêve pour vous.

Mon souhait le plus cher pour vous est donc que ma génération réussisse à atteindre le déficit zéro en environnement. L'équation pour y arriver est simple, mais dans le contexte actuel du Canada, sa mise en œuvre ne l'est pas. … Il faudrait que mes concitoyen(ne)s se sèvrent du pétrole et utilisent plutôt des énergies renouvelables comme l'hydro-électricité, le soleil et le vent. En plus de cette migration énergétique, il faudrait éviter de gaspiller l'énergie. Cela demanderait une transformation de nos villes et nos maisons pour que les villes soient plus denses et les habitations plus compactes. Il faudrait aussi repenser le transport en favorisant le transport actif et le transport collectif. Sachez qu'en 2014, les technologies pour opérer ces transformations existent. Cependant, je ne suis pas certaine que la volonté de changer soit au rendez-vous, car si on en croit les indicateurs de croissance durable de l'Organisation de coopération et de développement économiques, le Canada du début du 21ᵉ siècle est dernier de classe en la matière.[4] L'année prochaine, 2015, sera cruciale, car il y aura une conférence internationale d'importance à Paris sur les changements climatiques. Au moment où je vous écris, il est encore possible de limiter les impacts négatifs de ces changements en réduisant de façon ambitieuse les émissions de gaz à effet de serre. Cela ne peut pas attendre et demandera un effort de coopération internationale. Plus la lutte contre les changements climatiques sera efficace, moins il y aura d'impacts négatifs, mieux vous vous porterez. Votre regard sur nous dépendra beaucoup, je crois, de ce que nous choisirons en 2015 : l'avidité ou la solidarité. Je croise les doigts.

Avec espoir,

Catherine

1. This essay is available in English translation at the website *A Bold Vision*, http://aboldvision.ca/catherine-potvin.
2. L'index de développement humain est un index que les Nations-Unies ont développé pour mesurer le développement des sociétés de façon intégrale. United Nations Development Program, Human Development Index, consulté le 24 juin 2014, http://hdr.undp.org/en/statistics/hdi.

3. The Conference Board of Canada, *How Canada Performs*, consulté le 24 juin 2014, http://www.conferenceboard.ca/hcp/details/society/income-inequality.aspx.

4. The Organisation for Economic Cooperation and Development, OECD StatExtracts, consulté le 24 juin 2014, http://stats.oecd.org/Index.aspx?DataSetCode=GREEN_GROWTH.

NATALIE PANEK

Rocket scientist, explorer, and champion for women in engineering, Natalie Panek is an engineer at MDA Robotics and Automation, working on Canadian space robotics and other Canadian space exploration programs. She is on a mission to inspire the next generation of female game-changers to pursue careers in engineering and technology. She is the 2013 recipient of the University of Calgary Graduate of the Last Decade Award and the Northern Lights Award Foundation 2013 Rising Star in aerospace. She was named one of CBC's 12 young leaders changing Canada, and Canada's *Financial Post* describes Natalie as "a vocal advocate for women in technology."

Motivated by her dream of becoming an astronaut, Natalie Panek's love of space and aviation led her to obtain a private pilot's license to fly a single-engine aircraft, as well as build and drive a solar-powered car across North America. She has participated in internships at NASA's Goddard Spaceflight Center and at NASA's Ames Research Center, where she worked on a mission to Mars.

With degrees in mechanical and aerospace engineering, Natalie Panek has co-authored papers on microgravity combustion and on-orbit satellite servicing. She is a technology contributor for the *Next Women Business Magazine* and the editorial site Women You Should Know, where she was featured as a "STEM Rock Star."

Committed to paying it forward, Natalie Panek founded thepanekroom.com to encourage women to pursue challenging careers in typically male-dominated fields. She is a mentor and program advisor for Cybermentor, through the University of Calgary and also sits on the board for the not-for-profit HerVolution.

Natalie Panek is a popular speaker on topics of leadership, space exploration, and women in technology. She has given multiple TEDx talks and was invited to give closing remarks for Colonel Chris Hadfield at his first event after returning to Earth from the International Space Station.

INSPIRING FEARLESSNESS:

A Bold Vision for Women in STEM Careers

"*I want media to celebrate science and celebrate women advancing innovative fields. Paving the way for future generations of female engineers and scientists could be as simple as ensuring that the majority of youth can identify a female scientist, engineer, welder, or even fabricator instead of a reality TV star. There is a direct relationship between what young women are exposed to on a daily basis and what they believe they can be.*"

Every now and again I am asked why I enjoy what I do — why I enjoy working in science and space exploration. It is not just that I enjoy my job; it is that I love engineering change and using innovation and creativity to find solutions to complex problems or interacting with transformative technology.

Now, I am a Mission Systems Engineer working on the next generation of space robotics. I helped design and build a solar-powered car that I raced across North America, lying down on my back and driving the spaceship-shaped car as though it were a tank. I got my VFR (visual flight rules) pilot's license to fly a single-engine aircraft. During graduate school, I studied combustion in a microgravity environment. And I have worked on planning a mission to Mars. Through these projects, I have witnessed firsthand the positive impacts that technology can have on society, how we can revolutionize the way we live and work using innovation, and how rewarding this feels. Through these projects, it became so clear just how many diverse opportunities exist for women in technology and engineering, and how we need to make these opportunities visible. The challenge is harnessing the imagination and creativity of women at a young age and opening their minds to the possibilities of Science, Technology, Engineering, and Math (STEM) careers.

This inspiration needs to start at an early age, when children are first exposed to STEM subjects, both in school and at home. We should strive to increase the number of skilled female workers in science, engineering, and trades as part of Canada's future, specifically in terms of the status of women and economic prosperity. At some point in young women's development, there is an overwhelming decrease in their interest in STEM fields. However, success in STEM fields is not a question of natural abilities. It is about youth perceiving these fields as part of the norm, as providing career goals that are attainable by anyone. Female role models in science and engineering are fundamental to increasing the percentage of women in the field. While access to female role models and mentors is critical, educating parents regarding the diversity and rewards of STEM careers for their children is also a necessity.

My bold vision for Canada is to noticeably raise the level of participation of women in science, engineering, and technology. In my view, this will require at least five areas of action: First, increasing the accessibility and visibility of female role models in STEM fields directly through Canadian media; second, increasing the number of hands-on and experiential learning programs in engineering, trades, and technology, specifically targeting young women in elementary, junior high, and high school (which includes the awareness of such programs); third, increasing the enrolment of women in university programs in science and engineering in all Canadian universities and colleges and increasing the number of women pursuing technical trades at institutions across Canada; fourth, increasing the retention rate of women in science and engineering undergraduate and post-graduate studies as well as in employed positions; and, fifth, ensuring Canada is a leader in supporting and advancing women in non-traditional occupations.

The focus of my bold vision is to build Canada's leadership on women's advancement in non-traditional roles, specifically STEM. This can be achieved through facilitating mentor relationships with role models and encouraging the media to enhance the visibility of women working in science and engineering careers.

Direct access to mentors, role models, and sponsors could create a fundamental shift towards encouraging young women to pursue careers in STEM fields. Mentoring has the potential to revolutionize how we think of women in technology and showcase the incredible achievements of women in science, engineering, and technology careers. Mentorship provides a direct opportunity for women involved with technology to interact with the next generation of women. Mentorship can inspire young women to enter what have traditionally been male-dominated fields and to want to contribute to positively changing the world. We need generations of women to stand up and serve as role models, encouraging young women to develop the critical skills needed for the competitive workforce of tomorrow. This is about connecting the next generation of girls and young women with women already accomplishing amazing feats in their chosen fields of interest. This is about teaching the women of "Generation Y" to embrace challenge, failure, and fearlessness.

High visibility of and access to female role models in STEM fields — women such as metal fabricator Jessi Combs, race engineer Leena Gade, and aerobatic pilot Melissa Pemberton — help break stereotypes. They are proof of the value in breaking boundaries and disassociating from negative opinions of women holding traditionally "masculine" positions. As a female engineer, I recognize that we need to do a better job showcasing to the women of Gen Y the diverse opportunities available in the science and engineering worlds. Essentially, the goal is to generate excitement for young women to want to tackle challenging, hands-on problems that can transform the world. Role models and mentors offer high-quality opportunities for young women to engage with, ask questions of, and interact with experts in their possible field of interest. These opportunities provide a gateway to experiences these young women may not have otherwise had. Showcasing these opportunities — and why we women in STEM love what we do — is much more positive than discussing only challenges in these fields. We must inspire first, and then provide the resources necessary to overcome any of the challenges.

Access to women mentors in STEM careers provides opportunities for young women to ask questions about previously unknown career paths. From the perspective of a mentor, it really is rewarding to be able to pass along knowledge and information that may have otherwise been hard to come by and to build an ongoing relationship of bi-directional learning and communication. Mentors and mentees learn from each other, cultivating curiosity for science, engineering, and technology across generations, facilitating what women can accomplish in innovative disciplines. Canada needs to enable access to mentors for the next generation of women game-changers.

The fact that many women naturally mentor and nurture should be leveraged to achieve these visions for Canada. Fortunately, many women are very good at building communities and support systems. These abilities will trigger a very powerful shift in technology over the next few decades, as those who can build networks and provide access to mentors and experiential learning programs will be very successful.

One exemplary program I am involved with is called Cybermentor. It is an online (and soon to be mobile) platform that establishes an email relationship between youth and women working in STEM fields. Young women have the opportunity to get advice, whether to ask questions about university preparation and career options, or to hear about the daily activities of women in STEM. Access to women in STEM fields via Cybermentor, in addition to workshops, online resources, and other events, provides options for rewarding career paths while building confidence in girls and opportunities to discover new interests. Lack of confidence and limiting beliefs that there are boundaries to success in STEM careers together fundamentally promote lower potential for scientific achievement; they can be huge barriers to pursuing careers in STEM fields. Of course, it is always easier for youth to see themselves in a role if they can personally relate to someone or visualize someone doing the work. Seeing a successful woman in science or engineering contributes directly to giving young women the conviction to pursue careers in STEM fields. Role models connect youth with a career path they can visualize.

But mentorship is not the only method for showcasing female mentors; the media is and should be a huge asset. I am a tireless advocate for trying to get more women in technology and engineering at the forefront of the media. Networks such as Discovery, OLN, or SyFy need more women hosts on their shows discussing intelligent topics. Some already prominent women who immediately come to mind include Kari Byron, host of *MythBusters* and *Head Rush* and Ziya Tong, host of *Daily Planet*. We need the next generation of women to perceive STEM fields as part of the norm for their future, and shifting media focus towards smart, inventive women will help. Canadian media should be world leaders in diverse and innovative content in their programming, moving away from an era of reality television that offers little capability to inspire or motivate the next generation.

Unfortunately, society in general does not do justice to the vast number of women in the world doing really cool work and interacting with technology. As a Canadian, I want media to celebrate science and celebrate women advancing innovative fields. We need to eliminate societal biases completely to inspire Gen Y women to tackle challenging world problems that require imagination and ingenuity. Paving the way for future generations of female engineers and scientists could be as simple as ensuring that the majority of youth can identify a female scientist, engineer, welder, or even fabricator instead of a reality-TV star. There is a direct relationship between what young women are exposed to on a daily basis and what they believe they can be. A shift in media focus is also critical to improving the level of parental encouragement for young women interested in STEM careers. Parental support is oftentimes lacking for young women; often parents do not encourage their daughters to pursue careers in STEM simply because they are not aware of all of the possibilities. Educating adults to be supportive of young women and to encourage young women to pursue STEM disciplines is vital.

A better understanding of what engineers and scientists do will also help bridge the gap between childhood, when girls are engaged and curious about the world around them, and adulthood, when they are too often absent from the engineering profession. The stereotypical image of an engineer is so evident in society, and so clearly gendered male, that simply seeing women who are engineers on a regular basis can have a major impact. Visual messages are incredibly relevant today, when people grow up surrounded by information and visuals from the Internet and television and when information can be shared and accessed instantaneously with the click of a mouse. Media is a powerful informant and influencer for all generations.

By challenging the media to feature more positive women role models, we can inspire young women to enter what traditionally have been male-dominated fields and to want to contribute to positively changing the world. If girls grow up in an environment that naturally enhances their success in science and math, they are more likely to develop skills as well as their confidence, and to consider a future in a STEM field. Challenging the media can also be extended to challenging Canadian government and private industries to build support programs that connect students to environments and teachers in non-traditional occupations for their gender. This involves collaboration and partnerships with industry and organizations that can provide hands-on engineering or technological activities for women.

The ultimate goal is to engage a larger demographic with technology. Ultimately, technology can and will revolutionize the world. There is something fulfilling about being able to *build* and *design* technology that can change the way we live and work. The world would be wise to have a much more diverse population advancing what technology can accomplish.

So, I challenge Canadian media (and media around the world) to take responsibility, embrace a new era of change, and move towards more intelligent programming. Aim for a much higher ratio of women who are executing science and engineering work and feature them at the forefront of what people see on a daily basis. Aim for a much higher ratio of fearless women in the media challenging themselves in exciting and diverse STEM fields.

As a mentor and a role model myself, and as someone who tries to set an example of visibility for women in STEM, I am often asked how I navigate my career and what have been the keys to my success. It is not an easy question to answer, but I have identified a few key traits that have certainly been influential as I continuously work towards my goal of travelling to space. These are traits such as fearlessness, perseverance, and perspective.

As an engineer working in the Canadian aerospace sector, I want these traits to be taught to youth across the country. A key to encouraging young women to pursue science and engineering is to embrace fearlessness: Fearlessness in the decisions they make and fearlessness in the situations they embrace. There is definitely something powerful and self-revealing about thrusting ourselves into unfamiliar situations, which can teach fundamental life skills that are a foundation for success. These situations allow us to push beyond conceived limitations and build fortitude and resilience. We are not defined by our experiences, but how we react to those experiences and the attitudes we choose to adopt.

Fearlessness without a doubt also means embracing failure — appreciating what failure can teach us and learning how to recover. Working in the aerospace industry (or any other industry) proves firsthand the value of failing hard, failing a lot, and the sweetness of success that follows. Oftentimes, success is a direct result of creating our own opportunities and being fearless enough to seize them. Sometimes you luck out on opportunities because you were bold enough, and fearless enough, to fail. Embrace fearlessness to tackle challenge with an open mind and take risks: Ultimately, this is the path to realizing your wildest dreams. Recognize how to adjust to the challenges that life presents and plan a course of action to battle through it. Sometimes, it is worth diving head first into a situation and improvising as obstacles appear. After all, stormy seas make for skillful sailors; those who can ride out the storm and persevere will find success.

Perseverance teaches us how to do things better and learn from our mistakes: To make each of our initiatives better than the last and appreciate each one even more because of the hard work that is necessary for improvement. Determination is a trait well-learned and leads to experiences that can define the rest of your life. Among other opportunities, perseverance landed me two internships at NASA before my full-time job, internships which were extraordinary because of the dynamic relationships they developed and the challenge of being surrounded by like-minded, driven peers. But no matter how much we desire success, there is no escaping the power of perseverance. Persevering is how we innovate, create change, and become fearless leaders with the power to revolutionize the world. Perseverance allows us to facilitate powerful avenues to innovation and discovery and see the world from multiple perspectives.

There is incredible value to the insight that perspective can bring. Perspective fosters objectivity, which ultimately gives way to progress. Perspective also allows you to follow as well as lead, to sell your own vision, but also support and listen to the visions and dreams of others. This means respecting and utilizing the abilities of others, realizing that we work towards common goals. It is perspective, after all, that allows us to see the horizon from all directions and be prepared for opportunities when they arise. You will not be defined by your experiences, but how you react to those experiences and the attitudes you choose to adopt.

We need to foster the imagination and the drive of youth, especially young women, to develop traits such as fearlessness, perseverance, and perspective. These traits will help them strive for excellence and work towards positively influencing the world. Canadian youth need skill sets and support systems to thrive at every stage of their careers. These supports will also allow youth to seek out unfamiliar situations and challenge themselves, participating in activities that engage their imagination. When it comes to learning, nothing is off limits because there is always more to discover. There should never be a limit on what can be learned, on imagination, or on the power of a dream. Daring to achieve the impossible is how the next era of technology will be defined.

We need young women to realize that engineering, trades, manufacturing, technology, and science are rewarding professions and to understand at an early age what these careers really are. We need to encourage the next generation of women to embrace innovation. My Canada believes that women are a catalyst for change, with the abilities to revolutionize our world. My Canada fosters national communities that inspire, encourage, and support the next generations of women in non-traditional roles such as science, engineering, and technology. My Canada recognizes that we are ultimately responsible for our contributions to innovation, and that these contributions can help advance complex projects to be sustainable on Earth in an era of extreme change. I am certain that the next generation of women will be inspired to face challenge head-on, to thrive in unfamiliar situations, and to become leaders who will advocate for positive change. This is my bold vision for Canada.

.

MARGARET-ANN ARMOUR

Margaret-Ann Armour is Associate Dean of Science, Diversity, at the University of Alberta, a position she has held since 2005. Born in Scotland and educated at Edinburgh University (BSc, MSc) and the University of Alberta (PhD), Dr. Armour joined the Department of Chemistry at the University of Alberta in 1979. Her research and teaching have been in the area of environmental chemistry, especially methods for managing and disposing of small quantities of hazardous waste. Dr. Armour has presented talks on her work to academic and community groups throughout North America and Asia. She is a past member of the Board of the Pacific Basin Consortium for Health and Environmental Sciences and has been a Scientific Advisor to the Asian Association for Academic Activity on Waste Management.

Dr. Armour has been a leader in encouraging women to consider careers in the sciences as a founding member WISEST (Women in Scholarship, Engineering, Science and Technology), as a member of CCWESTT (Canadian Coalition of Women in Science, Engineering, Trades and Technology), and currently as President of the Board of the Canadian Centre for Women in Science, Engineering, Trades and Technology (the WinSETT Centre). She has been an active member or leader with groups including Rotary, Shad International, Beta Sigma Phi, St. Stephen's College, and the United Church of Canada.

Dr. Armour has received numerous awards for her research, teaching, and outreach activities, including a 3M Teaching Fellowship, the Governor General's Award in Commemoration of the Persons Case, and the Montreal Medal of the Chemical Institute of Canada. She was named an Innovator at the 2011 APEC Summit on Women in the Economy and was twice selected by Women's Executive Network as one of Canada's 100 Most Powerful Women. She is a Member of the Order of Canada and has received four honorary degrees.

She enjoys conversations with friends, reading, music, live theatre, and gardening.

SCIENCE WITH A SOCIAL CONSCIENCE:
The Leap-Forward Effect of Communities for Shaping Canada's Future

"*In my experience, there have been memorable occasions sitting around a table with my group of researchers talking about our recent results. As the conversation proceeds and all the members of the group become engaged, excitement mounts, and we generate rich ideas. Creativity flourishes and the research takes a leap forward. I know this transforming experience happens in many different communities.*"

What an imagination-soaring opportunity—to have a bold vision for Canada for the next 150 years! The prospect is also somewhat daunting. When undergraduate students ask me what courses they should take to be competitive in the job market in four or five years, my reaction is that technology is changing so fast it is hard to predict where the jobs will be even after that short length of time. But my dream of Canada's future 150 years from now is much more exciting, and, unlike the students' questions, it does not carry the same burden of accountability, since I do not expect to be around in 150 years' time.

My bold vision is shaped by my being educated as a scientist, by having spent most of my working life in a university, by the people with whom I have interacted, and by my life experiences. I am more of a dreamer than a planner, and so crafting a bold vision is a joy for me.

Where do I start to dream what I wish for Canada over the next 150 years? During my professional career, I have been engaged in activities to encourage women to consider careers in the sciences. In a recent paper,[1] Deborah Kaminski of the Department of Mechanical, Aerospace, and Nuclear Engineering at Rensselaer Polytechnic Institute and Cheryl Geisler of the Faculty of Communication, Art, and Technology at Simon Fraser University suggest that it will take 100 years for science faculties in North America to have 50 per cent representation of women as faculty members. However, with all of the initiatives currently underway, there should certainly be gender equity in decision-making roles in all areas of the sciences and engineering by 2164.

This is where my dream begins—diverse women and men working together in academia, in government, in industry, in all aspects of the life of our country, fairly represented, equally valued, and with equal voices. I have a vision of women knowing they belong and can contribute fully to workplaces where today, they remain a small minority. These would be respectful and inclusive workplaces where the differences between women and men are recognized, understood as important, and celebrated.

Why do I believe this is so important for Canada, and what difference will it make? Industry has discovered the benefits of having diversity on boards of directors and in management — increased productivity, increased return to investors, and increased social responsibility. Not only that, but a report in the *Harvard Business Review*[2] shows that the collective intelligence of a group of women and men increases with more women in the group. This is because mixed groups are less likely to exhibit "group think"; they generate more ideas, draw from multiple perspectives and experiences, and create more robust solutions to problems. By 2164, the people of Canada may be called upon to solve many complex problems, and maximizing collective intelligence will strengthen the development of creative ideas and lead to valuable technical innovation. But even in 2164, we will have to select the problems we choose to tackle. As a scientist, I ask the question, how will we make this selection? This brings me to the next stage of my dream of a bold vision.

My life has been shaped by a number of people whom I would describe as mentors, even though their mentorship was not formal, and I did not recognize it as mentorship at the time. One of the most influential of my mentors has been Ursula Franklin, a professor emerita of materials engineering at the University of Toronto. She shared a principle that for me is fundamental: "Do science as if people matter." This immediately provides a guide for selecting the problems we as scientists will solve. In his book, *Daily Planet: The Ultimate Book of Everyday Science*,[3] Jay Ingram shares an example of what this principle means in practice. He describes the work of Amy Smith, an engineering professor at the Massachusetts Institute of Technology. She says that her research is not to find new technology that will benefit the top five per cent of the world's population who can afford it, but rather to develop applications that will improve the lives of the 50 per cent of the world's population who need it. She went to Haiti, where there has been rampant deforestation since wood-burning stoves became the standard equipment used for cooking. Deforestation results in erosion and flooding when there are heavy rains, since there is nothing left to anchor the soil when the trees are cut down.

Professor Smith looked around and saw sugar-cane waste left after the sugar had been extracted. By heating them in sealed oil drums, she made charcoal from the spent sugar canes. She then wanted something to make the charcoal powder into bricks, and one of the students she was working with suggested the sticky porridge made from locally grown cassava that he used to eat as child. They formulated the mixture of charcoal and porridge and formed bricks from it, and these made an excellent fuel for the stoves.

It is estimated that women in developing countries spend 20 billion hours a year hand-grinding grain. Professor Smith also developed a practical, air-driven hammer mill for grinding grain. The mills currently available require regular maintenance and often jam. The uniqueness of Amy Smith's mill is that since it is air-driven, the flour is blown out, and although it does require electrical power the mill requires little technical support. What a huge release of women-power if they can spend fewer of these 20 billion hours grinding grain. As Canada moves into the 22nd century, may its scientists and engineers balance curiosity-driven and industry-sponsored research with a commitment to doing science as if people matter.

I have talked of diversity and the sciences, but underlying everything is the expectation that people will still be around in 2164. That brings me to the last stage of my bold vision dream.

Canada will always be a land of rich natural resources, fresh water being one of the most enduring and precious. But the most valuable resource we have is our people. As a woman and a human being, the most important aspect of my life has been loving, respectful, and trusting relationships. These relationships have not only been with individuals, but within many and varied supportive communities. It seems that especially women value and thrive in such communities. The community-inspired aspect of my dream is that over the next 150 years there develops in Canada a strong societal recognition of the fundamental human need to belong to supportive, interacting communities where we are nurtured and fostered.

What a variety these communities can have, from educational circles to teams in the workplace, to professional and social societies, to common-interest groups, to sororities, to collectives, to political bodies, to faith-centred, philanthropic, and advocacy gatherings. Such communities empower those who are engaged in them; they enable us to reach towards our potential as human beings.

In my experience, there have been memorable occasions sitting around a table with my group of researchers talking about our recent results. As the conversation proceeds and all the members of the group become engaged, excitement mounts, and we generate rich ideas. Creativity flourishes, and the research takes a leap forward. I know this transforming experience happens in many different communities. Social communities develop a supportive network of their individual members that encourages a positive attitude, even when life is difficult. Not only that, but many communities reach out to support those outside their group, locally, nationally, and internationally. They are sensitive to the needs of others and generate a social conscience that leads to action to promote social justice. In parallel with concern for people comes respect for nature and a sense of the community of all living things.

You may comment that groups such as these have been in place for many years, and I would agree. My dream is that in the future, the *value* of these groups is celebrated and that they are seen as enriching the lives of all those engaged in them. The communities would interact so that members of each community gain knowledge and understanding of the values and aspirations of members of other communities. When understanding grows, so does tolerance of differences. Furthermore, as members of the group come to know and trust one other, they make decisions by consensus and for the common good. Thus, they provide a model for settling disputes by listening respectfully to each point of view, then arriving at agreement through discussion and compromise rather than confrontation and conflict. Canada has had a reputation as a peacekeeper. As we move into the future, may we take the peace-making model of the communities to the national and international arenas.

Why do I believe this to be possible? We are an evolving society. I know that the experiences of yesterday made some change, large or small, to the person I am today. We can recognize evolution as inevitable, as movement towards increased knowledge, increased understanding, greater compassion, and stronger community. Two books have been published recently which suggest societal evolution is leading towards a more peaceful future for our world. They are Steven Pinker's *The Better Angels of Our Nature: Why Violence Has Declined*[4] and Doug Roche's *Peacemakers: How People Around the World Are Building a World Free of War.*[5]

If these visionaries can write in this way about our world in 2014, imagine the possibilities for 2164 with Canada leading the way.

---

1. Deborah Kaminski and Cheryl Geisler, "Survival Analysis of Faculty Retention in Science and Engineering by Gender," *Science* 335 (2012), 864–6.

2. Anita Woolley and Thomas Malone, "What Makes a Team Smarter? More Women," *Harvard Business Review* 89.6 (2012), 32–3.

3. Jay Ingram, *Daily Planet: The Ultimate Book of Everyday Science* (Toronto: Penguin Canada, 2010), 12.

4. Steven Pinker, *The Better Angels of Our Nature: Why Violence Has Declined* (New York: Viking, 2011).

5. Doug Roche, *Peacemakers: How People Around the World Are Building a World Free of War* (Halifax: James Lorimer & Co., 2014).

HAZEL MCCALLION

Hazel McCallion was elected Mayor of Mississauga in 1978 and is currently serving her 12th term. She is the longest-serving mayor in the city's history.

Mayor McCallion was born Hazel Journeaux in Port Daniel on the Gaspé Coast of Quebec and educated in Quebec City and Montreal. While a student, she played for a professional women's hockey team in Montreal.

She began her career in Montreal and later in Toronto with the Canadian engineering and contracting firm Canadian Kellogg. She married in 1951 and settled with her husband, Sam McCallion, in Streetsville, Ontario. In 1967, she decided to leave the corporate world and devote her career to politics.

Mayor McCallion was appointed Reeve, and then elected as Mayor of Streetsville in 1970, serving until December 1973. When the Region of Peel was established in 1974, Hazel McCallion was elected to the Mississauga and Peel Regional Councils. She served two terms as a councillor prior to her mayoral campaign in 1978. By the time she was elected mayor, she had sat on virtually every committee at the Region of Peel and the City of Mississauga.

Hazel McCallion has been recognized numerous times for her contributions to public service and has received the Order of Canada. Among a long list of honours and firsts, in the last decade she was conferred with an Honorary Doctor of Laws degree by the University of Toronto, was named among the top 100 of Canada's Most Powerful Women by the Women's Executive Network, and received the Queen Elizabeth II Diamond Jubilee Medal. In addition, numerous education and health centres have been named in her honour.

Hazel McCallion continues to live and work in Mississauga, Ontario. She has three grown children and one granddaughter.

DOWN WITH THE PEOPLE:

A Conversation with Hazel McCallion

"The time has come that if you live in Vancouver, or you live in St. John's, Newfoundland, you should know the responsibilities of the three levels of government. And it should have some consistency."

In May 2014, Her Worship Mayor Hazel McCallion spoke with retired foreign correspondent and Bold Vision nominee Doreen Kays of Charlottetown. The interview took place several weeks before the June 2014 provincial election in Ontario, and the roles of provincial and municipal governments were very much on the Mayor's mind. During their warm conversation, the Mayor shared with Doreen her bold ideas about how to enhance democracy, strengthen local governments, and increase citizens' understanding of civics to transform the next 150 years in Canada.

....

DK: Hello, Your Worship, and I am delighted to be talking to you. I realize how very busy you are. I spent ten years in Toronto — I'm an ex-TV correspondent and anchor — but I never got the opportunity to meet you, and I had so wanted to, so it is a treat for me to talk to you.

HM: Yes, thank you. The thing I wanted to deal with in my bold vision for Canada was *government* and what changes have to occur in the structure of government in Canada. It's interesting, it came up at our Council meeting this morning, how little the citizens know about the responsibilities of the three orders of government in Canada, so they are completely confused. They do not know who to call.

The roles of the three levels of government have never been clearly defined, and changes have occurred over the years since 1867— they make deals to transfer this or another responsibility from the federal government to the provincial government. For instance, social housing was transferred from the federal government to the provincial government, and then the Province of Ontario downloaded it to the municipal government, the only government in the country that did that. So how do people know who is responsible for social housing?

DK: You have been involved in municipal affairs for almost 50 years. What was your vision when you were there in 1978, for example, and up to today, how have things changed?

HM: The cities of Canada—and more cities have been created in the last number of years—have become more responsible for more services over time, but our authority has not changed and our sources of revenue have remained the same. We are not recognized in the Constitution. We are considered children of the provinces. But we've grown up and assumed many additional responsibilities.

In practice, we are no longer children of the province. And, as such, we *have* to have more authority. We should not be governed by the Municipal Act, if democracy is what we believe in.

So those are the things that I'd like to cover in my bold vision, with my experience in local government and having to deal with provincial and federal governments for all these years.

DK: It makes you wonder, how is this downloading and the heavy burden on municipalities such as yours manifested now?

HM: Well, I was a member of a task force about three years ago that got the Liberal government in Ontario to start taking back or uploading social costs, such as uploading security costs at provincial courts. We didn't succeed in getting them to upload the costs of social housing that the province downloaded on us. But we wanted to make it consistent across the country; we're the only province where it is at the local level.

The time has come that if you live in Vancouver, or you live in St. John, Newfoundland, you should know the responsibilities of the three levels of government. And it should have some consistency. So, what happens now, if you move from one province to another, is you're completely in the dark as to who administers what.

DK: That's an excellent point. There's no consistency.

HM: Right. No consistency. And then people complain about people not voting? They don't vote because they really don't know the issues, they don't know who is responsible for what. I've gone to meet-your-candidate meetings for the upcoming June provincial election where a person will want to know why they can't have a traffic light on the end of their section of the street.

DK: [Laughs.] Well, there you are!

HM: You know, they call us with issues— and the local government gets most of the calls— and then we'll say, "That's a provincial matter, and you should be talking to your MPP." They will say, "Who is that?"

DK: So, how have you managed then?

HM: It has been very difficult. In fact, you are forever explaining to people that you don't have the authority to do what they ask. Or that your decision is appealable to the Ontario Municipal Board. They'll say, "Oh, you're in control of development," and we'll say, "No, we're not." Yes, we're in control of processing the application that comes in for growth or development, whether it's industrial or residential or commercial. But, our decision can be appealed— appealed by the developer or appealed by the citizens. So, we really don't have the final decision. It is made by the Ontario Municipal Board, and this is not an elected body. So that is contrary to democracy.

DK: So, what are you recommending? And how will we get that message across?

HM: I feel that my role, involved as a mayor of a municipality and involved in municipal politics for 46 years, I feel like I should talk about what should happen to the structure of government in Canada, and what is my bold vision of what has to happen in government, in the structure of government. Because it doesn't *work*. It really doesn't work for the people.

For one thing, I think the Senate should be eliminated. Because it is undemocratic. When you elect the federal government, you elect them democratically, and if they don't do a good job, you toss them out the next election. Why should the legislation that they pass have to be endorsed by an unelected body?

DK: So, when you think about it, in the 150 years of Canada, the citizenship role, the role of citizens, has never been clarified.

HM: Yes. Secondly, that is why people don't vote. I believe it should be legislated that you have to vote. Again, because the federal government election gets around 51 per cent voter turnout, and local government gets 30 per cent and below of eligible voters. That situation sends a clear message.

DK: Really!

HM: So, in my opinion, you must vote. In Australia, you have to vote. It's mandated. So I believe — that's my bold vision — that you should be mandated to vote in local, provincial, and federal elections, based on eligibility. I think voting should be mandated for provincial, local, and federal government, and it might encourage people to pay more attention to what the responsibilities of the three orders of government are and acquaint themselves with the issues.

DK: Looking back, Your Worship, we're in 2014. In 150 years from now, in retrospect, what might future Canadians think of us today? How do you imagine the values, the needs, and the hopes will differ in 150 years' time from what they are today?

HM: Well, society has changed so drastically, and the information technology has advanced so much that Canadians should be better informed than they are on the issues and the challenges, but they are not. The information is *there*, and we're not getting it across. It's not getting across to the people.

DK: Well, if they don't know what services fall under which jurisdiction...

HM: Exactly. Let me give you a concrete example: We had a councillor tell me this morning — he went doorknocking, I guess, and he knocked on the door and he talked to the gentleman, and the gentleman raised four questions, all of provincial significance. He raised them one by one, and the councillor said, sorry we're not responsible for that. Four issues that the gentleman raised that he thought the councillor was responsible for. And on the property an election sign, a sign for the June 12 election in Ontario. And he didn't know those four issues were provincial issues. The councillor said to him, "You know, the person that you're supporting in the provincial election is responsible for the four things that you asked me, that we're not responsible for." The gentleman said, "Oh, really?!" [Laughs.] So, there you are. That's a concrete example that came up at our meeting this morning. So it gives you an idea of how uninformed people are.

DK: *Is there a reason why you stuck to municipal government? You would have made a great Prime Minister of this country, if I may say so.*

HM: I'm not a party person. If you are in a party, you have to toe the party line—and if the Opposition came up with good legislation, I'd be the first to vote for it. And therefore, I would be eliminated, as many politicians have been, from their caucus. At the local level, you can make your decision based on what research you've done or *your* knowledge of the issue. You are far more independent.

DK: *Well, you must have done something right with Mississauga, with almost 760,000 people, I think. So, the values that drive your vision would be what, would you say, Your Worship?*

HM: Well, I feel that the system of government isn't working. It just isn't working. That's what is driving my desire. And I believe that the three orders of government have to sit down and determine what the roles and responsibilities are of each order of government and then determine what revenue they need to implement their responsibilities.

Responsibilities are all over the map. Welfare is partly financed by the federal government, the provincial government, and the municipal government. Housing is all over the map. The financing of the three orders of government is all over the map, and in many cases divided. I often ask people when I am speaking, who pays for welfare? And I have never yet gotten the right answer.

DK: And, of course, change also depends on which government is in power in Ottawa, in terms of downloading or not downloading. And they've pawned off responsibilities on the provinces who then pawn off responsibilities on the municipalities...

HM: Yes, and the province can challenge the federal government's position. We municipalities can't challenge — or we can *challenge* but we have no *authority*.

It is because we are children of the province. We are not an order of government according to the Constitution.

You know, municipalities were first designed to provide grass-cutting, winter maintenance, garbage, roads. Our responsibilities have expanded. We're into economic development in a big way, promoting our cities and encouraging economic development. And that's still financed based on property taxes, and property tax is a regressive tax. And that's the only source of revenue that we get other than user fees.

There are some differences which the provinces can allow, because we operate under a municipal act in each province (and they are not all identical). But, again, confusion. It's just a can of worms, the way government operates in Canada.

DK: Does the Constitution need to be changed?

HM: Yes. And the Constitution should clearly determine what the federal government is responsible for, what provincial governments and territories are responsible for, and what local government is responsible for.

DK: Well, you know it's interesting that this arrangement has existed for almost 150 years, then.

HM: I was on the commission that was set up to look at the Municipal Act of the Province of Ontario, and it hadn't been looked at for 100 years. Now, things have changed in 100 years, I can tell you! So, that's a good example.

And we at the local level can't change that. The Province has to decide whether they wish to make any changes.

DK: You've obviously discussed this, or maybe you haven't yet in any detail, with your provincial or federal counterparts. Have you discussed any of this?

HM: Nope. I've often made the statement that the three orders of government in Canada should be looked at and clearly defined so that people would know who to call when they had a problem. And what happens is, what is the practice, people call local government, because it is closest to the people. And therefore, we have to say to them, "Well, that's a provincial matter." And, "That's a federal matter." So, we get the *calls*, and the province and federal government do not get the same calls that we get at the local level on items that are not our responsibility.

DK: Right. Well, that's very interesting. I would not have imagined that this would be your vision, and that is a great, great vision. And I didn't realize the situation. And you're right. If the citizens don't know such elemental things about their own governments, then you're right, it does affect our democracy.

HM: I'm sure people are going to vote on June the 12th in Ontario, and they'll be voting because a transit shelter wasn't put at an intersection in Mississauga. [Laughs.] And they think that's provincial! Or they'll think the airport, the noise that the airport causes, is the responsibility of the Mayor of Mississauga. We have no control over federal airports at all. Absolutely none.

But it's not just a lack of clear definitions, the point is on some issues all three orders of government are involved. So how do the people know who to call?

DK: Gosh, yes, exactly. Has there been a period of time, Your Worship, during your many years, when one period of time was more difficult than another?

HM: It's more difficult now, far more difficult now, because the municipalities of the country are more involved in the development of their community than they were ever before because of the growth that is occurring in the municipalities across the country and the immigration that is coming in. We have to provide the services and the homes and the jobs for people. And that is ending up on the table or on the plate of the local mayor and members of council. Climate change is another challenge we are facing. Major disasters in our communities cannot be funded by the property tax.

DK: *And it can only be more so, then, in the next decades…*

HM: Well, the big thing that has to happen is how the order of local government is financed. I mean, that's the big change that has to occur. We can't continue on handouts, because a municipality has to plan financially — and not from year to year. We have to plan ten years down the road. And if you don't know what you're going to get, it's pretty hard to plan.

DK: *Sure is. I don't know how you've managed to go without a deficit. Unbelievable. That's good governing on your part, because I can't imagine Mississauga being deprived of anything. It seems to be an incredibly well-functioning city. That's vision of enough right there, and that is your purview, is the municipal level of government.*

I want to congratulate you, and your name, apparently, was the first one that came up everywhere when they were looking at possible visionaries.

HM: Really?

DK: *Your name was number one, and rightly so. To tell you the truth, I read through your bio, several pages — I was exhausted by the bottom of the second page. Your energy! You're phenomenal. I can't imagine anyone having done more than you. I don't know how you've managed it. It's unbelievable.*

HM: Well, I've enjoyed it. That's why I've stayed at the local level. You can accomplish more. You can be independent. You don't have someone telling you how to vote on the issue. And you're down with your people. You're there, in front of them, you're in their face every day, either at church or shopping or events in the municipality. So you can't hide from them.

DK: You've got an excellent point there, and I'm glad that you didn't.

HM: I felt that's the role I should play, to talk about my vision for local government and democracy, and I'm sure all the other wonderful people that have been chosen as visionaries will cover all the other aspects of life.

DK: I don't think anybody else will be able to do this. . . . I'd love to be around to see the changes to the Constitution!

HM: I don't think I will be. Not at 93.

DK: Bless your heart! Ninety-three! Well, keep going, onwards and upwards, and thank you so much, Your Worship.

HM: Oh, you're most welcome. Take care.

R. IRENE D'ENTREMONT

R. Irene d'Entremont, C.M., D.Comm. h.c., is a successful Francophone business and community leader from Yarmouth, Nova Scotia.

Irene d'Entremont has been involved in businesses for more than 40 years, in diverse roles including sales, service, research and development, and manufacturing. She is the president of ITG Information Management Inc., consulting in business management. She is the past-president of M.I.T. Electronics Inc., president of Women's Up-To-Date Shop Inc., and secretary-treasurer of Wesmar Electronics Canada Ltd.

In the mid-1980s, Irene stepped into the political arena, serving as a Yarmouth town councillor. As a community leader, Irene d'Entremont has been actively involved with Chambers of Commerce at the provincial, regional, and national level. She is also vice-chairperson of the American Chamber in Atlantic Canada.

She is a director of Nova Scotia Power Inc. and has served on public- and private-sector boards for Revenue Canada, the Nova Scotia Business Development

Corporation, the Atlantic Canada Opportunities Agency, the Law Commission of Canada, and the Aerospace and Defence Industries Association of Nova Scotia. Most recently, she was appointed vice-chair of the new Nova Scotia Tourism Agency and to the Board of Governors for the Art Gallery of Nova Scotia.

Over the years, Irene d'Entremont has been awarded numerous honours and distinctions for her leadership roles in entrepreneurship and community development. She is the recipient of the Governor General of Canada Commemorative Medal. She was also inducted into the Nova Scotia Business Hall of Fame. In 2001 she was appointed to the Order of Canada, and in 2002 she received the Queen's Golden Jubilee Medal. Ten years later, in 2012, she was honoured to receive the Queen's Diamond Jubilee Medal.

Irene resides in Yarmouth, Nova Scotia, and was married to the late Theodore (Ted) d'Entremont. She has two sons, Wayne and Gary, and three grandchildren, Heather, Tanya, and Dylan.

CANADA 150 YEARS FROM NOW, AS ENVISIONED BY AN ACADIAN BUSINESSWOMAN

"We are only now beginning to see the huge potential that is unlocked when women are given freedom and support to fully develop their capacities as leaders, decision-makers, innovators, and entrepreneurs."

The experts tell us that the totality of human knowledge is now doubling with each generation, and that technological advance and innovative thinking will continuously transform how we live and make our livings. This is true now and was true in 1864 when, at the Charlottetown Conference, the idea of our country was born. Innovation comes in many forms, and the concept of a unified nation was a groundbreaking proposal. As we celebrate the 150th anniversary of this event, I'm reminded of just how much has evolved — and the opportunities just on the horizon.

My mother and father were born before the Model T Ford was on the road, and they lived to see men walk on the moon. At the current pace of change, I can anticipate that my grandchildren will see people living on other planets. I myself have experienced great change in every aspect of daily life, and I now live, work, travel, and communicate in ways that my grandparents could not have imagined. In the space of two generations my family has made the transition from subsistence-oriented activities in self-contained rural communities to active participation in diverse economic networks that link everything to almost everything else in a globalized marketplace.

In this almost chaotic environment I find it hard to imagine how people will live 25 years from now, let alone picture what life will be like for Canadians in 2164. We know there are exciting possibilities for positive outcomes. Continuing advances in scientific knowledge may soon lengthen our lives and generate better ways to treat or prevent serious diseases. We can hope that expanding research and development will provide new, sustainable energy sources for heating our homes, fuelling our transportation systems, and powering industrial production. And we can hope that families, communities, and governments will work together to educate successive generations of good citizens, creative entrepreneurs, and skilled workers. As the anthropologist Margaret Mead stated, "We are now at a point where we must educate our children in what no one knew yesterday, and prepare our schools for what no one knows yet."[1]

But we can also see real dangers in the not so distant future. Will the most advanced societies be able to change attitudes and behaviours in time to head off accelerating climate change and environmental degradation? Will we be able to reverse the trends to rising inequalities in wealth and opportunity within our own country and among the nations of the world? And will the nations of the world come together to resolve conflicts without resort to war and destruction?

Faced with these uncertainties, I can only think about the future through the lens of my own values and experience and the basic things I know to be true about people and everyday life. While many things will change — in particular, the hardware and software that support our work and everyday activities — I believe that certain basic human needs, capacities, and aspirations will remain constant. It is these things, I believe, that will most shape our future and, hopefully, lead to a better world.

Like most people, I look at the future from the vantage point of where I live and what I do. So I will begin with my story and try to draw lessons from it with which to imagine what life might be like in Canada 150 years from now.

I was born into an extended Acadian family in Southwest Nova Scotia with a long history in the fishery. For generations my community, survivors of the 1755 expulsion of Acadians, had relied on the sea for their livelihoods, exploiting rich fish resources that supported a lively trade with the United States and the Caribbean. Fishing is a tough life, filled with danger and uncertainty, so people had to be resilient and resourceful. You made the best of what you had, suffered through the lean times, and were quick to take advantage of opportunities that came along. I absorbed these attitudes and skills and, early on, learned that making progress in one's life is about facing and overcoming challenges and barriers.

The first barrier I faced was in my own community, where women had traditionally had little place in business. Our roles were generally restricted to the home and the social side of community life. This was part of my culture, and I accepted it. The opportunity to expand my horizons came, perhaps surprisingly, with my marriage at age 19. In the early 1970s, my husband came out of the Air Force with expertise in electronics, and he began to work for an American company, running its Canadian subsidiary for selling and servicing sonar equipment for fishing vessels in the eastern regions of Canada and the U.S. With two small children at home, I began to help out with the business side of his work. Within a few years, we were able to buy out the subsidiary and establish our own company. We had some good years, setting up distributor outlets all around the Atlantic Region. In the early 1980s, we started another company, with me as its president, to do research and development and then manufacture and market new safety products for fishing vessels.

When things later turned down in the fishing industry, we saw the need to diversify. I bought out a long-established ladies' clothing store in Yarmouth and purchased another commercial property. In the 1990s, I incorporated a consulting firm to provide liaison between the fishing industry and offshore energy developers. I still run that business today, with an expanded role in providing business management and consulting services.

After we had been living in Yarmouth for some time, I was increasingly recognized as a leader in my community. In the mid-1980s, I was elected to municipal government and became active on community boards and economic development councils. Because of our expanding business interests, I was drawn to the Chamber of Commerce, a largely male-dominated organization, and soon became President of the Yarmouth Chamber. This turned out to be a pathway to the wider world for me, as I developed links among business leaders in the province and beyond. Eventually I became president of the Nova Scotia Chamber, then Chair of the Atlantic Provinces Chamber, and then served two terms on the Canadian Chamber.

I pursued this path not because I was a radical feminist out to change the world, but because I was a businessperson trying to do real things to improve the climate for entrepreneurs across our region. There were barriers at every step, but I could see practical ways to make things better, and I just kept going. I worked hard, treated people with respect, and soon found that I was well accepted. There were so many meetings that I walked into for the first time and saw no other females, but I came to understand that I was there at the beginning of a great change that was rapidly gaining momentum.

Today, I am still very active in running my own businesses and on corporate boards and volunteer organizations. In 1995, I became a director of Nova Scotia Power Inc. and was a part of setting up Emera, its parent corporation, to invest in electricity generation, transmission, and distribution as well as gas transmission and other energy services in North American markets. I served on the board of Emera for seven years, and I just recently completed 19 years on the Nova Scotia Power board. On these bodies, we dealt with some of the most pressing public policy and business challenges facing our region.

I have also served as a director on the Atlantic Canada Opportunities Agency, ACOA (the federal economic development agency in the region), Marine Atlantic Inc. (ferry services), and Nova Scotia Business Development Corporation (a provincial economic development agency). Other engagements over many years included the Law Commission of Canada, Revenue Canada's Small Business Advisory Committee, and the boards of Université Sainte-Anne and the Art Gallery of Nova Scotia. Very recently, I served as a commissioner on the One Nova Scotia Commission on Building Our New Economy (the "Ivany Commission"). These and many other commitments provided me opportunities to lead and give back but also to expand my knowledge, build new relationships, and widen my horizons. This, I now understand, is how we grow, overcome barriers, and meet our challenges.

So what does all this tell me about the future of Canada? As I said at the outset, I can only look ahead through the lens of my values and experience as an Acadian businesswoman with deep roots in rural Nova Scotia. We all know that there will be continuous and dramatic changes in society driven by science and technological advance. What we need to understand better is the constants: The guiding lights and stabilizing values that will hopefully guide us through all this change and help us build a stronger, more peaceful, healthy, and prosperous Canada. I want to identify three basic areas of change that I believe can provide the solid foundations that will be needed.

First of all, continuing progress towards genuine equality for women is essential in our families, communities, public institutions, and the business world. We are only now beginning to see the huge potential that is unlocked when women are given freedom and support to fully develop their capacities as leaders, decision-makers, innovators, and entrepreneurs. It is my experience that in addition to new creative energies, women bring a more holistic perspective to the conduct of business and government, seeking a better balance between economic growth, social development, and environmental management objectives. These qualities will be increasingly important as we move forward into an uncertain future.

As a business leader, I believe that one of the most important places for women to be more strongly represented is on corporate boards. This is where key decisions are made that impact on all of society and shape our shared future. In 2012, only 11 per cent of directors on the boards of Canadian companies listed in the S&P/TSX composite index were female, and 43 per cent of these firms had no women directors at all.[2] This is not unique to Canada: Only about 15 per cent of board seats on Fortune Global 200 companies are held by women.[3]

To some extent this inequality results from continuing discrimination in the appointment of board members, but, on a more basic level, there are still not enough women getting into business and breaking through the glass ceiling from the grassroots level as I did. I have great hopes when I see the numbers of women in college and university business programs or pursuing professional degrees, but we need to do more in our families, communities, and schools to help younger women see their futures not just as employees but also as entrepreneurs and business leaders. They should be encouraged to volunteer on non-profit boards, chair committees, join Chambers of Commerce, and offer themselves for elected positions. Young women can learn through these experiences to be confident and to believe in themselves.

A second general theme for me in thinking about the future is the importance of our traditional rural industries and their links to the natural environment. Today, we have some 80 per cent of Canadians living in larger urban centres, and their values, attitudes, and lifestyle preferences are impacting heavily on public policy. With some exaggeration to make a point, it seems at times that urban dwellers see the future of rural Canada largely in terms of national parks, recreational facilities, and ever-expanding cottage country. Rural people are now a minority group, often seen as backward and out of touch with modern realities. Governments at all levels often make decisions that overlook rural economies or that materially impede them.

The simple reality is that Canada's national economy continues to rely heavily on production from rural-based mining, energy, agriculture, and marine industries. And these industries, in turn, depend on the continued vitality of rural communities to provide workforces, supporting services, and the environmental stewards that are all needed to maintain access to resources on a sustainable basis. This is true today, and I believe it will be true 150 years from now, even though the technologies involved may change dramatically.

I grew up beside the ocean. For hundreds of years people in my community made their livings by catching as much fish as possible and selling it off the wharf at the best price they could get. They were so successful at this that they overexploited important fish stocks almost to the point of extinction. Today, fish harvesters approach their work in very different ways — they participate in policy and science forums and work to rebuild fish stocks and establish sustainable harvesting levels. They see their future prosperity coming not just from catching fish but also from doing everything they can to add value and market it in expanding global markets. And when they look out at the ocean today, they see not just the traditional fisheries but also huge potential for new development of aquaculture, transportation, and energy production.

In short, rural regions are changing rapidly as we learn to manage and nurture our productive environments. With our huge capacities in forestry, mining, fisheries, and agriculture, Canada today is feeding the world and supplying it with many of the essential materials for daily life.

Over the next century, water will become increasingly important for human sustenance but also to generate energy and support food production and transportation. With abundant water resources of all types, Canada is well positioned to benefit from such developments. My region of Atlantic Canada will emerge as a major energy producer with continuous expansion in offshore oil and gas, tidal power, hydroelectric generation, and wind farms. The Lower Churchill hydro complex in Newfoundland and Labrador is comprised of two proposed installations, Muskrat Falls that is now under construction and Gull Island to be developed later. When completed, the overall project will generate 3,074 megawatts of electricity and utilize a new power grid to support local use and exports to the U.S. Tidal energy holds equally exciting potential. Every day, 160 billion tonnes of water flow in and out of the Bay of Fundy — more than four times the quantity in all the freshwater rivers in the world — and we are only just beginning to harness them for energy production.

With these and other developments, the rural resource economy can and will expand and grow dramatically over the next 150 years, and, as we grow, we will apply ever greater knowledge and expertise to nurturing and protecting the natural environment and its immense productive capacities. The current imperative is to value, support, and revitalize rural communities so that the expertise and commitment to manage natural resources sustainably is there when and where we need them.

A third area of significant change is population. Our current demographic outlook is not positive for maintaining workforces and viable communities, particularly in rural regions. In most of Eastern Canada we are now at a stage where more workers are retiring from the labour force than young people are coming up to replace them. This means that the continued viability of many communities and key industries will depend on expanded immigration. Over the next century or more, we will of necessity be welcoming many, many new Canadians from many different backgrounds into our communities.

The challenge associated with this change will be to pursue it in ways that allow us to become a more culturally diverse and tolerant society while maintaining the core values, freedoms, and institutions that make us uniquely Canadian. This raises sensitive issues, but I believe we can manage them if we are open and respectful in our approach. Again, it is my personal experience as a change leader that people and communities will more easily embrace new attitudes if they feel their shared histories and cultures are neither threatened nor devalued. As in business, social change is as much about continuity and nurturing our roots as it is about transformation and renewal.

In my vision of Canada 150 years from now, we will have true equality for women, and their contributions as entrepreneurs and business leaders will have helped immensely in building an economy that is fair and sustainable in contributing to peace and prosperity throughout the world.

In my vision, rural Canada will be a hugely productive environment for generating the food, water, energy, and material resources that the world needs, while doing it on a sustainable basis. Rural citizens will live full and rewarding lives in healthy and growing communities, no longer isolated and neglected, with the same high standard of living and quality of life enjoyed by urban Canadians.

And in my vision for 2164, we will be a much more ethnically diverse society, in rural as well as urban regions, but we will still be distinctively Canadian. We will maintain our core values and our founding cultures and traditions while we welcome many new groups as they come to us from around the world. The global village will have within it many vibrant, vital communities that are uniquely Canadian, including those that are proudly Acadian.

My vision is less a prediction than it is a hope and an aspiration. In my own life I have seen great change on many fronts, and I have been able to grow with such change by confronting the challenges I faced as a woman and by nurturing my roots in a rural fishing community in Acadian Nova Scotia. I hope that all Canadians will face their challenges and build on strong cultural foundations as we grow together through the next 150 years.

....

1. This and other Margaret Mead quotations are available at
   http://en.wikiquote.org/wiki/Margaret_Mead.

2. Janet MacFarland, "'We still have work to do' to topple barriers, says RBC's
   Taylor," *Globe and Mail*, September 19, 2013, accessed July 2014,
   http://www.theglobeandmail.com/report-on-business/we-still-have-work-
   to-do-to-topple-barriers-says-rbcs-taylor/article14403352/#dashboard/
   follows/.

3. Corporate Women Directors International, *Women Board Directors in the*
   Fortune *Global 200 and Beyond*, 2013, accessed July 2014,
   http://www.boarddiversity.ca/sites/default/files/2046_001.pdf.

LANA PAYNE

Lana Payne is the Atlantic Regional Director of Unifor, Canada's largest private-sector union. She was elected to this position in September 2013 and is currently one of the six top officers with the union.

Lana found her home in the labour movement in 1991 as a member of the Canadian Auto Workers/Fish, Food and Allied Workers. She worked for CAW/FFAW for 17 years in research, servicing, public policy, campaigns, and communications. During that time, she worked with the women of the union to make the union's structures more inclusive, to ensure women were part of the union's decision-making bodies, and to make sure policy issues were examined with a gender lens. She also led the union's campaign work on issues such as minimum wage, childcare, employment insurance, and violence against women. She was a driving force in the province around the National Women's March Against Poverty. She also participated in many committees and coalitions at the provincial and national level.

In 2008, Lana Payne was elected president of the

Newfoundland and Labrador Federation of Labour and was re-elected in 2010. During her time as president, she continued advocacy on the issues she had been a voice for with CAW/FFAW, now advocating on behalf of all workers, with a special focus on women's equality.

Before joining the union in 1991, Lana Payne was a journalist for *The Sunday Express* and the St. John's *Telegram*. She continues to write a bi-weekly column for the *Telegram* and appears as a regular panellist on the provincial CBC TV political program *On Point*.

Lana Payne is a proud feminist and activist. She lives in St. John's with her partner, Ed, and her daughter Kate.

A FAIRER, MORE EQUAL CANADA, A BETTER CANADA, IS POSSIBLE

"We cannot discuss a world that is fairer or more equal in 2164 if we don't ensure a dynamic, vibrant, and strong trade-union movement that has the tools, including legislative support, to counter the growing power of capital and corporations in a globalized world."

"Another world is not only possible, she is on her way. On a quiet day, I can hear her breathing." – *Arundhati Roy (Indian writer)*

In 2164, we will be judged by the kind of leadership and change we provide today on two of the most pressing issues facing our nation and the planet: climate change and rising social and economic inequality. How we deal with these inconvenient truths will determine the kind of nation we will have in 150 years.

They are, of course, intertwined. And they need earnest attention. The poor feel the impact of climate change more severely; disasters deepen inequality. The gold-rush mentality of resource development also fuels inequality.

More and more experts agree: Widening income inequality erodes democracy and weakens democratic participation and engagement. In other words, economic inequality begets political inequality. Of course, the negative impacts of inequality are more deeply felt by women, immigrants, Aboriginal peoples, persons with disabilities, the sick, and the elderly.

There is little doubt that a more egalitarian society is better equipped to build a broader social consensus on issues such as the environment and wealth redistribution. If the Scandinavian countries of the late 20th and early 21st centuries are any example, more egalitarian societies certainly lead to stronger democracies.

When the founding fathers of Canadian Confederation came together in 1864 in Charlottetown, their meetings were about creating a new country by uniting peoples and lands. Strength through unity was their battle cry.

Strength through unity is no less relevant today. Unity, though, is a collective response. Reversing the damaging impacts of inequality and climate change will require collective action as well as defining and bold leadership. Collective action will mean governing for the future and not just for today, governing with something more in mind than political expediency and power for power's sake. Nations are about the collective — what we can do together to make our world better. Collective-building is, in essence, nation-building.

What do we want Canada to look like 20, 30, 50, even 150 years out? Every generation should ask this of itself. Will we be a country where equity, strengthened democracy, environmental defence, and fairness define us? Will these be the principles that guide us? My bold vision for Canada is of a country that has these principles at its core, at its heart.

Advancing Canada as a progressive nation requires thoughtful discussion and action around inclusion, how wealth from our economy and vast resources are shared, how we develop those resources, how we build a more equal and equitable country, how we enrich democracy, and how we harness our collective values to ensure we protect, enhance, and build institutions, laws, and systems that act as an equalizing force. Such as universal public health care. Such as charters of rights. Such as fully accessible, public post-secondary education. Things that, together, build a vibrant civil society.

If we are to progress as a nation so our world is a place where democracy and fairness trump uncontrolled corporate power and unrestrained oligarchy, we must take concrete steps today to address rising inequality. We must take concrete and bold steps to stop or reverse the harmful destruction of the planet.

How we deliver justice and equality to women, to Aboriginal peoples, to newcomers, and to the vulnerable, and how we truly share economic wealth while protecting the environment for future generations: These will tell the tale of the kind of country we have built and the kind of society we have created. This is how we will judged 150 years from now. Not by what we consumed, or what we owned, but by the kind of world we have left for future generations.

These are big matters of public policy. The solutions will not happen if we leave the decisions up to the "haves" and the outcomes up to the so-called "markets" in an economic system rooted in greed and selfishness. They will happen if people care and act boldly to challenge what in 2014 is a disgraced economic system that allows wealth to be accumulated by the few, that fuels unsustainable resource development, and that deepens inequality by discrediting those organizations and civil society groups and institutions meant to deliver or advance equality and democracy.

Reversing climate change cannot be left up to markets or chance, either. Equality and inequality do not just happen, but rather are a product of what we do and what we don't do — a matter of government policy or lack of government action. Another inconvenient truth.

And no matter how willing governments may be to act, they still need progressive forces in society acting to counterbalance unprecedented corporate power. A vibrant civil society that includes strong unions, a diverse and equally strong feminist movement, and powerful institutions whose job it is to protect the environment and advance equality, human rights, and social justice. These are essential if we wish to build a better world.

Others in this wonderful group of 23 bold women of vision, experts in the field, address the issue of climate. This is also true for how Aboriginal people, especially women, achieve justice — both social and economic. I look forward to learning from their visions, and I deeply commend the Bold Vision committee on its diversity of choices.

As the only trade-union leader among the 23, I feel compelled to make a clear statement about the role of unions in our society as a force of good, as a catalyst for wealth sharing, as a progressive force for equality in an economic system that has tipped the scales so lopsidedly in favour of the "haves."

Unions have played a significant role in advancing women's economic and social equality and in making our workplaces safer and more democratic. Unions have also forced wealth to be shared generally and have raised the standard of living for all workers. Through collective bargaining, unions have made the distribution of wages and incomes significantly more equal than would otherwise be the case. Unionization serves to increase the share of national income going to workers, but also, as economist Jordan Brennan of my union, Unifor, reported in a 2014 study, unions ensure that the national wage is divided more equally among workers.[1]

The growth of shared prosperity, he found, was a partial consequence of the growth of trade unions and collective bargaining coverage. Conversely, the erosion of unions has also meant a partial erosion of that shared prosperity.

To reverse this erosion so that by 2164 we are not a country of great inequality run by oligarchs, we need to consider the fundamental principles and values that prevent such an outcome.

Unions have championed income and economic security programs for all, including public pensions and public health care. They share prosperity through their collective bargaining and political bargaining demands. Nations where prosperity is best shared have strong trade unions, committed to working for progressive social change for all. There is no disputing that unions are among the greatest equalizing forces on the planet. And no nation in 2014 had achieved shared prosperity without a strong trade-union movement. Therefore, we cannot discuss a world that is fairer or more equal in 2164 if we don't ensure a dynamic, vibrant, and strong trade-union movement that has the tools, including legislative support, to counter the growing power of capital and corporations in a globalized world.

Numerous studies and even Nobel Prize–winning economists have lauded the important role played by unions and the state in reducing income inequality. Indeed, as the power of unions was weakened through regressive laws and mass globalization and concentration of wealth, income inequality began to rise rapidly — often as a result of trade agreements that did little to put people first.

But in 2014 inequality is also on trial. The Occupy Movement, born as a response to the devastating financial crisis and subsequent recession of 2008, focused the world's attention on the problem that the majority of the wealth in the world is owned by the few. The GINI Project, a three-year project conducted by researchers in over 30 countries, noted that "inequalities are not inevitable ... governments play a key role in determining domestic levels of inequality even in a set of highly globalised rich countries."[2]

The researchers asked: "Why does inequality matter and why should governments be interested in seeking to contain inequality increases? Put very simply: People don't like inequality."[3]

People don't like inequality! And yet most countries have done little to address its growth. With their models of social democracy, the Scandinavian countries have perhaps achieved and done the most to narrow the rise in inequality. They also have significant union density and collective bargaining coverage for their citizens.

In Canada, there is very little doubt that in addition to unions, important collective actions such as public health care, seen as a great equalizer in society, and other public programs have helped to share prosperity especially to women. But in 2014 these, too, are under assault.

Interestingly, but not surprisingly, the GINI Project discovered that increases in inequalities have gone hand in hand with lower political participation and engagement by citizens, with decreased voting. In other words, there is a relationship between inequality and damaged democracy.

One of 200 researchers involved in the study, Abigail McKnight of the London School of Economics, notes:

> concern has been growing about increases in concentration of income and wealth among a small group of people and the relationship between this group and an emerging privileged political elite. This new evidence on inequality trends, political participation and evolving public policy is a concern for all democracies.[4]

In other words, inequality will be at the root of much social and political upheaval. So if we care about a nation built on social consensus and equality, reversing the trend towards inequality is essential.

In 2014 unions in Canada are under unprecedented attack by those who foster inequality. Their legitimacy is being threatened by those with power. Reversing this and allowing unions to do the job they were designed to do requires innovation and legislation: a supportive policy environment. It means designing and modernizing labour legislation to ensure the rights of workers are protected in this new global world. It means designing labour laws that enable unions to lift people up, including in those sectors where wealth is very unequal and where wages remain below what would be considered a livable wage.

Unions, too, must be prepared to renew themselves because by resisting the inclination to turn inwards, to be defensive, when they are under attack, they can play a more profound role. We need unions to become even more democratic, more inclusive, and more activist in future.

All this is what will be required to challenge an economic system that is designed to deliver the most to those who already have the most. As noted Nobel Prize–winning economist Joseph Stiglitz proclaimed in 2014, "An economic system that only delivers to the very top is a failed economic system."[5] Yet the political will, the courage, to change such an unfair system been for the most part entirely lacking.

We must never forget the lessons of the workers' movement or the struggle by feminists for equality for all women. Rights, gains, and progress were never given. They were achieved through struggle, through courage, through conviction, and often through collective action, through solidarity.

Certainly, the growth of women in the workforce and in turn in the trade-union movement has forced positive change on our workplaces and changed the demands of unions. The outstanding role played by women in unions has pushed them to be about more than justice at work.

In 2014, women make up more than half of the unionized workforce in Canada. Women in unions earn on average $5 more an hour than women without a union. Unionized women working full-time earn 95 per cent per hour of wages earned by unionized men; the wage gap for non-unionized women is considerably and stubbornly higher. Unionized women are more likely to have retirement security, a pension, and decent hours of work, including good vacations, paid leave, and family time.

Working side-by-side with feminist organizations, women trade unionists are bold voices in the call for universal childcare, considered a necessary building block in the path to advance full equality for women. They are also champions of a better work-life balance for all.

As noted by the Broadbent Institute in a 2014 report, social movement unionism, as opposed to narrow workplace-focused unionism, has helped build a much more inclusive, equal, and democratic society: "If we want to pursue a Canadian society of greater equality, social justice and social democracy, we would be better served by strengthening, not weakening, our unions."[6]

But you first have to want that kind of society. That kind of world. Perhaps this is the biggest challenge: Those who hold power appear to not want that kind of country. Unions and their social allies must challenge that way of thinking at every turn.

But unions must also challenge our own conventional wisdom and include a feminist lens to how we propose developing our economy and addressing inequality.

Following the giant recession of 2008, Marjorie Griffin Cohen, a Canadian feminist economist, noted that governments needed a more inclusive response by "including women in the picture of job creation" and that shifting government funding to building the social sector would be a stepping stone to a more inclusive, egalitarian society.[7]

Cohen wrote: "Those who design economic policy for governments should have a wider perspective than relying on the deepening exploitation of resources. Attention needs to shift to economic activity that meets the needs of people within this country."[8]

This makes so much sense. A simple concept and yet, in the context of the state of the world, a radical thought: a people-centric approach. Radical, but completely necessary, if we are to build a more inclusive and equal country.

Politically in 2014, more and more women have risen through the ranks of the trade-union movement to take on leadership roles. But we must also acknowledge our shortcomings. For example, at this point in its history, only one woman has led the Canadian trade-union movement's central labour body. As in politics, there is still much work to do to ensure women and other equity-seeking allies in the labour movement are also breaking through the glass ceiling.

Few would argue against the statement that women in unions have made unions stronger. In my opinion, women have been chiefly responsible for the growth of social unionism in Canada. As mentioned, social unionism takes the union out of the workplace and broadens its purpose to include social justice aims. Social unionism translates into more community-based activism, and it means involvement in politics. Women in the movement have understood that fully advancing women's equality can't be done through collective bargaining alone, as important as collective bargaining is to lifting people up, improving their workplaces and their lives, and building a middle class.

Social unionism speaks to the kind of world we'd like to see outside of our workplaces. It understands that we do not operate in a vacuum, but as catalysts for good in the workplace, the community, and our country.

It sometimes means advocating for broad-based achievements such as higher minimum wages, public health care, accessible education for all, and justice for First Nations peoples. It means using our collective power in the workplace to effect change in our communities. It means being involved in the struggle to end violence against women and to advancing reproductive rights for women. It means taking our collective bargaining gains, including improvements to work-life balance, maternity leave, and same-sex benefits, and advancing them for everyone — because until social progress is advanced for all, it remains fragile. Social unionism is not just about our workplaces; it is about our lives, about our society. And it has a place in a more inclusive Canada. Indeed, it can be one of the catalysts for building an inclusive nation.

But none of the gains of social unionism can happen if unions are constantly under attack, if their legitimacy is threatened by those who resist shared prosperity and by those who resist the role unions play in reducing poverty.

If you share my vision of a fairer, more equal Canada, we need a vibrant, strong, and dynamic trade-union movement to realize that vision.

In 2164, I want my Canada to be a nation that is more equal, more inclusive, and more democratic, where human rights are truly respected. Where unions are valued as important and woven into the social fabric of our nation, and where decisions are made with an equality and equity lens.

Canada in 2164 will be that way because we build the structures today, including a fair tax system and laws and institutions that foster a more egalitarian society. It will be that way because today we support a vibrant civil society and renew and update the social contract with citizens—all citizens, not just the "haves." It will be that way when wealth is shared and when no one is left behind. We can build this kind of country with guts, with determination, with compassion, and by understanding that it is indeed possible.

Social progress is not a guarantee. It is a result of action.

And if we are a successful nation in 2164, if Canada is indeed a more equal and just place, it will be because forces in civil society such as unions and environmental organizations, citizens' groups, anti-poverty advocates, feminists, and all progressive groups worked together in solidarity, in sisterhood, and in common cause.

It will be because we mobilized for a different kind of world. It will be because citizens found the courage needed to challenge conventional wisdom and failed economic systems. It will be because we were willing to truly share prosperity and deliver on the promise of full equality. The only thing holding us back is our unwillingness to dream that this kind of Canada is indeed possible and achievable. Together we can act with the conviction required to get us there. Strength through unity: A powerful reminder of what indeed is possible.

1. Jordan Brennan, *The Creation of a Shared Prosperity in Canada: Unions, Corporations and Countervailing Power,* Canadian Centre for Policy Alternatives, April 17, 2014, accessed July 2014, https://www.policyalternatives.ca/publications/reports/creation-shared-prosperity-canada.

2. Abigail McKnight, London School of Economics and Political Science, British Politics and Policy, accessed July 2014, http://blogs.lse.ac.uk/politicsandpolicy/rising-inequalities-not-inevitable-according-to-new-research/.

3. Ibid.

4. Ibid.

5. Quoted by Lorraine Woellert, "Stiglitz Says Growing Inequality Betrays U.S. Moral Values," *Bloomberg News*, accessed July 2014, http://www.bloomberg.com/news/2014-05-08/stiglitz-says-growing-inequality-betrays-u-s-moral-values.html.

6. Andrew Jackson, *Union Communities, Healthy Communities: The New Attack on Unions and Its Threat to Shared Prosperity in Canada* (Ottawa: Broadbent Institute, 2013), accessed July 2014, https://www.broadbentinstitute.ca/sites/default/files/documents/union-en.pdf.

7. Marjorie Griffin Cohen, "The Global Economic Crisis—Part 2: A Canadian Dimension Roundtable," *Canadian Dimension* (10 January 2012), accessed July 2014, http://canadiandimension.com/articles/4405/.

8. Marjorie Griffin Cohen, "The Staple Theory @ 50," *The Progressive Economics Forum* (22 November 2013), accessed July 2014, http://www.progressive-economics.ca/2013/11/22/the-staple-theory-50-marjorie-griffin-cohen/.

MARIA MOURANI

Maria Mourani, the independent Member of Parliament for Ahuntsic, Quebec, is a Francophone sociologist, criminologist, politician, and author.

Born in Abidjan, Ivory Coast, of Lebanese descent, she later immigrated to Canada with her family. Maria Mourani attended the Université de Montréal, where she received a bachelor's degree in criminology and a master's degree in sociology. As part of her studies and her work, she conducted research on street gangs. She is the author of *La Face cachée des gangs de rue* (Les Éditions de l'Homme, 2006), a book about the hidden side of street gangs, and *Gangs de rue inc. : leurs réseaux au Canada et dans les Amériques* (Les Éditions de l'Homme, 2009), a book on street gang networks in Canada and the Americas.

Maria Mourani was elected Member of Parliament for Ahuntsic in 2006, becoming the first woman of Lebanese heritage to be elected to the Canadian Parliament. She was re-elected in 2008 and again in 2011. A former member of the Bloc Québécois, she is an independent MP since September 2013 due to her opposition to the discriminatory measures in the Quebec Charter of Values introduced by the Parti Québécois government. In December 2013, after careful consideration, Maria Mourani broke with the Quebec separatist movement.

Both in Canadian society and in Parliament, she has worked on various high-profile portfolios, including street gangs, organized crime, human trafficking, and the sexual exploitation of women and children.

In 2008, Maria Mourani was awarded an honorary medal in Beirut, Lebanon, by the World Lebanese Cultural Union. In May 2014, she received from the President of Lebanon the National Order of the Lebanese Diaspora, awarded by the Lebanese Minister of Foreign Affairs and Emigrants.

DANS CE MONDE NOUVEAU... SACHONS ÊTRE UN PEUPLE DE SŒURS ET DE FRÈRES/

In This New World, Let's Find a Way to Be Brothers and Sisters[1]

> « Anglophones et francophones, nous avons tous droit de cité. Chez moi, « We are all Quebecers because Quebec is our home » et partout au Canada, je peux entendre le français se dire et se chanter. »

Je ne peux penser le Canada qu'en rêvant mon Québec et je ne peux rêver mon Québec que dans le Canada. Le Québec se doit d'être productif, prospère et solidaire; leader en matière de droit de la personne, de soutien envers les plus démunis, de développement durable.

Je vois mon Québec et mon pays, partenaires des premières nations, où ces femmes et ces hommes prendront part, dès les premières ébauches, à tout projet qui oriente et détermine notre avenir. Ces magnifiques et riches terres, où nous sommes installés, nous sont prêtées par le destin pour vivre ensemble dans le respect.

Je vois mon Québec et mon pays, sécuritaires pour tous. Une femme autochtone disparue ou assassinée suscitera autant l'outrage que toute autre femme ou enfant du pays disparu ou assassiné. Je vois un Québec et un Canada où le corps des femmes et des enfants ne s'achète pas. Non, on ne peut pas tout acheter en ce pays!

Je vois un Canada où tous les détenus, d'un océan à l'autre, bénéficient de programmes de réhabilitation de qualité, peu importe la durée et le lieu de leur détention; et où les victimes ont droit à la compassion et à la réparation. Je vois mon pays et mon peuple détester le gaspillage et la corruption, mais encore plus la dissimulation et le mensonge.

Je nous vois libérés des rapports vainqueurs-vaincus où les symboles d'inégalité trouvent leur place dans les musées. Les générations futures apprécieront l'histoire, mais comprendront qu'on ne fait plus, ici, l'éloge de ce qui blesse et divise.

Anglophones et francophones, nous avons tous droit de cité. Chez moi, « *We are all Quebecers because Quebec is our home* » et partout au Canada, je peux entendre le français se dire et se chanter.

Je nous vois constamment négocier pour moderniser le Canada. Les citoyennes et citoyens, au cœur des préoccupations. Que la négociation de notre constitution, pacte de notre vie commune, devienne à ce point banal qu'aucun politicien ne puisse en faire un enjeu électoral; qu'il devienne normal de la modifier à souhait. Qu'on ne fasse plus dérailler notre avenir en opposant les gens ordinaires qui, dans le fond, veulent tous paix, sécurité et possibilité de gagner dignement leur vie.

Le Québec signera la Constitution, nous sommes ensemble un grand pays!

....

1. This essay is available in English translation at the website A Bold Vision, http://aboldvision.ca/maria-mourani.

CAROLYN BENNETT

Carolyn Bennett is a self-described "accidental tourist" in politics, serving as the Member of Parliament for Toronto-St. Paul's, Ontario, since 1997.

Carolyn grew up in Toronto and attended Havergal College. She earned a degree in medicine at the University of Toronto, and, prior to her election, she was a family physician at Wellesley Hospital and Women's College Hospital in Toronto from 1977 to 1997. She also served as an assistant professor in the Department of Family and Community Medicine at the University of Toronto. She also served as President of the Medical Staff Association of Women's College Hospital.

As a member of Paul Martin's cabinet, Carolyn served as the first ever Minister of State for Public Health. During her tenure, she established the Public Health Agency of Canada as well as the Public Health Network, which provides a framework for provinces and territories to work collaboratively with the federal government on matters related to the health and well-being of Canadians. She also appointed Canada's first Chief Public Health Officer.

While in opposition, Carolyn served as the Liberal Party of Canada's health critic and the critic for democratic renewal. She is currently the Liberal critic for Aboriginal affairs and the chair of the Liberal Women's Caucus.

Carolyn Bennett is the recipient of numerous awards and recognitions including the Royal Life Saving Society Service Cross, Equal Voice's Award, the College of Family Physicians of Canada Award of Excellence, the Federated Press Women Leader of the Year Award, and the Queen's Diamond Jubilee Medal. She is also the author of *Kill or Cure? How Canadians Can Remake Their Health Care System*, published in October 2000.

Dr. Carolyn Bennett and her husband, Canadian film producer Peter O'Brian, have two sons and a chocolate Lab named Marley.

GOING FORWARD IN A "GOOD WAY":
My Bold Vision

"Here are seven of my learnings, seven 'aha!' moments that made me realize that, for Canada to move forward, we will need the voices and wise practices of First Nations, Métis, and Inuit leading the way."

OK, we're supposed to be bold, so here goes!

My vision starts at the top, at Rideau Hall, where Canada's Head of State would always be an Indigenous person. This would send the message that Canada did not have two "founding nations"; rather, Canada was built upon the good will of the First Nations, Métis, and Inuit peoples who chose to enter with the settlers into a partnership in which the land would be shared fairly.

As we all know, something went terribly wrong. To reset the relationship, the 96 per cent of Canadians who are not from an Indigenous background must understand and be proud of the wisdom of the people who were here first. Going forward in a "good way" means once again learning from First Peoples: "Idle KNOW More."

All New Zealanders have Māori culture as an integral part of their identity. Māori studies are taught from Kindergarten to Grade 8 and integrated into all subjects. The famous Māori Haka[1] dance is part of the ritual of the New Zealand national rugby team and is even seen performed by members of the New Zealand Armed Forces. They have found a way forward in the reconciliation and repair of the essential relationship between First Peoples and settlers. Canada needs to do the same. It is urgent.

Over my years as a family doctor, a Member of Parliament, a Minister of State for Public Health in the years leading to the Kelowna Accord, and especially during the past three years when I have had the honour and responsibility to be Aboriginal Affairs critic for the Liberal Party of Canada, I have been inspired by the teachings of the First Peoples, teachings that could so easily have been lost when the colonizers sought to replace them with Victorian ideas of "civilization." Fighting side by side with First People on the greatest social injustice Canada — manifest in the unacceptable gap in health, education, and economic status between Indigenous people in Canada and the Canadian average — I have made such wonderful new friends and coaches. They have a right to be angry and frustrated.

The ways of the colonizers are now proving to be wrong-headed. I have always loved the t-shirt slogan, "Fighting terrorism since 1492." I believe that before we get to Nation to Nation governance, Canadians must open their minds to the basic principles that First Peoples had right and that we would be wise to consider anew. All Canadians need to have new friends and heroes who are First Nations, Métis, and Inuit: interpersonal relationships based upon respect. There cannot be respect when so much ignorance remains.

So here are seven of my learnings, seven "aha!" moments that made me realize that, for Canada to move forward, we will need the voices and wise practices of First Nations, Métis, and Inuit leading the way.

1. Sustainability — Seven-Generation Thinking

In my bold vision, we would begin with sustainability of the planet.

Indigenous people lived "sustainability," and many continue to do so. They knew not to clear-cut a forest or fish out a lake. The land, the water, and the air together were a gift from the Creator. The Creator expected humans to take care of Mother Earth. As Mariano Auilaarjuk of Aivilingmiut said: "The living person and the land are actually tied up together because without one the other doesn't survive and vice versa … That's why we treat it as part of ourselves."[2]

The Iroquois taught, "In every deliberation, we must consider the impact on the seventh generation … even if it requires having skin as thick as the bark of a pine," and they made this principle central to "The Constitution of the Iroquois Nations: The Great Binding Law."[3]

James Freeman Clarke once said, "A politician thinks of the next election. A statesman, of the next generation."[4] With an election coming every four years or less, it is clear that present political thinking has been unable to tackle major threats such as climate change.

Seven-generation thinking should become the norm. If citizens were judging policies on what they would mean to their children, grandchildren, and great-grandchildren to seven generations, cynical short-term thinking would be punished. Decision-makers would broaden their perspectives enormously.

2. The Medicine Wheel, Not the Medical Model

Tommy Douglas said the goal of medicare was to keep Canadians well, not just to patch them up when they get sick. In some ways, this is a reaffirmation of the First Nations medicine wheel, which teaches us that wellness means keeping people well physically, mentally, emotionally, and spiritually. A bold vision for Canada would mean putting in place real strategies for wellness, including a sense of belonging.

As Minister of State (Public Health), I used to give a speech called "Fleeing the Medical Model, Embracing the Medicine Wheel." I would quote Sir Michael Marmot: "The worst thing for a physician is to help someone get well and then send them straight back into the condition that made them sick in the first place."[5] He talks about the *causes*, and the *causes of the causes*, of health outcomes. The *causes* are factors such as poor nutrition, lack of physical activity, tobacco, alcohol, and drugs. The *causes of the causes* are much broader social issues: poverty, violence, unhealthy environments, inadequate shelter, lack of education, and inequality.

It was clear during the H1N1 crisis that First Nations in northern Manitoba with 14 people living in one house and no running water needed housing and clean water, not more medevac trips to Winnipeg.

It is imperative that we understand that we want more *health* in order to need less *health care*. The sustainability of our cherished health-care system depends upon it. In order to keep Canadians well, we will have to have "whole of government" solutions that cross many government departments and many jurisdictions, as well as the private sector and civil society. We will need to cultivate an Indigenous approach to life—holistic and balanced.

During our hearings on Health Goals for Canada 2005,[6] people across Canada added their advice to our "Healthy Canadians Tree": identifying the causes, the causes of the causes, and the outcomes.

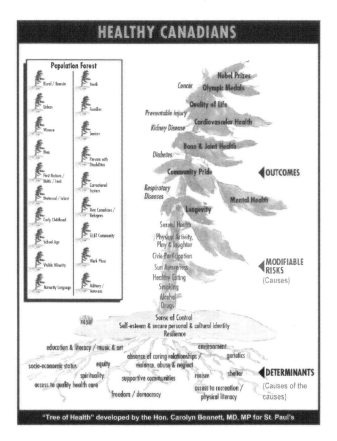

"Tree of Health" developed by the Hon. Carolyn Bennett, MD, MP for St. Paul's

They were clear that a sense of belonging was essential to keeping Canadians well. Bill Mussell from the Native Mental Health Association told me that my "tree" needed "ground." He taught me that healthy choices only come when an individual has a secure personal and cultural identity. Self-esteem and a sense of control over your life provide resilience, which results in good health, education, and positive economic outcomes.

3. Leadership and Democracy

In our dining room we have a "quote tree" where we hang our favourite quotations. My most treasured is from the late Jose Kusugak, the Inuit leader, that reads, in Inuktitut syllabics, "Pause before you speak."

Traditionally, Indigenous cultures were based upon genuine respect for one another, shown by listening. The Iroquois Confederacy has been described as the oldest participatory democracy in the world and an inspiration to the United States Constitution. I remember one day in the very successful West Bank First Nations Band office, Chief Robert Louis explained that sometimes, in order to get support for a project, they would have to have four community meetings in one month until all the questions had been answered and there was real consensus to move forward.

Canadian politicians are going to have to do more active listening to rebuild trust in our political institutions. More inclusive decision-making — once viewed as a feminist model of leadership, and now taught in all the MBA schools — is actually Indigenous leadership: "asking not telling." Professor Ursula Franklin defines good governance as that which is "fair, transparent and takes people seriously."[7] Jane Jacobs said that good public policy comes when the decision-makers can see in their minds' eye the people affected.[8] Indigenous leadership never lost sight of the people affected; they clearly saw and continue to see their responsibility to ensure that no one goes hungry.

The Haudenosaunee say: "He who wants to be chief, will never be chief." I've always taken that to mean that people can see through those who seek power for power's sake. In 1975, Nellie Cournoyea, the first woman Premier of the Northwest Territories, was quoted in *Speaking Together*: "Paternalism has been a total failure."[9] Talking sticks and sitting in a circle are more than symbolic; they demonstrate the very essence of respect for one another. They are the antithesis of hierachy, paternalism, and "father knows best" attitudes.

The cynicism that is eroding our democracy can only be healed with a commitment to meaningful consultation with Canadians. We must *all* develop structures and processes through which public policy taps into the lived experience of those affected by the policies and those with real expertise. As an elected representative of the citizens of Toronto-St. Paul's, Ontario, I have tried to build the kind of relationship I had with my patients as a family doctor: "Ask what's wrong, listen, and together we make a plan." We have tried in St. Paul's to be a model for a real "democracy between elections," a two-way accountability.

We have a constitutional "duty to consult" Indigenous people on the laws and policies that affect them. I think First Peoples could be very helpful as we try to design the processes and structures for a real "democracy between elections" for all Canadians.

4. Pedagogy — Learning by Doing

It's time to reassess education in Canada. Our schools are having trouble serving the needs of our students. More and more students are labelled "special needs." We know adult education is more effective when it is interactive. Lack of interactivity may be one of the reasons boys are doing worse than girls at school in some areas; apparently, they have difficulty sitting still!

It is important as we look back at the horrors of residential schools — the abuse, the nutritional experimentation, the sickness, the deaths — that we better understand the deficits of Western pedagogy. Children sitting in tidy rows having information poured into their heads to be memorized was anathema to Indigenous learning, and perhaps remains anathema to children of any culture.

As it states on the Aboriginal Education Resource Centre Indigenous Education website:

> The distinctive features of Indigenous knowledge and pedagogy are learning by observation and doing, learning through authentic experiences and individualized instruction, and learning through enjoyment... It embraces both the circumstances people find themselves in and their beliefs about those circumstances in a way that is unfamiliar to Eurocentric knowledge systems.[10]

At this time, when reform of First Nations education has become so politically charged, it seems important to all First Nations to develop successful education systems based upon Indigenous pedagogy and ways of knowing. There are many examples across the country: the First Nations Education Steering Committee in British Columbia; the Oskayak School in Saskatoon;

the work of Brian Stonefish and the Indigenous Education Coalition in Ontario; the highly successful programmes in Kahnawake in Quebec and the Mi'kmaw nation in Atlantic Canada. Canada needs to build on these successes.

The focus on language and culture is working. Courses on the land, outside the classroom work; "Mother Nature" is an excellent teacher. As someone who used to say everything I needed to know I learned at summer camp, I am reminded that there weren't any blackboards there!

I believe that the Indigenous pedagogy of learning by doing can teach us all a great deal. We now know that everyone learns differently. Expression of intellect, emotions, and spirit through art, music, culture, and sports should not be afterthoughts. It's through participating in a well-rounded educational experience that children find their souls and their many talents. It's only then that they are able to succeed in life.

5. The Strength of Women

Although not all Indigenous societies were matriarchal, there is no question that, as the "lifegivers," women were held in tremendous respect. From the days of hunters and gatherers, women and men had different roles. Most hunter-gatherer bands had strict gender roles; men hunted and fished while women gathered roots, seeds, and berries. This was apparently an effective pattern for survival, since 97 per cent of hunter-gatherer cultures were organized similarly. Aside from strict gender roles, these were largely egalitarian cultures in which everyone worked to survive and neither gender, nor typically any one individual, had a higher status or more political power than anyone else.

Doug George-Kanentiio explains the role of Iroquois women:

> In our society, women are the center of all things. Nature, we believe, has given women the ability to create; therefore it is only natural that women be in positions of power to protect this function ... We traced our clans through women ... Our young women

were expected to be physically strong… The young women received formal instruction in traditional planting… To us it made sense for women to control the land since they were far more sensitive to the rhythms of the Mother Earth… Our women decided any and all issues involving territory, including where a community was to be built and how land was to be used… In our political system, we mandated full equality. Our leaders were selected by a caucus of women before the appointments were subject to popular review… Our traditional governments are composed of an equal number of men and women.[11]

The Indigenous cultures recognized what Louann Brizendine documented in *The Female Brain*:

Outstanding verbal ability, the ability to connect deeply in friendship, a near psychic capacity to read faces and tone of voice for emotions and states of mind. The ability to defuse conflict. All this is hardwired into the brains of women.[12]

In her bestselling book *Why Women Should Rule the World*, Dee Dee Myers says: "There is no unisex brain, there is no unisex norm. There is only the male norm. And it undervalues the powerful, sex-specific strengths and talents of the female brain."[13]

We need to recognize that women have always been able to embrace and understand complexity. As Ursula Franklin explains, their bodies are complex, their families are complex, and their communities are complex. They have so much to teach the linear thinkers who obstruct the real solutions to complex problems.[14] As H.L. Mencken said, "There is always an easy solution to every human problem—neat, plausible, and wrong."[15]

At Women's College Hospital in Toronto the motto is "*Non quo modo, sed quo modo*"—it's not what you do but how. The founders believed that the patients were always full partners in their care. I have always been inspired by this example of how our democracy would be improved if we could have citizens acting as true partners in their democracy. For that attitudinal shift to happen we may well need at least 50 per cent of MPs to be women.

As Doris Anderson asked: "Isn't it time women stopped holding up half the sky and began making at least half the decisions right down here on earth?"[16]

6. Elders, Not Elderly

I once asked elders at the Elders Centre in Iqaluit, "Why are you called 'elders' when in the south older people are called 'elderly'?" They said: "Because we are the survivors. Our lives were tough, and we were the ones that survived." They were respected for their expertise and their lived experience.

As a family doctor, I have always been aware that age had nothing to do with date of birth. There are "old fogies" who are 30 years old — they already think they know it all. I remember being told, "If on any given day you haven't taken to yourself a new idea and let go of a hard held idea, you should check your pulse, you might be dead."

I didn't have any grandparents alive as I grew up. It was only as a family doctor that I became aware of the wisdom of older people. I believe that, as a society, we should understand that wisdom comes from having made mistakes and learning from them. If we don't listen to the lessons of the past, we will make the same mistakes again.

Respect for elders is indeed an example for a bold vision for Canada. I want to grow up to be an "elder," not "elderly."

7. Children at the Centre

I have always been inspired at the ceremonies in Ottawa in which Elder Courchene participates. He always talks about the "little ones." He explains that Mother Earth (sustenance — water and food) is at the centre, then the children, and then everyone else.

Dr. Cindy Blackstock, the amazing activist for Aboriginal children with the First Nations Child and Family Caring Society of Canada,[17] has made it clear that putting children first can help shape all public policy. If we put the children first, everything else will make sense. Children are the future. Children need to have the best possible opportunities to succeed.

Putting children first could help us break through the gridlock that impedes progress on all the complex issues that cross government departments and cross jurisdictions. As Chair of the Sub-Committee on Disabilities, I remember thinking that if we could solve the problem of Aboriginal children with disabilities, we could solve all the problems of Canada.

Shortly after that, Jordan's Principle was passed in the Parliament of Canada.[18] It was to ensure that the needs of children would transcend jurisdictional squabbles. The work of former Senator Landon Pearson on children's rights is also truly important.[19]

Cindy Blackstock has pointed out that in the United States, children are not allowed to be apprehended into care because their parents are poor. We now have more Aboriginal children in care in Canada than were in residential schools at their height. Imagine if every time there was a risk to a child because of poverty, the community was able to wrap supports and services around that family in order to keep them all together.

Putting children first is a bold vision for Canada. If we can ensure children have all they need to be safe and have the opportunities they need to succeed, their families, their communities, and our country will all benefit.

Going Forward in a "Good Way"

So, in proposing how we can go forward in a "good way," I have focused on the First Peoples; my new First Nations, Métis, and Inuit friends who have taught me so much.

I am also inspired by my Francophone teachers and coaches who have allowed me to share the beauty of their culture, language, and values which have shaped our truly wonderful Canada.

My wonderful friend and co-conspirator Cynthia Wesley-Esquimaux reminds me of how important the "International Caravan" was to her growing up, a multicultural event put on in Toronto which celebrated the melting pot; how much she enjoyed being part of the culture portrayed at the Native Canadian Centre; but also how much she enjoyed learning about the other cultures that make up the modern Canada. The medicine wheel celebrates the four directions but also recognizes those from all races—"white," "red," "black," and "yellow." It really is about inclusion!

Cynthia and I share a bold vision for Canada in which all Canadians would "Idle KNOW More," truly celebrating the teachings of the First Peoples of Canada. What's exciting to us is that our friendship allows us to work together to build a Canada that would build a Nation to Nation relationship founded upon the trust that we have as friends who have nothing but respect for one another.

This journey will start with changing the curricula throughout Canada, but also the programmes in camps, Scouts, and Guides and taking every opportunity for First Nations, Métis, and Inuit to be able to share their stories. Cynthia has founded Canadian Roots in order to begin the work of having Indigenous youth share their culture with non-Indigenous youth.[20]

The Great Canadian Bus Tour, run out of the Native Canadian Centre in Toronto, takes participants to all the important sites of the First Peoples in our area, from portages to Huron villages. Imagine if it was just normal to have plaques and QR codes at every Indigenous site, as proposed in the LINK Moccasin Identifier project.[21]

Cynthia and I have loved speaking together at Rotary Clubs and town-hall meetings. We generally prescribe John Ralston Saul's *A Fair Country*, Thomas King's *The Inconvenient Indian*, Richard Wagamese's *Indian Horse*, and CBC's four-part television documentary *Eighth Fire* for those who want to get started on their journey of learning and understanding.

The bold vision of "Idle KNOW More" will take the kind of leadership and commitment that recognized this may take 30 or 40 years to complete. In New Zealand, where they have been educating everyone about Māori history and culture, the Māori population is 20 per cent; First Nations, Inuit, and Métis here in Canada are only four per cent. The founding document of New Zealand is a treaty, the Treaty of Waitangi (*Tiriti o Waitangi*); in Canada, numerous meetings and documents, and more numerous treaties, preceded Confederation. In New Zealand there is really only one Māori language; here we have over 60 Indigenous languages and many that are almost extinct. Still, we can emulate their success.

Bold visions are not for the faint of heart. We need to commit now and then put in place real and tangible strategies to make our visions happen. In our hearts and minds, it could be possible within a generation to achieve knowledge and understanding. My life is so much richer because of my new friends and my greater understanding of what it is to be Canadian. I wish it for you, I wish it for everyone!

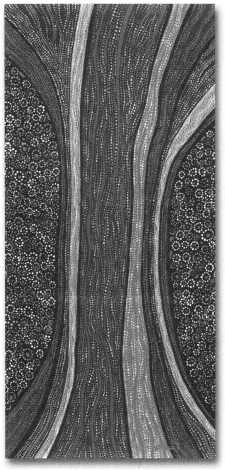

"The Path" 2002
Métis Artist Christi Belcourt
Used by permission of the artist

Chi-Miigwetch!

1. "Haka," Wikipedia, accessed July 2014, http://en.wikipedia.org/wiki/Haka.
2. John R. Bennett and Susan Rowley, *Uqalurait: An Oral History of Nunavut* (Montreal and Kingston: McGill-Queen's University Press, 2004).
3. "The Constitution of the Iroquois Nations," accessed July 2014, http://www.indigenouspeople.net/iroqcon.htm.

4. "John Freeman Clarke Quotes," Brainy Quote, accessed July 2014, http://www.brainyquote.com/quotes/authors/j/james_freeman_clarke.html.

5. "Interview with Michael Marmot," Unnatural Causes… Is Inequality Making Us Sick?, accessed July 2014, http://www.unnaturalcauses.org/assets/uploads/file/MichaelMarmot.pdf.

6. "Health Goals for Canada/Objectifs de santé pour le Canada," accessed July 2014, http://carolynbennett.liberal.ca/files/2014/07/Health-Goals-for-Canada-2005.pdf.

7. Ursula Franklin quoted in *Advancing Change Together: A Time to Act, The Report of the Change Commission of the Liberal Party of Canada*, April 2009, accessed July 2014, https://www.liberal.ca/files/2010/05/change-commission-report.pdf.

8. Jane Jacobs, *The Death and Life of Great American Cities*, Modern Library Edition (New York: Random House, 1993).

9. Nellie Cournoyea quoted in *Speaking Together: Canada's Native Women* (Ottawa: Secretary of State, 1975).

10. "Indigenous Pedagogy," Aboriginal Education Research Network, accessed July 2014, http://aerc.usask.ca/education/pedagogy.html.

11. Doug-George Kanentiio quoted in "Matriarchy — A Social System that Benefits Mankind," Britain's Land Policy, accessed July 2014, http://www.womenslandrights.org/index.asp?pageid=437940.

12. Louann Brizendine, *The Female Brain* (New York: Broadway Books, 2006), accessed July 2014, http://www.drlumd.com/wp-content/uploads/2011/12/The-Female-Brain.pdf.

13. Dee Dee Myers, *Why Women Should Rule the World* (Toronto: Harper Perennial, 2009).

14. Mary Jane Mossman, review of *The Ursula Franklin Reader: Pacifism as a Map*, by Ursula Franklin, *Osgoode Hall Law Journal* 45.4 (Winter 2007): 821–7, accessed July 2014, http://digitalcommons.osgoode.yorku.ca/cgi/viewcontent.cgi?article=1226&context=ohlj.

15. "H.L. Mencken Quotes," Brainy Quote, accessed July 2014, http://www.brainyquote.com/quotes/quotes/h/hlmencke141512.html.

16. Rosemary Speirs, "The Last Obsession," *Canadian Woman Studies/Les cahiers de la femme* 26.2, 109–12, accessed July 2014, http://pi.library.yorku.ca/ojs/index.php/cws/article/download/14918/13970.

17. "Who We Are," First Nations Child and Family Caring Society of Canada, accessed July 2014, http://www.fncaringsociety.com/who-we-are.

18. "Jordan's Principle," First Nations Child and Family Caring Society of Canada, accessed July 2014, http://www.fncaringsociety.com/jordans-principle.

19. Landon Pearson Resource Centre for the Study of Childhood and Children's Rights, accessed July 2014, http://www.landonpearson.ca.

20. "About Canadian Roots," Canadian Roots, accessed July 2014, http://www.canadianroots.ca/.

21. John Allemang, "New Credit First Nation Gets a 'Thank You' 200 Years Later," *Globe and Mail*, June 21, 2013, accessed July 2014, http://www.theglobeandmail.com/news/national/new-credit-first-nation-gets-a-thank-you-200-years-later/article12758245/.

PAMELA D. PALMATER

Dr. Pamela D. Palmater is a Mi'kmaw citizen and member of the Eel River Bar First Nation in New Brunswick. Her great-grandfather was a Chief; her grandmother, a traditional healer; and her father a hunter and World War II veteran. She comes from a large family of eight sisters and three brothers, and has two children of her own. She has been a practising lawyer for 16 years and currently is an associate professor and Chair in Indigenous Governance at Ryerson University.

Pam Palmater completed her Doctorate in the Science of Law (JSD) in Aboriginal Law at Dalhousie University in 2009. She also holds a Master of Laws in Aboriginal law, a Bachelor of Laws with an award in environmental and natural resources law, and a Bachelor of Arts with a double major in Native studies and history. She stays grounded through traditional ceremonies and practices, while constantly learning more about traditional Indigenous knowledge.

For over 25 years, Dr. Palmater has worked and volunteered in First Nations legal, political, and social issues including housing, child and family services, treaty rights, education, governance, and legislation affecting First Nations. She works extensively with First Nation communities, and, in July 2012, she was runner-up in the election for National Chief of the Assembly of First Nations. She was also one of the spokespeople and organizers for Idle No More.

Pam Palmater also engages with Canadian society by speaking and delivering training sessions to unions, universities, high schools, governments, and businesses with a view to educating the public about the historical context and facts behind inaccurate myths and stereo types that affect First Nation and Canadian relations. As a result, she has been nominated for several prestigious awards, including the 2012 YWCA Woman of Distinction Award in Social Justice, the 2012 Women's Courage Award in Social Justice, the Bertha Wilson Honour Society 2012, and the Top 25 Most Influential Lawyers in Canada 2013.

CANADA:

As Long As the Grass Grows and Rivers Flow

"My vision for Canada is one which gets back to the original vision of the treaties and ensures our future generations get to enjoy the best of who we are as diverse Nations and of the life-sustaining gifts of the territories which make up Canada."

From time immemorial, Turtle Island (what is now known as North America) was an island of rich, vibrant, proud Nations. Indigenous Nations all over Turtle Island drummed, sang, and danced in celebration and gratitude for the bounty which surrounded them: For the ancient forests which provided shelter, materials for canoes and weapons, and animals for food; for the lakes, rivers, and oceans that offered convenient trade routes, life-saving water, and fish. The Sun warmed our spirits in the summer and the snow cleansed the earth in the winter. The shifting stars and changing flight patterns of the birds let us know when the seasons were about to change.

For some, a change in season meant we packed up our homes and travelled inland for shelter from the coming winter. For others, it meant preparing food to last for the season. While some of us survived the winter on salmon, others lived on dried moose meat or berries. Whether we spoke Mi'kmaq, Cree, Mohawk, or Haida, we shared a common appreciation of the territories we used to sustain our Nations. Our Nations had different ways of celebrating and honouring the gifts of our territories, but we all knew that we had an obligation to protect the lands, waters, plants, animals, birds, fish, and resources by which we sustained ourselves. Our ancestors, in their spirit forms, walked with our peoples during their struggles and their good times. Our collective focus was the well-being of our future generations, and we secured that future by protecting our territories.

The symbiotic relationship Indigenous peoples had with their lands was not an accident. It was based on traditional Indigenous knowledge passed down from generation to generation, sometimes in songs, dances, ceremonies, teachings, or stories. Traditional Indigenous knowledge systems were place-based and based on how the world actually worked, as opposed to theories about how it *should* work. The name of a river could indicate whether the water was safe to swim in, whether it contained edible fish, or whether it was suitable as a trade route between Nations. The visions our ancestors had for our Nations were focused on protecting our children seven generations into the future by ensuring a proper balance in all things.

We could not enjoy the land's life-sustaining gifts without first living up to our responsibility to take care of it.

It is within the context of these diverse — but similar — worldviews, values, and belief systems that Indigenous Nations on Turtle Island approached their relations with newcomers. In the spirit of kindness and caution, Indigenous peoples extended a hand in friendship, while also protecting their Nations and territories. Some of the first treaties between Indigenous Nations and the Queen were called "Peace and Friendship" treaties; for example, the Treaty of Peace and Friendship 1760.[1] These treaties were meant to establish peaceful relations — legal commitments not just to forgo hostilities, but to encourage friendly relations where Indigenous Nations and the Queen's settlers could exchange ideas, trade goods, engage in mutually beneficial economic endeavours, and intermarry. We did not give up our sovereignty as Nations when the newcomers came. We were strong, confident Nations, and because of this we extended our hands in trust and, in the words of Treaty 1752, used our "best Endeavours to save the lives and goods of any People Shipwrecked on this Coast."[2]

These Indigenous and newcomer Nations, meeting for the first time, dared to dream a bold vision of a partnership based on respect, non-interference, and mutual prosperity. But more than that, Canada (or Kanata) would not exist without some foundational treaties such as the Peace and Friendship treaties signed in the Maritimes which ended hostilities; or the Treaty of Niagara 1764 which set out an agreement to share the land on the condition of recognition and respect of our mutual sovereignties.[3] The "peace and goodwill" (as described in Treaty 6) espoused in these treaties were not time-limited contracts or MOUs — they represented a powerful vision of how we would share this land and work together for as long as the sun shines, the grass grows, and the rivers flow.

Sadly, if we look around at Canada today, we see vast areas of land, formerly covered in grass and other plants, turned into wastelands by oil sands or open-pit mining. We see mighty rivers whose flows have been halted or significantly altered by dams, drastically changing the health of plants, animals, fish, and people. We see large, forested areas clear-cut by irresponsible timber companies. The sun that used to shine on us is now blocked by the pollution of large corporations. We used to think that our treaty relationship would last forever, but one treaty partner is killing the grass, stopping the flow of water, and affecting the effects of the sun on our planet. While one treaty partner destroys the earth and enjoys the profits today, both treaty partners will suffer in the future if we don't take action. If we don't take steps to set things right, our whole ecosystem is at risk — and setting things right starts with the original vision of our treaty relationship.

The most amazing thing about human beings is that we have the power to create the world we want around us. As humans, we can choose to create a healthy, safe, sustainable world for our future generations or one which condemns our grandchildren to live on a desolate, polluted planet — devoid of food, water, and life. Canada does not have to be this way. We promised one another that we would work together in peace and friendship for our mutual prosperity. Our understandings were based on respect for the sovereignty of our respective Nations and the desire of our Nations for their citizens to live safe, healthy, prosperous lives. Our understandings were meant to ensure our future generations would have the same opportunity that our ancestors did to enjoy the benefits and obligations of living on Turtle Island. Indigenous peoples made promises to our treaty partners "with hearts full of sincerity."[4] We fully expected we could count on the Queen's promised "bounty and benevolence"[5] (promised, for example, in Treaty 1725) and that her representatives would live up to commitments made in good faith, in her name.

While there is beauty in the words of the treaties — and also in the great speeches made by our leaders without treaties — who wanted to work together in peace and friendship, the words were not meant to be admired as prose: They were significant commitments meant to last forever. In this throw-away society, where we upgrade cellphones faster than we can figure out how to use them, where the job turnover rate is on the rise, and where 40 per cent of all marriages end in divorce, our treaty commitments, which according to Treaty 1752 bind all of our "heirs and the heirs of their heirs forever"[6]—are something special. These treaties force us to put effort into the relationship. They are meant to act as guideposts in case we lose our way; they are meant to provide a way to ground each other so that we can refocus on our collective vision. My vision for Canada is one which gets back to the original vision of the treaties and ensures our future generations get to enjoy the best of who we are as diverse Nations and of the life-sustaining gifts of the territories which make up Canada.

Going forward together in a good way is going to take some effort. No bold vision can be realized without hard work and sacrifice. Indigenous Nations have lived up to their end of the treaty promises; now, it's time for the other treaty partner to do the same. Canada's genocidal policies against Indigenous peoples—which included scalping bounties; forced sterilizations of Indigenous women; the rape, torture, and abuse of Indigenous children in residential schools; the impoverishment of our people through the theft of our lands and resources; and the over-incarceration of our men and women—all have intergenerational impacts which still affect us today. One can't celebrate the wonderful parts of our treaty relationship without acknowledging and addressing the problematic parts. To gloss over these harsh realities for Indigenous peoples would be like telling the family of the eight-year-old girl who committed suicide that their loss doesn't matter. We can't paint a better future for Canada by ignoring the problems—our great efforts must go towards addressing the problems. Thankfully, most Canadians are stepping forward in support of Indigenous peoples because they want their Canada to go back to its original intention—to become a place for all to share in mutual prosperity and freedom.

While we all have to come together to find a way to heal from abusive aspects of our relationship as Nations, this can't start without good faith on Canada's part. It is going to take more than empty political apologies: It will require real restitution and reclamation. The continued theft and destruction of Indigenous lands and resources must end. The legal, social, and economic control and impoverishment of Indigenous Nations must end. The criminalization of Indigenous peoples for hunting, fishing, and trading must end. The theft of Indigenous children from our homes and the murder of our women must end. What will our children, seven generations into the future, think if we allow these injustices to continue? Will they be proud to be Canadian? Will they stand up to defend such a Canada? We have a legal and moral obligation to make sure we learn from the past and give our present and future generations a chance to live the treaty relationship on which Canada was and is based.

Going forward is not an exercise in relieving the guilt of the colonizer. Neither is it about cementing the harms of the colonized as the basis of the relationship. It is about mutual healing and finding a way to restore the original intention of the treaty relationship; that is, the original intention for Canada. Canada was never intended by its citizens to be a genocidal or destructive country. On the contrary, the people who came to Canada believed in the promises of freedom, democracy, and justice. They believed that this country would be free from oppression, it would be governed by the people, and its laws and policies would treat everyone fairly. Newcomers dreamed of a place to enjoy the good life for their families. They grew attached to the vast landscapes, open waters, and beauty of these lands. The newcomers wanted to protect and enjoy these lands alongside Indigenous Nations — not in opposition to them. The treaties were about respecting each other's autonomy to live the good life as we saw fit. They were about respecting each other's governments, laws, economies, traditions, and customs — with no one legal system trumping the other.

In the end, it will be the Indigenous governments, legal systems, practices, and customs that end up protecting Canadians. Everything that matters to Canadians depends on the rights and interests of Indigenous peoples being recognized and respected. Canada's very sovereignty is entirely dependent on the fact and recognition of Indigenous sovereignty. What required the newcomers to make treaties with us is that we, as Indigenous Nations, lived here for millennia, occupying and defending our respective territories — the real land owners. Without those treaties, Canada would have no rights here at all. Think about the implications of this basic fact along the United States border or in the high Arctic near Russia.

The same can be said for other issues which concern Canadians: Treaty relationships are not part of our past, but the foundation of our present and our hope for the future. The social services upon which Canadians rely are paid for with Indigenous resources. The ability to provide free education and healthcare comes from the wealth of Indigenous lands. If we don't protect these resources now, there will be no benefits for Canadians in the future. Similarly, the forced impoverishment of Indigenous peoples costs Canadians billions of dollars every year. Reversing that poverty would bring billions in gross domestic product to Canadians. Addressing outstanding land and treaty rights would benefit Canadians and Indigenous peoples alike. We all win if justice is restored in Canada.

In the very near future, the most valuable commodities will not be oil or gold, they will be farmable land and clean drinking water. Every human, animal, fish, and bird requires food and water to live. This holds true regardless of which side of the treaty you are on. The future generations of both Indigenous peoples and Canadians will require food and water. Indigenous Nations have constitutionally protected Aboriginal, treaty, and inherent rights that offer the last defence against complete destruction of our precious environmental resources. However, the trend in Canada has been to make more and more unilateral, profit-focused decisions while only conducting superficial consultations with Canadians and Indigenous peoples.

The United Nations and various international think tanks are alarmed at the declining relationship between Canada and Indigenous Nations, a decline that is linked directly to a decline in Canada's own governance practices. Parliament is prorogued at will to avoid accounting to Canadians; MPs and Senators are charged with assaults, fraud, and theft; debate over legislation is halted; and large omnibus bills are rammed through the House of Commons and Senate before Canadians even know what is in them. These practices threaten the very democracy upon which Canada was built, as well as the constitutionally protected rights of Indigenous Peoples to have their consent obtained before using Indigenous lands, waters, or resources.

Canadians can use the current situation of Indigenous peoples as a predictor of what is to come for them. In the last ten years, we have already seen, to name just a few examples, the escalation of police violence (G20 Summit 2010 in Toronto); prison populations at an all-time high; an increase in government scandals (F-35 fighter jets, Senate expenses); the slow erosion of the rights of Canadian citizens to exercise their voices (omnibus bills pushed through Parliament); and lack of government accountability (Parliament prorogued, misinformation exposed by the Auditor General). So long as governments are not kept in check, the gross injustices that have happened and are happening to Indigenous peoples will flow to Canadians. The treaty relationship offers balance: We promised to take care of one another as allies, as traders, and as friends. It is never too late to realize this vision.

My vision for Canada can only be realized if Canada gets real about the fundamental flaws in its current system of governance, the morals and values it represents, and its failure to abide by its own laws and the laws of Indigenous peoples as envisioned in the treaties. If we are to stop government from selling our resources to large international corporations, it will be the rights of Indigenous peoples that do it. If we are to protect our lands and waters from environmental destruction, it will be the rights of Indigenous peoples that get it done. Indigenous peoples are Canadians' last, best hope at protecting the lands and waters for all of our future generations. Despite all of the abuses, hardships, and broken promises, Indigenous peoples are still on the front lines trying to protect the lands and waters over which we have stewardship—not just for our children, but for those of our treaty partners as well. We live in paradise, and it is worth saving.

In 150 years, I hope that our great-grandchildren can look back at 2014 and be proud that we came together as Indigenous Nations and Canadians and did what was necessary to put our relationship back on track. That we made amends, that we forced federal and provincial governments back to the basics of democratic governments, that we amended the laws to be just and fair, and that we worked out a mutually beneficial sharing of the lands and resources as intended by the treaties. Our great-grandchildren won't want to look back at 2014 and hear that "we tried," or "we had every intention to do better," or "we gave it our best effort." Those are cop-outs. We have the power to turn this ship around and make the fundamental changes required of our respective governments, laws, and practices that will protect our lands and waters for future generations. If we can come together and do this, then we have a chance at saving our collective futures and enjoying the wealth and beauty this land has to offer. But if we can't stand up and save this generation from injustice, then we won't have a seventh generation in the future to worry about.

We have survived every government attempt to eliminate and assimilate us. Despite the many harms we have suffered, we have kept our faith in the treaty relationship and continued to try to find ways to work together. Indigenous Nations are standing up to protect all of our future generations — to protect the original treaty vision for Canada. We can get this treaty relationship back on track if more Canadians rise to the challenge and stand beside us as they have done in recent years. Canadians have the power to take their governments back and not only right the wrongs of the past, but forge a new way forward that offers a just Canada for all.

I believe in the power of our people. Our ways are beautiful. Our customs and practices were designed to protect the world around us. Our resilience and our refusal to give up in the face of grave injustices are testament to our strength and our commitment to the treaty vision for Canada. In the treaties, we promised to be good allies and defend these lands — and we have lived up to our promises. In the treaties, we promised to save the shipwrecked newcomers who had lost their way — and once again Indigenous Nations are rising up to protect these lands and defend the rights of Canadians to a just society. The treaties will not only keep Canada from losing its way again, they offer the best hope at a prosperous future for all of us.

....

1. *Treaty of Peace and Friendship concluded with the Delegates of the St. Johns and Passamaquoddy Tribes of Indians at Halifax, February 1760* (Treaty 1760), available at Cape Breton University, Mi'kmaq Resource Centre, accessed July 2014, http://www.cbu.ca/mrc/treaties/1760-1761.

2. *Enclosure in Letter of Governor Hopson to the Right Honourable The Earl of Holdernesse 6th of Dec. 1752 Treaty or Articles of Peace and Friendship Renewed* (Treaty 1752), available at Cape Breton University, Mi'kmaq Resource Centre, accessed July 2014, http://www.cbu.ca/mrc/treaties/1752.

3. The text of the Treaty of Fort Niagara 1764 is not available online, but the context is described at Canadiana.org, accessed July 2014, http://www.canadiana.ca/citm/themes/aboriginals/aboriginals4_e.html#niagara.

4. Treaty of 1752.

5. *Copy of Treaty No. 6 between Her Majesty the Queen and the Plain and Wood Cree Indians and other Tribes of Indians at Fort Carlton, Fort Pitt and Battle River with Adhesions* (Treaty 6), available at the Office of the Treaty Commissioner, Saskatchewan, accessed July 2014, http://www.otc.ca/ABOUT_TREATIES/Treaty_Map/Treaty_6/.

6. *Treaty of 1725: The Submission and Agreement of the Delegates of the Eastern Indians (December 15, 1725, Boston, New England, British possession)* (Treaty 1725), available at Cape Breton University, Mi'kmaq Resource Centre, accessed July 2014, http://www.cbu.ca/mrc/treaties/1725.

EL JONES

El Jones is the current poet laureate of Halifax, Nova Scotia. She is also artistic director of Word Iz Bond Spoken Word Artists Collective and teaches in the Women's and Gender Studies and English Departments at Acadia University, in the creative writing program at Dalhousie University, and in the African Canadian Transition Program, the only black-focused adult learning program in Canada, at Nova Scotia Community College.

El Jones was born in Cardiff, Wales, of a Trinidadian mother and a Welsh father. Jones first immigrated to Canada with her family and lived in Winnipeg. El made her way to Halifax, Nova Scotia, to pursue her PhD in English at Dalhousie University. In Nova Scotia, she found her political heart in the African Nova Scotian community, which gave her voice and purpose.

El Jones is deeply committed to community work and has worked with numerous organizations on issues including sexual violence, poverty, racism, and engagement in global issues. She is particularly committed to youth work and work with incarcerated people. She believes in the power of art to move communities and to empower marginalized communities. She sees poetry as a tool of resistance that can speak back to power.

El Jones is the recipient of a number of scholarships and awards, a published author, and a highly sought-after public speaker. She has a book of poetry forthcoming, *Live from the Afrikan Resistance!* (Fernwood, 2014). Her work in various capacities all over Canada lends to her knowledge and experience of the complexities and challenges that Canadian women face — as well as an understanding of our strengths and gifts.

MY VISION OF CANADA IS NOT FANTASY, BUT FRUITION

"*I believe in a Canada where transition is possible*
Where we can hold people responsible
But where justice is transformative
And we collectively support people over obstacles"

My vision is for a Canada where we honour our beginnings.

Where in the spirit of the treaties we live in

Respect and harmony with each other, nature, and land.

Where we remember the promises on which we stand

And which we swore to never abandon

While rivers were running and birds were singing.

I believe in the value of a nation that is Indigenous;

Not a nation of the past, but one that values knowledge systems

And wisdom, that looks beyond colonialism,

That gets rid of the myth of two founding European nations

As the only source of civilization.

A Canada no longer dependent on capitalism, genocide, and racism.

A Canada where women are given equal place.

My vision is for a Turtle Island where resources are sustained

And where communities are maintained

And where the wealth gap is restrained.

Where safe housing is available

And where there is free access for all to education.

There may be some cynics who are reading this wincing

Imagining that this is a fantasy I am bringing

But I do not believe that a Canada where more than one in seven children

Are living in poverty should be the height of our ambition.

I believe the poverty cycle can be finished.

My vision is for a Canada of community building—

Come to Centre Line Studios where there is music spilling

Out of the windows, and youth are chilling

In the rooms and stairways,

Where despite poverty conditions our young people are resisting

The stereotypes and refusing to be statistics.

This is not just something I am wishing

Because I have seen it come to fruition,

When we refuse to give up on our youth or give in,

Allow them space and time and respect their vision

They will deliver, and communities will follow.

I believe in a Canada that prepares for tomorrow.

Not by placing youth in debt and forcing them to borrow

Upon their futures, but by building

Healthy relationships between the generations,

Where elders are respected as the foundations,

Where pensions are adequate for seniors to live on,

Communities formed from the labour of women,

Where grandmothers and single mothers get recognition,

Where development in communities is envisioned

Not in terms of condos but in terms of relationships

And health, and quality of living.

My vision is for a Canada beyond prisons—

Prisons for the body, the mind and spirit,

A Canada where we replace punishment with forgiveness—

Because I have seen too many of my own community

Become lost within the system.

I want a just Canada where the colour of your skin

Does not determine your existence,

Where we treat instead of punish mental illness,

Where we acknowledge that too many Afrikans

And Indigenous people and poor women

Are marginalized, abused, abandoned, and then hidden,

Given lifelong sentences of social stigma

In Nova and Burnside and Springhill.

I have seen so many struggling to change their positions,

So many families and communities destroyed by our insistence

On harsher and harsher sentencing.

It is time for a Canada that is committed to rethinking

A system that punishes based on wealth divisions,

Based on race and class and social victims.

I believe in a Canada where transition is possible,

Where we can hold people responsible

But where justice is transformative

And we collectively support people over obstacles.

A Canada where even those who transgress are not forgotten

And where we measure our progress

By the treatment of those at the bottom.

My vision is for a Canada of paperless citizens,

Where refugees and immigrants are not limited,

Where we accept all who are willing—

A Canada where lessons in French and English and Indigenous languages

Are free, a Canada where multiculturalism

Is not just lip service, but a purpose and a mission.

A Canada where diversity extends below the surface,

Beyond quotas and tokenism

And where qualifications and educations from back home are admitted.

The Canada I believe in will never be perfect

But I believe we can work towards a Canada

Where respect for all is not just words but a reality.

Nothing I have envisioned is a fantasy,

For in actuality I have seen all these things happen.

I have seen families and communities connect,

I have worked in prisons with those who have transformed,

I have seen youth perform and create in the projects,

I have seen people drop weapons and pick up pens—

If it can happen here with one person or program creating success

It can happen somewhere else, everywhere else.

Because my Canada is a work in progress

But my vision is for a Canada where we ask the right questions,

A Canada where we make decisions that are collective,

A Canada willing to make corrections.

A Canada where equality is our chosen direction.

BONNIE BRAYTON

Bonnie Brayton is the National Executive Director of DAWN-RAFH Canada (DisAbled Women's Network of Canada). DAWN Canada is a national feminist-disability organization whose work for almost 30 years has focused on advancing the rights of women with disAbilities and Deaf women in Canada and internationally.

Bonnie is the youngest of five children from a small village in Northern Quebec near the tip of Labrador. Her earlier career was in the private sector, in sales and marketing and as an entrepreneur. Before joining DAWN Canada in 2007, her work history also included almost ten years in the educational sector, primarily in administration, human resources, and fundraising at McGill University.

Since joining DAWN Canada, Bonnie Brayton has shown tremendous leadership in ensuring the voices and needs of women with disAbilities and Deaf women in Canada are put at the forefront of policy change across Canada. She works to highlight key issues that impact the lives of women with disabilities with regard to health, equity, housing, employment, and violence.

In addition to her work with DAWN, she is also the president of *Coup de Balai* — Clean Sweepers, a social economy organization providing home care services to people with disabilities and seniors in her community in Montreal while also creating employment, income, and job security for women who were previously unemployed (primarily immigrant and racialized women).

Bonnie Brayton is the Vice-Chair of the Feminist Alliance for International Action, serves on the Making Women Count Advisory Group with the Canadian Centre for Policy Alternatives, and is a member of the Steering Committee of *La Maison Parent-Roback*, a Quebec feminist collective in Montreal.

Bonnie Brayton lives in Montreal with her partner Delmar Medford. She has two adult daughters, Leah and Virginia. Bonnie also proudly wears the "disability" label; having had mild polio as a child, she developed post-polio syndrome in her late forties.

A FEMINIST HISTORY LESSON OF THE 21ST CENTURY

"Social movements and social change are about a convergence of ideas and a moment in time."

Note to the Reader — This fictional depiction looking back to the Vision Conference is my expression of a vision for Canada 150 years from now. I chose to write it this way because my work through DAWN-RAFH Canada and my leadership of that organization has always been informed by possibility, by thinking and being bigger than we are.

– Bonnie Brayton

....

From September 24 to 26 of 2014, in Brudenell and Charlottetown, Prince Edward Island, a small group of women's organizations, together with the Government of Prince Edward Island, brought together a Conference of Women. Each year on September 26, we remember them, and we recall not just one but two turning points in our Nation![1]

We remember not the kind of turn one can see with the eye, like a clay pot turning on a potter's wheel. Rather, this was a slow turn that a century-and-a-half of determined, focused, and honourable words and actions can do to shape a nation, our nation. And this is how it happened.

It was a turning point and a tipping point in the struggle for gender equality. By 2014, with millennia of oppression and a mere century of real advances in women's rights, the stage was set for a bold vision in the truest sense. Every woman among the Visionaries had in some sense already been made ready. They came determined and focused, of honourable words and actions, each in their own right.

At this juncture in history, the struggle for gender equality had two tracks, with Canadian women still both socially and economically situated well below their male counterparts. This was before we adopted the Pay Equity Act (2017) and the Caregiving Act (2020), before we had moved to equal representation, and long before the Governance Reforms of the mid-21st century were fully implemented.

At the time, the United Nations had declared gender equality the greatest and most important challenge of the times, and in Canada, violence against women crimes were consistently the most serious and common in the courts.

Millions were calling for an inquiry into the thousands of missing and murdered Indigenous women, and the rights of sex workers had finally made their
way to the Supreme Court. Women from Prince Edward Island and right
across Canada were still fighting for access to reproductive health care (referred to as the "Pro-Choice Movement"), despite a Supreme Court decision
from several decades earlier that had, they naïvely assumed, enshrined our
right to choose what happened to our bodies.

In reality, women at the turn of the 21st century in Canada were carrying
the weight of oppression on their bodies and their minds, and the "progressive" realization of their rights was only recent.

At that point, women had been entering the workforce in large numbers since the Second World War of the 20th century. The Women's Rights
Movement had entered a Third Wave, so there was a multi-generational con-
sciousness-raising occurring. However, issues around child care and caregiving were still completely unresolved. Consequently, women were paying with
their health and their pocketbooks.

Depression, anxiety disorders, extreme body issues, Alzheimer's disease
and other forms of dementia, multiple sclerosis, arthritis, lupus, and fibro-
myalgia were common, and at least one in four women in Canada was living
with a chronic illness or disability. Rates of breast cancers were not diminishing despite decades of research and millions upon millions in "pink" dollars.

The "Men's Movement" was on the rise, fuelled by an uneasy public purse
that had all but shunned a human rights framework in favour of jobs in the
resource sector. They perceived a patriarchy under attack by an intelligent,
rational "enemy" that had begun to understand the rules of engagement. And
men from this "movement" began pushing scholars and students alike to debate a new notion of gender equality that had some young women speaking
with an air of certainty about the Gender Wars that lay ahead.

In sharp contrast to the United Nations' call to action on gender equality
at the time, this Vision Conference in Canada was set against the knowledge
and quiet terror that all the injustices these women shared with their sisters

in development — from the daily reports and almost banal media coverage of acts of public rape and murder, to the mass kidnappings of schoolgirls. Therein lay an irrefutable but frequently denied truth — that gender equality *truly* remained the greatest and most important challenge of their times.

Social movements and social change are about a convergence of ideas and a moment in time. The women attending the Bold Vision Conference of 2014 appear to have had that kind of impact on one another, and so the sands of gender equality began to shift yet again.

The Conference was designed to bring together women in leadership, and it would appear, by design, that the organizers were seeking a particular type of leadership profile in the women they named as the "Visionaries," as these were all women who had distinguished themselves in very specific ways. Some by being the groundbreakers for the women who have followed, some for their innovation, each of them for their focus on the greater good, and *all* of them for seeing past the obstacles in their paths to the promise of a brighter future — thankfully, to our future.

They set us on the path of Intentional Leadership and Community First principles — with a vision for a Canada that includes everyone. Some of the key outputs from the Vision Conference of 2014 can only be appreciated when they are explained against objectives and frameworks of the time.

The Social Determinants of Health[2] had been in existence as a concept by that point in time for several decades, but the GTT (Global Tax Treaty of 2024) that eventually came out of the OECD tax reforms had not yet been imposed when the Visionaries recommended them as a key framework upon which to build a healthy nation. The Vision Network took as an important focus, first, advancing and protecting the right of each Canadian to a birth, life, and death of equal quality and opportunity to thrive; and, second, recognizing the Social Determinants of Health as being central to building a healthy society.

Using existing human rights conventions of the United Nations as a tool for advocacy, the Vision Network also strongly supported Canada's dramatic reengagement in the UN following the 2015 federal election.

Many of the community, regional, and federal programs and benefits we enjoy today are rooted in the fact that this first Vision Conference took on the Social Determinants of Health and many other key recommendations for reforms that shaped the policies and direction of our country coming out of this very tumultuous era. Significant reforms in labour law and both family and criminal justice are, to this day, strongly linked to the application of the Social Determinants of Health lens to which these women were so faithful.

The global effects of climate change had already begun to impact on the world economy in 2014. The era of the individual, the car, and the mobile was beginning to unravel under mounting evidence that it was an unsustainable and fundamentally unjust digression in human development.

In 2014, Canada's opportunity to take a leadership role in the environmental sector was being undermined by a government that at the time was still clinging to fossil fuel and a resource economy. A pipeline leak in British Columbia in 2022 damaged a huge tract of protected marine shoreline and resulted in the extinction of two bird species and the destruction of key areas of killer-whale habitat. The legal actions taken by the First Peoples' Trust following the disaster established important new precedents in affirming the ownership, protection, and stewardship of lands previously appropriated under 19th and 20th century "treaties."

The agents of the First Peoples' Trust used the disaster to argue for the first of many negotiations that led to Governance Reforms (2048–2053) and the eventual annexation of specific territories to Kanata and the Great Territories of the People. The strong presence and voice of Indigenous women at the first Vision Conference are widely seen as another of the key reasons that the Vision Network had such a significant impact going forward as a credible driver for social and economic change on a large scale.

Increasingly extreme weather caused by climate change had pushed the insurance and investment sectors to a point of extreme fragility. By that time, the Vision Network was one of the key policy drivers recommending responses to unprecedented shifts in the geopolitical, environmental, and economic direction of the country when a fractured coalition government led by the Green Party had just taken power.

The lead up in the Post Millennium (2015) era, to the "Tax it where the activity occurs" principle being applied, and to subsequent Tax Treaties was punctuated by labour unrest, a resurgence in organized labour's power, massive protests, and a tax and wage revolt driven by middle- and low-income families, bankrupt municipalities, and small business owners, under mounting pressure to address social and economic inequities. Trillions of dollars were being lost through tax evasion, and the growing practice of "double non-taxation" by multinationals and dictatorships had created a divide between "the many" and the "One Per Cent" that had us headed for all-out gender war, collapse of the world food supply, and environmental disaster.

So why do we still refer to the Vision Conference of 2014? What was it about this particular conference that set it apart? It was, of course, the beginning of the Vision Network, a non-partisan group focused on social and economic inclusion and the application of the Community First principles. In addition, the Conference was, for many to this day, the moment in time when Canadian women's leadership came into its own. At no time before in Canadian history had we set out to celebrate women in leadership, invited them to come together to consider the state of the country, and asked them to vision a new way forward.

The power of this idea may seem lost today, but at that point in time it was seen as radical or fantastical, depending on one's point of view. In describing the underlying tensions of the time, the stage was set in a critical pre-election year in Canada. Political agendas bankrupted by lobby groups and leadership apathy had left us with a party system that was uninspiring and driven by individualism, capitalism, and the status quo — the absence of vision, like a gaping hole in our future!

Before the Governance Reforms of the late-2040s and early 2050s were fully implemented, equal representation was being applied in some regions. Demographic shifts because of immigration and an aging population had begun to change "the face" of our nation. The concept and reality of globalization was manifesting in tangible shifts in both geographical and societal boundaries. Quebec's preoccupation with nationhood throughout the second half of the 20th century fell away as the collective conscience of the *"francophonie"* gradually regained its place of leadership as a distinct society within Canada. Early in the 21st century, Quebec showed leadership as the driver of social development and social change. In this regard, we owe to Quebec much of the substance of the Pay Equity Act, the Caregiver Act, and the shift in healthcare towards a social enterprise model.

One of the unexpected outcomes of the Bold Vision conference of 2014 was that it led to the Vision Network's annual Vision Conference. The Reformists managed to impose a gradual shift on the health and social services sector. Reorienting to a social economy model was one of the first tangible examples of how we found our way out of what had become an increasingly dark period in human development. Evidence of the successes associated with social enterprise in the goods and services sector and in new infrastructure projects led to measurable shifts in terms of quality of life (and therefore the Social Determinants of Health) of all Canadians. These reforms have gradually favourably repositioned Canada/Kanata and the Great Territories of the People in terms of global leadership.

Sustainable development, significant reforms in education, and a major shift towards "horizontal or networked" governance and fiscal reform, with a view to deconstructing the ability of the wealthy to control the few—these were some of the big ideas that began to take shape at the Vision Conference.

The act of bringing those particular women together, women who had given their lives purpose through service to others, through acts of kindness, through acts of defiance, and through dedication to their craft, their science, their experience, and their knowledge—this was a selfless act, driven by other women of vision, the women of Prince Edward Island.

The first decision they took was to commit themselves to an annual Vision Conference to be held in each of the provinces and territories. The second decision they took was to turn the conference and all its participants into a network and to keep their dialogue and their dream relevant and evolving—like a nation.

They celebrated and supported the evolution of Intentional Leadership in Canada—leadership not driven by self-motivation, self-aggrandizement, or greed. The annual Vision Conference and the Vision Network were driven by optimism, vision, and determination and by the commitment to equality for which our country has become known.

....

1. The first was the original Charlottetown Conference of September 1864, and the second was the Bold Vision Conference of September 2014.

2. In 2014, a key reference for the social determinants of health was Juha Mikkonen and Dennis Raphael, *Social Determinants of Health: The Canadian Facts* (Toronto: York University School of Health Policy and Management, 2010), accessed July 2014 http://www.thecanadianfacts.org/.

ACKNOWLEDGMENTS

We owe much gratitude to A Bold Vision's Honorary Board members Honourable Gail Shea, federal Minister of Fisheries and Oceans and MP for Egmont; Honourable Catherine Callbeck, former Premier of Prince Edward Island and recently retired Senator; Honourable Valerie E. Docherty, PEI Minister Responsible for the Status of Women and MLA for District 17 Kelly's Cross–Cumberland; Chief Matilda Ramjattan, elected Chief of the Lennox Island First Nation; Councillor Irene Dawson, elected Councillor of the Town of Cornwall; and Jessie Inman, Chief Executive Officer of the Confederation Centre of the Arts. They are extraordinary leaders who were generous with their time and support for all aspects of the project.

We thank Jane Dunphy Cudmore who first suggested a meeting of 23 women to match the Charlottetown Conference meeting of 23 men. She was generous with her vision. We thank all the organizations and women who took part in brainstorming about a potential project.

Thank you to everyone across the country that got involved with A Bold Vision. We know that nominators put a lot of time and effort into the nominations. And as the nominations rolled in, we were amazed and humbled by the extraordinary accomplishments of women across the country. It was a pleasure making connections and getting to know more about the efforts of women to improve their communities from coast to coast to coast. We look forward to imagining ways to continue build on these connections.

We truly appreciate the contributions of our 23 visionaries to this project. Thank you for your words, your time, and your visions. The collective work presented in this book makes us hopeful.

Thank you to the anthology project team. To Catherine Ronahan at Women's Network PEI, for publication coordination. To Dawn Wilson of the PEI Coalition for Women in Government, for drafting biographies and coordinating with visionaries. To Jane Ledwell and the PEI Advisory Council on the Status of Women for editing and additional writing. To Lee Ellen Pottie for proofreading and to Kirstin Lund of the steering committee and Becky Tramley of the PEI Advisory Council on the Status of Women for assistance. To Senja Djelouah for translation. To Valerie Bellamy, Dog-ear Book Design, for stellar work. To author Patti Larsen for generous advice in the planning stages. To our three interviewers, Doreen Kays, Kate McKenna, and Dawn Wilson, two Bold Vision nominees and a steering committee member, for accommodating visionaries who preferred an interview and for sharing your lively intelligence.

Thank you to our major funder, PEI 2014 Inc. As women's organizations, our work often focuses on the challenges women still face in our society, so this unique community grant program was a wonderful opportunity to take a step back and acknowledge how far women have advanced in society in the past 150 years. Taking the time to celebrate women's leadership and include these diverse voices in thinking about the future is something we simply would not have endeavoured without this explicit opportunity to "honour the past, celebrate the present, and plan for a bold tomorrow."

Thanks to steering committee members and partner organizations Sara Roach-Lewis (Women's Network PEI), Dawn Wilson (PEI Coalition for Women in Government), Jane Ledwell (PEI Advisory Council on the Status of Women), Michelle Harris-Genge (PEI Interministerial Women's Secretariat), Hannah Bell (PEI Business Women's Association), and Kirstin Lund (Programming Chair) for ongoing project direction and dedicated work. Thanks also to the members of the boards and councils of the partner organizations for their support and for making this work possible.

We would also like to thank our other funding agencies, the Atlantic Canada Opportunities Agency (ACOA) and Canadian Heritage, as well as project sponsors.

Finally, we would like to thank our friends and family for their support and encouragement. Launching a national project that includes coordinating a national search for visionaries, publishing an anthology, and hosting a national conference doesn't happen without early mornings and late nights. Our family members are not simply passive supporters, but active participants and champions of *our* Bold Visions.

Author Photo Credits

pg. ix	Dr. Roberta Bondar	Carlyle Routh
pg. 15	Crystal Fraser	Charlie English
pg. 67	Becka Viau	Stephen Harris / crown by Leigh Elliott
pg. 89	Kluane Adamek	Heather Jones, photographer, 'hpj photography'
pg. 103	Nazanin Afshin-Jam MacKay	Karolina Turek Photography
pg. 119	Kim Campbell	Gunnar Freyr
pg. 141	Eva Aariak	Legislative Assembly of Nunavut
pg. 157	Dr. Catherine Potvin	Guy l'Heureux
pg. 181	Dr. Margaret-Ann Armour	Richard Siemens, University of Alberta
pg. 251	Dr. Pamela Palmater	Ryerson University
pg. 263	El Jones	Riley Smith
pg. 271	Bonnie Brayton	Madeleine Pare

All other photos credited in captions or used by permission of the author

15861355R10172

Made in the USA
San Bernardino, CA
10 October 2014